English
Influences in Dutch Literature

English
Influences in Dutch Literature
and Justus Van Effen
as Intermediary

An Aspect of
Eighteenth Century Achievement

By

W. J. B. PIENAAR

M.A. (STELLENBOSCH)
PH.D. (LONDON)

Le plus grand Génie de l'Univers n'ira jamais loin s'il ne
tire ses pensées que de son propre fond.

JUSTUS VAN EFFEN
La Bagatelle XCIII,
1719

CAMBRIDGE
AT THE UNIVERSITY PRESS
1929

CAMBRIDGE
UNIVERSITY PRESS

University Printing House, Cambridge CB2 8BS, United Kingdom

Cambridge University Press is part of the University of Cambridge.

It furthers the University's mission by disseminating knowledge in the pursuit of education, learning and research at the highest international levels of excellence.

www.cambridge.org
Information on this title: www.cambridge.org/9781107487376

© Cambridge University Press 1929

First published 1929
First paperback edition 2015

A catalogue record for this publication is available from the British Library

ISBN 978-1-107-48737-6 Paperback

PREFACE

IN writing the following account of English influences in Dutch literature and the work of Justus van Effen in this connection, I was actuated by the sense that the whole story of English literature cannot be told as long as its vicissitudes abroad, and especially in Holland, are insufficiently known. The adventure of English letters there is of great interest, and I have endeavoured to give some coherent, if abbreviated, account of it up to the time when English literature may be said to have become a settled, though fluctuating, living force within the Dutch *milieu*.

From the point of view of Dutch literature, if it is to be understood rightly and chronicled fully, the subject has an importance at least equally great as for English literature. The hope that I have added something to the knowledge also of Dutch literature gives me a particular gratification.

The period is the early eighteenth century when a pushful English culture penetrated to the continent, and cosmopolitan Holland was an effective broadcast station relaying the newly-discovered island culture. And this fact invests our subject with a European importance beyond the domestic literary interests of Holland and England.

But I have further attempted to do the science of comparative literature a modest service, by giving also an account of the activities of Justus van Effen. Some account of him, especially in English, as an ambassador of English culture abroad and as an international literary figure is long overdue. His name constantly recurs in modern reviews and studies. Here we find him discussed as the first translator of *Robinson Crusoe*, there of *A Tale of a Tub*, and as the first imitator of Swift; or, again, as the translator of Mandeville, of Shaftesbury, of the *Guardian*. Goldsmith coolly plagiarized him, as several investigators have recently shown; he was the inaugurator of the "Spectator" movement on the continent; the part-editor of a number of

influential reviews; an acute observer and chronicler of
English literature and culture, and finally the Addison of
Holland by his own "Spectator" in Dutch. His noteworthy
record, about which I hope I am right in assuming that
there exists some curiosity, suggested him as the central
figure for our study.

The great field of comparative literature into which I have
here made an excursion is perhaps the most legitimate field
for literary research to-day. The chronological historian of
literature is open to the charge of empiricism so long as
the comparative point of view is ignored. The dogmatism
of the aesthete, which is apt to be repeated *ad nauseam*, is
out of date. Yet the history of any one of the great
groups of European literature is open to profound modi-
fication if the accumulated researches of comparative
scholars during the last half century be properly utilized.
To form a true and proper estimate of a writer or of
a literature, we must obviously have all the ascertainable
facts at our disposal. Among these, an analysis of indebtedness home and foreign, its origin and extent, use and abuse:
of the forces that went to the making of great literature,
may legitimately claim a place. To consider how an
author combined originality and imitation in both construction and expression, to consider the nature and extent of
his original contribution, is a necessary, but much neglected,
task for which we must have all the cards on the table.
Genius has eluded definition, but we may be pardoned for
wanting to see how it works. If, then, we may discover
where genius went to quarry for much of its material,
what it collected and rejected and what value, if any, was
added in the workshop, it seems clear that this fascinating
enquiry should be the first object of the methodical student
of literature; for upon him the onus rests of constructing
a reliable account of what happened in the making of fine
literature. As regards the authors themselves, it is neither
right nor fair to leave the general reader with distorted ideas
of their inventiveness. To study, say, Goldsmith, without
due attention to his sources, to ignore in *The Vicar* (in

many respects so original) the obvious imitations of, e.g., Richardson and Fielding, is to deny merit to those to whom it is due, to blind oneself to the continuity of literature and the patent facts of its development. Instead of urging exaggerated claims of a false kind for a writer's creative capacity, a fuller consciousness of the necessary derivativeness of art may well be cultivated side by side with reverence for genius and originality. To attribute to Coleridge the bulk of the critical ideas which he used in the process of discovering Shakespeare for England is to deprive certain German critics of their just distinction, and yet to see what Coleridge made of his borrowings is to gain a finer appreciation of the true quality of his style and taste. In fact, authors themselves have invited us to compare, and discover if or how they have improved upon their originals.

In following the track of an author's reading, the student soon realizes the exhilarating fact that he is in the full swirl of European literature, and has crossed national boundaries. European literary criticism has always been comparative. The classical literatures particularly were long the norm by which modern products were measured. In the days of Addison, as we see in much of his criticism, at which Matthew Arnold sneered, the old comparative method was still strongly in vogue. But in that age also it became more and more customary to compare modern literatures openly, especially English and French. Comparison then usually took the futile and even odious form of mutual depreciation. The conflict between these two literatures during the eighteenth century was, in fact, much more heated than the famous *querelle* of the previous century. But apart from the mere contentious and idle aspects, conscious comparison was one of the most fruitful and stimulating things that could have happened to literature. Comparison enabled men, as nothing else could, to taste the peculiar flavour, to appreciate the different quality, method and point of view of each, and to make such widening of the literary horizon a real benefit to the home product. Indeed, so much interaction has taken place that ignorance of some main features of European literature as a whole must make any component part of it almost unintelligible except in a dilettante and empirical sense; and appreciation of this kind, though it may yield much enjoyment, is not sufficient for any scientific study of literature.

As the reading and borrowing of the individual must be examined for the full understanding of his achievement, so the national indebtedness must be assessed in its nature and extent before anything like a true conception of its growth and character can be gained. The comparative study, in fact, brings a fuller sense of the realities of literary evolution in Europe. Yet the fascinating play of light between groups, interfertilization and its far-reaching effects, are things rather more tacitly admitted in general, than allowed to direct the study of literature in practice. If the high achievement of the Greeks owes not a little to the accident that they were the last to receive opportunely a culture already bearing deep scores left by several successive groups, so the remarkable achievement of the modern European during the last millennium or more owes no less to the marvellous and significant way in which he has been able to hand on from one national group to another the forms and processes of artistic expression. But the international and cosmopolitan aspects of art have elsewhere received that inspired reference which is their due. It remains only to call attention to a persistent wraith which will not be laid. It is the facile theory of a cosmopolitan literature where the national equation will count for very little, if anything. And it is when this attitude is struck towards the literary records of the past that too much foreign influence is usually read into them. To begin by assuming that even in imitation any nation would neglect to put its characteristic stamp on whatever it attempted is always wrong. However much Italian influences may have been at work it is easy to discover that Surrey and his group are purely English in almost every way—but not entirely, which is important. The Dutch tried, during the eighteenth century, to step into the wide stream of world literature with excessive orientation to French, English and, later, German literature. The result was an object-lesson in decadence to the rest of Europe. If such were the common practice, European literature would be deprived of the very condition of its existence as a great literature or group of literatures. Nationality and national character are but a sort of distinctiveness and individuality in the larger sense, and are precious things.

This work incorporates the greater part of a thesis prepared by the author and approved for the Degree of Doctor of Philosophy in the University of London. Although it may therefore be thought to be of a somewhat academic nature, I have tried to write for the general student and reader as well as the specialist. I venture to express the hope that my book may be of service and some value to younger students in the universities, especially of the Netherlands and of South Africa, where English and Dutch language and literature are studied side by side.

As the field which I have covered is so wide that a really useful bibliography would fill a volume by itself, I have had to confine myself to an index containing references relevant to the text only. The extent of my indebtedness to previous workers is, I hope, fully indicated everywhere. In particular, my introductory chapters owe much to J. T. Bense's *Anglo-Dutch Relations*. Upon questions such as the relation of *Elckerlijk* and *Everyman*, Vondel and Milton, *Krinke Kesmes* and *Robinson Crusoe*, Spenser and Van der Noot, etc., I pronounce rather summarily, but only after careful original investigation as well as a due consideration of the literature of the subjects. Unfortunately, I was forced to omit any real discussion of them.

I must thank Dr P. Geyl, Professor of History and Dutch Institutions in the University of London for some fruitful ideas—and fruitful ideas are valuable things—suggested at the commencement of my work, and his interest and assistance since. To Dr P. Harting, now Professor of English in the University of Groningen, I am grateful for advice and assistance. My thanks are due to Professor R. W. Chambers, Quain Professor of English in University College, London, and especially to Professor Herford, Emeritus Professor of English in the University of Manchester, for good advice and encouraging remarks. I have much appreciated the kind interest Professor J. G. Robertson, editor of *The Modern Language Review*, has taken in my work, even to the extent of reading the MS. I must finally express my gratitude to my wife for her devoted encouragement and assistance, including some months' work in the British Museum. The greater part of the index was compiled by her.

To the trustees and officials of the great libraries of the British Museum and of Bodley I must express my sense of obligation for the wonderful facilities, entertainment and instruction I have been privileged to enjoy in their respective institutions.

Oxford,
4th June, 1926.

W. J. B. P.

CONTENTS

CHAPTER I

INTRODUCTORY

The last quarter of the seventeenth century seems a peculiarly convenient starting-point for any survey of Anglo-Dutch relations during the eighteenth century. It was then that two of the most momentous events between the regicide of Charles I and the French Revolution took place: first, the religious persecutions in France, which, spreading some half-a-million of her best sons and daughters over the civilized world, had a most powerful influence upon European civilization; secondly, the English Revolution with Monmouth's rebellion as prelude, and the *coup d'état* of William of Orange as climax.

In this period, moreover, the spirit of progress, after a temporary quiescence, began to shine out in a fresh splendour of rejuvenation. It was a period in which the tentative intellectual movements of the past were established on firmer foundations, and it is to this age that we must refer to understand the periods of Queen Anne in England, of Van Effen in Holland, and of Voltaire in France.

But we must, above all, and particularly for the purpose of this study, regard the age as one which gave birth to a new conception of international relationships and exchange in the permanent things of our common civilization. It was this spirit of cosmopolitanism which led to an interchange of national cultures and so stimulated the second European Renaissance of the early nineteenth century. The Dutch seem from very early times to have been one of the most, as the English were one of the least, internationally-minded of great nations. This is a virtue which Sir William Temple would have qualified by making it a necessity, as other Dutch virtues appeared to him, and it certainly was partly the product of political and economic circumstances. It is, moreover, a virtue that contains within itself the danger of denationalization, as the Dutch found too late to their cost; but it is also a virtue which had enabled them to absorb the finest qualities of the various types of foreign culture and enlightenment that lay beyond their borders, and frequently to take the lead themselves.

From the times of the Middle Ages the Netherlands had shared, though in a more conspicuous degree perhaps, with Germany, England and other countries, the privilege of being educated in literature and culture by France[1]. "C'est la France qui porte à l'Europe occidentale la Renaissance littéraire; l'Humanisme, en son caractère cosmopolite, a bien vite conquis le monde, la Renaissance s'infiltre plus lentement. C'est la France qui inspire la Renaissance à l'Angleterre, aux Pays-Bas, à l'Allemagne," says J. Prinsen with truth. It cannot be questioned that the Dutch inclined more to France than to any other country in respect of literary art, fine culture and perhaps even thought and religion[2].

And yet of all international intimacies, that of the Netherlands and England was one of the closest. Indeed, the very fact that these two Germanic groups stood so directly under the tutelage of France, only made their literary culture more intelligible to each other in the end. And so it happened in the eighteenth century, when both England and Holland had reached the climax of their French period of influence, that the Dutch were readily able to appreciate English literature, in spite of the blurring prepossessions into which the French traditions finally degenerated.

With such deeper spiritual significance William's conquest of England was fraught. When Admiral Herbert, in the beginning of July 1688, handed William of Orange the historic request at Honselaarsdyk to speed and save English liberty, the heart of the English people was really offering a confidence to which the Dutch magnificently responded. It was, of course, neither the first nor the last time that the

---

[1] *Vide*, e.g., Sir Sidney Lee, *The French Renaissance in England*.
[2] *Vide* the remarkable enquiry conducted by the *Revue de Hollande*.

Dutch stood loyally by their *outre-manche* neighbours. Viewed superficially, it was simply another of those political alliances contracted for the sake of ephemeral self-interest and mutual convenience. If it did contain so much of dross, it contained also an element of the purer gold. After centuries of contact in trade and of political intercourse the two nations were at length in a fair way to remove masks and penetrate to the reality of each other's culture. Masks had, of course, been lifted before. In the long history of continuous Anglo-Dutch intercourse from the time of the separation of Anglo-Saxons and Jutes from their continental kinsfolk to 1688, when an Anglo-Dutch king united the now distinct peoples of the British Isles and the Netherlands, many intermittent confidences had been exchanged. There had indeed been brief moments of cultural *rapprochement* divided by long stretches of spiritual, though never material, isolation.

Of these, the first may be said to have been the splendid missions of which Willibrord and Boniface were the central figures. It was the period of the remarkable Northumbrian civilization, that belated flower which grew in the shadow of the great Roman Wall. Happily the Northumbrian culture did not remain confined to this central area but spread southwards to London and eastwards to Frisia, Flanders and France. Active relations had of course been maintained between the Anglo-Saxon adventurers and their old homes, and the note of wistful reminiscence in Old English literature tends to show that a real feeling still existed. It is certain that it was partly the spirit of brotherhood that actuated those fine characters from Britain to undertake the evangelizing of the German and Low-German territories. "And so also were there holy and learned men that were careful and had compassion for the souls of the heathen dwellers in the lands whence they themselves had come," says the chronicler Govoerdt Schoevaerdt[1], and he adds that the success of the Anglo-Saxon missionaries was no doubt due to the similarity of language: "so then St Willibrord preached in

[1] *Nederlandsche Antiquiteyten*, p. 33.

these lands in the same tongue as he preached in England, which without doubt was at that time the natural language of both these countries[1]."

Boniface, in attempting to revive an almost obliterated Roman Christianity, called for books and more books in his letters home. But, better still, scholars and willing helpers flocked to him. "He had brought unto the Lord a vast people among the Frisians and many educated by him, and from the parts of Britain an exceedingly great multitude... had come unto him, readers and writers also, and men learned in other arts," says his biographer Willibald[2]. His aim was clearly enlightenment as well as conversion. His murder by the Frisians emphasizes the element of heroic sacrifice with which this picturesque episode in international relations was fraught, and cannot but be associated with that other tragic romance of Anglo-Dutch friendship, namely that of Sir Philip Sidney.

The lifelong activities in Frisia and Denmark of Willibrord and his many disciples who included Liudger, a Frisian trained by Alcuin at York, are a no less interesting and important chapter in the steadily growing intercourse, which after this brief missionary period seems to be mostly of a political and economic nature.

When the Normans came, relations with the Low Countries must have been greatly stimulated. The Gallicized Teutonism of Norman culture was at least as near to Low-German as to English civilization, further removed from France, which was the sphere whence cultural influences then radiated. The Conqueror's army, of course, contained many Low-German mercenaries, and during his reign large numbers of Flemish weavers were imported into England to provide Norman grandees with something better than the coarse homespun of their adopted country. In fact, an era was beginning in which the Dutch peoples were no more to be recipients as they had been in the eighth century, but were

---

[1] *Nederlandsche Antiquiteyten*, p. 33.
[2] Willibald's *Life of Boniface* (Robinson). *Vide* also *The English Correspondence of St Boniface*, ed. Edward Kylie, etc.

themselves to exert influence in the trades, arts and sciences up to the end of the seventeenth century. The Anglo-Dutch trade was the most vital to the growth of the commerce of each country. England was a backward country in the Middle Ages. She had a considerable export trade of which the Dutch were the carriers up to the time of Elizabeth, when English shipping began to supply the necessary freightage. Dutch fishermen, a race of intrepid sea-rovers, were allowed to exploit the wealth of English coasts for nearly a millennium. The fishing trade became the very backbone of Dutch seafaring prosperity and trade, and was of great importance to the economic life of mediaeval England. The periodic markets of Yarmouth and other towns could not be held if for any reason (and there were many) Dutch fishermen absented themselves[1].

The fourteenth century is conspicuous for the establishment of closer relations between England and the Netherlands. English trade policy grew less grotesquely protectionist especially with respect to the Dutch, Edward III definitely attempting to divert English trade to the north and away from France. At the beginning of the Hundred Years' War we find the English and Dutch opposed to France, a position often repeated later and most notably when William III pitted his whole strength against Louis XIV. The fourteenth century is a time of frequent intervention by the Dutch in English politics and *vice versa*. A fleet of 140 herring-boats and others assisted Isabella and her son in their *coup d'état*, and Edward, realizing the importance of Dutch shipping, contemplated laying claim to Zeeland, of which the temporary overlordship had been granted him. Other links, such as the alliance of William V of Flanders with Matilda of Lancaster, the assistance Richard II afforded the Flemish against their count in 1382, the extensive importation of Flemish weavers whose industry excited the jealousy of "Jacke Strawe & his menye,"

---

[1] J. Ruinen, *De Oudste Handelsbetrekkingen van Holland en Zeeland met Engeland*.

are no less interesting and important. For it was then that the foundation of a regular English textile industry was laid from which the "merchant adventurers" were to rise[1] and become perhaps the most important and regular link with the Netherlands, a link invaluable to England if only for the priceless Caxton who, a century later, sent over as their *Governour* "beyond the see," returned after thirty years' residence with a printing-press.

And it is this period of Caxton which is perhaps the most remarkable of all. In the quarter of a century on each side of the year 1500 fall some of the greatest historic events in Anglo-Dutch cultural associations. Caxton, a descendant it seems of a Flemish family settled in Kent during the fourteenth century, is a highly important and characteristic figure of this age, who represented English interests in the Low Countries in politics, business and learning. He played an important part in the negotiations that led to the marriage between Charles the Bold and Margaret, sister of Edward IV, a union that was a considerable factor in developing amicable relations of all sorts between England and the Low Countries. It was the time of the great economic treaty of 1496 between England and the Netherlands, significantly called the "Intercursus Magnus" and as significantly nicknamed "Intercursus Malus" in troubled days later on. England was at this time mostly receptive. Sons and apprentices of the Merchant Adventurers were, as Wheeler[2] tells us, sent to the "mart Towns beyond the Sea," "there to learn good facions and knowledge in trade."

But this period is especially noted for the book trade that sprang up between the two countries. Caxton inaugurated a new era for England too by turning his experience as a printer in Flanders to such good account at Westminster. But his former associates and successors in the Low Countries continued to print for the English market, and it is to their enterprise that England owes two of the most astonish-

[1] *Vide* C. te Lintum, *De Merchant Adventurers in de Nederlanden.*
[2] *Treatise of Commerce.*

ing literary productions—*Everyman* and *Reynard the Fox*, both translations from the Dutch. But there was much besides. Jan van Doesborgh with his pupil L. Andrewe, who set up in England, was alone responsible for some eighteen extant translations from Dutch into English. From his press issued an English version of that most exquisite Dutch "miracle" play *Mary of Nemmegen*. Doesborgh was also the printer of Richard Arnold's curious book (Antwerp, 1502) which gave us the famous *Ballade of ye Notte Browne Mayde*. This period of steady cultural influence from Flanders, in which Thomas à Kempis also figures, broadens out into the humanistic cosmopolitanism rendered glorious in the history of Dutch-English connections by the classic association of Colet, More and Erasmus. This celebrated Dutchman owed a great deal to the classical scholarship and spirit of the "Oxford Reformers," but himself came to stand as the embodiment of humanistic culture in the North. And it must be particularly noted that this commanding figure sprang from the intimacy of Anglo-Dutch culture of the early sixteenth century. For Sir Thomas More[1], nothing was more natural than to place the dialogists of his *Utopia* at Antwerp. *Utopia* became a well-known book in the fictitious country of its birth, inspiring imitations at least up to 1708 in the *Krinke Kesmes*, and this in turn may have been utilized for the production of *Robinson Crusoe*. This is the period of Coverdale and the bible translations into the vulgar tongue in the printing of which Dutch printers were active[2]. Coverdale's translation was published at Antwerp largely at the expense of a Dutchman, Van Meteren. The cultural stream was

---

[1] He was one of the first English writers to gain a great continental reputation.

Pitsius, one of the early chroniclers of English art and learning, says of him among other things of splendid panegyric: "Denique licet patriae fines studiorum causa nunquam fuerit egressus maximam tamen Europae partem singularis eruditionis & ingenii fama replevit. Guilhelmum Grocinum, Ioannen Coletum, Thomam Linacrum viros pietate & eruditione insignes in studiis habuit praeceptores. Utopiam nouam insulam, idem Erasmus in epistolis ad Morum vocat Nusquammam, scripsit Latine, quod opus translatum invenitur in linguas Anglicam, Gallicam, Italicam, Germanicam."

[2] *Vide* Introduction to Coverdale's Bible, also J. T. Bense, *Anglo-Dutch Relations*, p. 98.

flowing from the Low Countries in the direction of England, and that Englishmen were sensitive to this is indicated by the following naïve deposition[1] in the mouth of the English translator of *The Comedy of Acolastus*[2]—"a very curious and artificial compacted nosegay":

I wold be glad to move into the hartes of your graces clerkes of whyche your noble realme was never better stored, some lyttell grayne of honeste and vertuous envye, whiche on my partie to confesse the verye truthe unto your grace hath contynually in all the tyme of these my poore labours takyng, accompanyed me and styred me onwardes to achieve this matter in this wise by me attempted. For thus have I thought to my self. Shal Fullonius an Hollander born, thus many yeres after the decay of the latyne tongue by the Gothes, Vandales and Longobardes most barbarous nations, be able to make so fine and so exact a piece of work and I shal not be able at these yeres of myn age to do so moche as to declare what he meaneth in my natyve tongue?...In very dede I shal thynke myselfe moche fortunate if this myne enterprise or at the least fyrst settynge on maye gyve occasion unto other your graces wel lerned clerks....

Translations from Dutch continued throughout the century; missals and emblem books—a forgotten but very popular form of literature—Van der Noot's *Theatre*, the famous *Beehive* of Marnix of St Aldegonde, a book as sensational as the *Praise of Folly*, are some of a considerable body of translated literature which still awaits full investigation.

The days of "Bloody Mary" in England and of the Spanish Terror in the Netherlands mark a new period of sympathetic relations to be indelibly charactered with the name of Sidney at a later date. The loss of thousands[3] of good subjects who streamed to that land of liberty in the dark days of Mary was more than compensated for by the influx of excellent Dutch citizens at other times. Hundreds of thousands flocked into England, and their feelings are reflected in the

---

[1] Preface addressed to *Henry VIII*.
[2] John Palgrave, London, 1540.   [3] Weiss gives 30,000.

following words addressed to Elizabeth by one of their number[1]:

Neuer was it seene in any age or time heretofore that this your realme of *England* hath flourished as it dothe at this present under your maiesties moste happie gouernement. Firste in all kinde of liberall Artes and sciences. Secondarily in the abundance of treasure. Thirdely in the free passage and trafike of all kinde of Merchandise: Besides this, in good and politike lawes and ordinances.... The worde of God is purely preached here in six or seven languages.... Finally every countrey and nation that will liue here according to his holy worde is receiued and findeth good entertainement. O how happy and blessed is that king or kingdome where these things are in force. For here is peace and quietnesse where as the moste parte of foraine countreys are full of great tumultes.... We a numbre of vs are arriued in saftie in this your maiesties realme of Englande as into a moste safe and sure harborough, where we liue (God be thanked) vnder your maiesties protection and safeguarde in great libertie to serue God in eyther language, the Frenche or the Dutche, without al feare of tyrantes.

Elizabeth is panegyrized for her learning and eloquence "as well in Greeke, Latine, Italian, Frenche, Dutch as in your owne natural English," and her skill in "the divine arte of Poetrie[2]."

In addition to the crowded foreign quarters in London, there were the Dutch settlements at Norwich, Rye, Colchester, Canterbury, Southampton, etc., to the incalculable benefit of English trade and prosperity. "Shoulder of Mutton and English Beere make the Flemmings tarry here," they sang "in the sea-towns of England," tells Moryson[3], which witticism the Dutch countered with: "English Beere, English Verstant" (wits)[4]. But the good citizens were in right earnest glad to have the industrious foreigners. Clarendon remarks that "the wealth of those places marvellously increased," adding that Queen Elizabeth "made use of them in her great transactions of state in France and the

[1] J. J. van der Noot—*Epistle, Theatre for Worldlings.*
[2] Dated: "At London your Maiesties Citie and seate royal. The 25 of May, 1569."
[3] Fynes Moryson, *An Itenerary* (London, 1617), vol. IV, p. 63, ed. 1907.
[4] Part III, book 2, chap. 4.

Low contries[1]." Dutchmen were employed in engineering and drainage schemes in many parts of the country. In London, as Stow tells us in his *Annals*, the Dutch taught the English many industries and useful household arts, amongst which was starching[2]. Coaches were also introduced by the Dutch, Guilliam Boonen becoming the Queen's coachman in 1564, and soon after "divers great ladies (with as great jealousy of the Queen's displeasure) made them coaches and rid in them up & down the countries to the great admiration of all the beholders[3]." But the refugees did not merely increase economic prosperity and the amenities of life[4]. They shared the intellectual life of the time. The pastors and elders of the Dutch Church were men of enlightenment, Jan Alasco, who was appointed as first official pastor, being described as "homo propter integritatem et innocentiam vitae ac morum et singularem eruditionem valde celebris" in Edward's Letter Patent of 1550. A manuscript of the end of the century among the papers of the Dutch Church shows that there was a liberally supported fund for maintaining young Dutchmen at Cambridge and other centres of learning. But the seventeenth century is the age of reciprocal patronage of the great Dutch and English universities by students and scholars of each country, and from Sir Thomas Browne to Oliver Goldsmith Leyden alone counted some thousands of British *alumni*. Among the refugees from Antwerp was Jan Jonker van der Noot, who was a true harbinger of the French Renaissance and who, as a careful examination[5] of their association has revealed, must be held not only to have fired Edmund Spenser with the artistic enthusiasms of the Pléiade, but also to have fertilized the genius of the young poet. The collaboration of the ardent Dutch poet with the youthful Spenser to produce an English version of

[1] *History of the Rebellion*, vol. II, p. 141 (cit. Burns).
[2] "The best & most curious wives of that time observing the neatnesse & delycacy of the Dutch" soon discarded "cambric" and introduced the mode of starched ruffs of lawn, "which was at that time a stuff most strange & wonderful."
[3] *Collection of Divers Curious Historical Pieces*, Burns, p. 189.
[4] *Vide* also J. T. Bense, *op. cit.* chap. 4.
[5] *Vide English Studies* (Amsterdam), April and June 1926.

the *Theatre for Worldlings* is one of the most interesting of international literary connections, especially in view of the direction Spenser's work and tastes took, and of the vital part played by the French Renaissance in the forming of the great Elizabethan literature. But there were others of Van der Noot's school, the poet-painters Van Mander, Lucas d'Heere and Cornelius Ketel, who visited England and laid the foundation of that appreciation of Dutch art which the English had from the very first. This is an important factor in the cultural relations of the seventeenth century when so many great Dutch painters worked under the stimulus of English patronage. The formidable Elizabeth established a precedent of royal patronage of Dutch artists; she sat to Ketel and employed Lucas d'Heere.

It is to the mid-sixteenth century, too, that we must look for the development of political and religious traditions which were to mould Anglo-Dutch relations. Spenser has impressively and heroically sung the affliction of a sister-country and its championship by Gloriana's knight, Leicester. Churchyard gave his *Lamentable & Pitiful Description* in 1578. It was the tradition of the maintenance of the Protestant succession that steadily formed Anglo-Dutch sentiment. Many pamphlets in the strain of *Reasons why England should protect the Low Countries* show how strong this feeling was. Diplomatic relations were established for the first time[1] with the Northern Netherlands, and the action of the crafty Elizabeth in sending them aid highly impressed the imagination of the mass of the people of both countries who were innocent of diplomatic chicanery. The letters of Sir Thomas Gresham, who was very popular and influential amongst the Dutch, contain repeated assurances of the affection of the Dutch for England. This is also the time of literary pilgrimages. From Heywood who fled to Antwerp in 1564, scores[2] of English writers find themselves for one reason or another in the Low Countries, which were, for one thing, a regular military school. Gascoigne, Churchyard, Marlowe, Ben Jonson, the

---

[1] Brit. Mus. Harleian MSS. 1877, fol. 67. (From about 1575.)

[2] Cp. J. T. Bense, *op. cit.* p. 196, who has mentioned "some fifty."

gossipy Howell, Donne, are amongst the better-known ones. And their presence was not unregarded by Dutch poets. In the *Nederduytsen Helicon*, 1610, a miscellany after the style of *England's Parnassus*, and redolent of the French Renaissance atmosphere, appears a poem: "Of the Englishman who sings so lustily in imitation of the Nightingale[1]." "The story of Pandion has received support from the marvel that has happened lately among us," says the writer. The spirit of Philomela has entered the person of an Englishman, a mean and seemingly disreputable cavalryman in the service of Bellona. Yet his singing is as lively and clear as a gushing fountain that even the nightingale would swear "that who sings thus is rightly naméd Nightingale." He has been offered fair meed by "great lords," but prefers sweet liberty of song to the thraldom of princes. As a felicitous line expresses it: "His freedom, then, to him his kingdom is." It would be extremely interesting to know which of the Elizabethan adventurer poets is here intended. If an identification can be made it will point, I think, to Gascoigne, whose adventures in the Low Countries were famous. He was actually in favour with the great Prince of Nassau, is represented in English miscellanies similar to the *Helicon*, and is, of course, author of a poem *The Complainte of Phylomene*.

Many of these literary adventurers did not return empty-handed in respect of new subject-matter or of literary ideas. Churchyard did translations from the Dutch, Gascoigne's *Glasse of Government* is a product of the *Acolastus* type, and for well over a century the Netherlands and its history provided matter for literature. But these were not the only class of men, besides regular soldiers and traders, that formed a counter-stream to that of Flemish refugees, artists and artisans. It was in the last decade of the sixteenth century that a band of Puritan pilgrims "resolved to goe into ye Low Countries, wher they heard was freedome of Religion for all men; as also how sundrie from London & other parts of ye Land had been exiled and persecuted for ye same cause &

---

[1] "Van den Engelsman die den Nachtegael soo levendigh naesingt."

were gone thither & lived at Amsterdam & in other places of ye Land[1]." At Amsterdam they found several English religious communities strongly separatist. There were disputes in which the celebrated Junius was consulted, and later the historic party left for Leyden. Their cause had been widely advertised so that "yet many more came on with fresh courage" from England, says Bradford. At Leyden "a fair & bewtifull citie and of a sweete situation," and "the most famous Protestant seat of learning in the seventeenth century," as Bradford and Mullinger, the Cambridge historian, refer to it respectively[2], "they continued many years in a comfortable condition, injoying much sweete & delightfull societie." A number of them matriculated at the University and otherwise shared in the intellectual life of the day, for Leyden was throbbing with intellectual activity and artistic enthusiasm as well as industrial bustle. Robinson, the pastor of the group at Leyden, and writer, amongst other theological works, of the well-known *Defence of the Doctrine propounded by the Synode at Dort,* is described in a petition of Amsterdam merchants as an "English preacher versed in the Dutch language." It was evidently an unusual accomplishment for an English preacher in Holland. At his funeral in 1625 "many universitie professors & other eminent citizens were present," Dexter relates. His widow and children became members of the Dutch Church and so with many others were absorbed by the Dutch. From this fate a section of the party had saved themselves by timely departure, and so made history. They were the "Pilgrim Fathers" of the good ship *Mayflower,* and left Leyden on Friday, July 31, 1620. One of the number, Winslow, gave as one of the reasons for their departure the consideration: "how like we were to lose our language & our name of English[3]." Two other members, Brewer and Brewster, had commenced a printing business which Carleton, the English ambassador in succession to Winwood, was instructed to nip in the bud; for, as he said, "most of the Puritan books sent

---

[1] W. Bradford, *History of Plymouth Plantation.*
[2] Cit. M. Dexter, *The Pilgrims in Holland.*   [3] Cit. Dexter.

over of late days into England" hail from Dutch soil. This was the surreptitious source of "prohibited books to be vented underhand in his majesty's kingdoms." But the association of the "Pilgrim Fathers" with Holland is merely a characteristic episode in the growing relations between the two countries. The good King James, with characteristic fussiness, saw to it that England was represented at the celebrated Synod of Dort, whether the proceedings were intelligible to the English representatives or not.

It would be strictly outside our purpose to survey the crowded economic, political and social relations of the seventeenth century, but they are often a prelude to intellectual and cultural intercourse. The vicissitudes of that most important association known as the Merchant Adventurers were of the greatest significance in this direction. We have noted how it played a large part in establishing amicable relations with the Low Countries. On January 16, 1598, the Dutch delegates of the town of Middleburg, who had been sent to London to make proposals that would attract the Merchant Adventurers to their town, were entertained by Essex, who took them to a dramatic performance played before the Queen and her Court. Perhaps they may have seen Shakespeare on the boards! They had audience with Lord Robert Cecil and were interviewed by the Queen herself. In the general meeting of the Merchants, a delegate claimed that the English at Middleburg were looked upon as "bons voysins, aussi en communion de Religion d'Alliance et quasi de tout ce que dieu a départé a la société humaine." An Englishman, Mr Fletcher, rose and responded in Latin, for those were the days when neither English nor Dutch had acquired an international status[1].

The end of the sixteenth century was a notable period for closer relationship between England and Holland. It was a part of Elizabeth's policy to extend English trade in North Holland and divert it out of the sphere of the German Hansa. From the time of Henry VIII, Holland, the financial centre of Europe, was a sort of Bank of England, as the

---

[1] *Vide* C. te Lintum, *De Merchant Adventurers in de Nederlanden.*

lifelong activities of Sir Thomas Gresham illustrate so well. On both sides there was a desire to cultivate the best relations. By the "octrooi" of 1598 the States General granted the Fellowship substantial privileges which were the basis of many years of renewed and close relations.

Dutch towns vied with one another in offering English merchants the best terms. Embassies were despatched to England, considerable sums of money changed hands, the recipients being generally influential members of the Merchant Adventurers, an association that knew how to stimulate competitive bidding among the foreign towns for the coveted prize of their "court." Charles I, like his predecessor Edward III, who had used the wool staple in the Netherlands as a powerful persuasive, made political capital out of the influence of the company. In 1634 Rotterdam offered Charles the sum of £60,000, besides the usual bribes, if the Merchant Adventurers would only establish their headquarters there. No item was ignored. The Middleburg authorities contracted for the provision of a "large and adequate church." But the agreement of 1635-6 with Rotterdam may serve as a specimen of the remarkable concessions and advantages which the Rotterdamers were prepared to grant the English merchants, who had always been a favoured class. The article of agreement begins by stating the object of the city fathers in attracting this merchant company, viz. "the upkeep of the common trade, the advantage of the generality, and the maintenance and increase of the mutual friendship with the celebrated English nation[1]." We find that the members of the company were fully and adequately housed, their particular form of religion protected against the other English dissenting sects in the town, and a church was built specially for them. All these buildings and houses provided were kept in a proper state of repair at the public expense. Fuel, provisions, wine and beer were admitted duty free, a privilege which they were

[1] "Het onderhouden vande gemeyne commercie, het voordeel van onse gemeynte ende onderhoudinge ende vermeerderinge van de onderlinge vruntschap met de vermaerde Engelsche natie."

not slow to abuse and which cost the city thousands of pounds every year, as it was required by the States General to make good whatever duties had been relaxed in favour of the English. The Adventurers were protected from the competition of "entrelopers" and their ships were protected by Dutch men-of-war.

Wars interfered, contracts expired and the States General abolished some of the Adventurers' most cherished privileges (all of them in 1688); but Rotterdam remained one of the chief centres of English commerce in Holland. No less than three churches were required to accommodate the British colony there. The Adventurers relaxed their monastic discipline, and members, instead of living in barracks, lived with their wives and families amongst the inhabitants[1]. A large number of free English and Scottish merchants settled there. No wonder then that an English consul could write of Rotterdam: "many of its citizens speake good English[2]." "A long line of distinguished men served as ministers of the Scottish church which still stands in the town[3]." And so there was scarcely a town of any importance which did not have its English quarter, a source of wealth and prosperity to the citizens and therefore regarded as no small blessing. When in 1621 the Adventurers settled at Delft, it was solemnly recorded of the active Mr "Carlton" that "next to God he had contributed most towards getting the Court within Delft[4]." When the Fellowship was attacked by antagonistic Dutch manufacturers, especially from Amsterdam, they said in their defence that they had been "the sole authors of her welfare & prosperity" (Bruges); that they had found Antwerp "a poor fishing town" and had left it "the wonder and admiration of all the world." They reminded their critics that during the Spanish Terror they had shared the "afflictien" of the Dutch, and pointed out that

---

[1] In 1648 thirty-six members of the company are listed as living independently at Rotterdam with their families. This does not refer to the many other English and Scottish traders and visitors who lived there.

[2] G. N. Clarke, *N. Gids*, Oct. 1923.

[3] *Ibid. Vide* also W. Steven, *History of the Scottish Church at Rotterdam*.

[4] Soutendam, p. 27 (cit. Te Lintum).

while a century before there were only a few Dutch merchants of note doing business in London, "England was now full of prosperous Dutchmen" who had captured the English continental trade from other foreigners, so that it was the enterprise of the Adventurers that opened markets for the Dutch. In answer to these high claims, the Amsterdammers stated that the Dutch were letting in the Trojan horse, that the Adventurers were their direst competitors "to the decay and ruin of many inhabitants," objections which, with others, were stamped as "rotte calumnien," "practycque van den Satan" that would merely alienate the people from the English merchants. But this passage carries us into mid-century antagonisms. Perhaps the general sentiment of the opening years of the century is best expressed by the noble note on which Fynes Moryson closes his classic travels:

Therefore if perhaps the united Prouinces forgetting their old league with England and our late merit in defending their liberty, shall at any time resolue to have warre with England (which for the good of both Nations God forbid) then are such bloody fights at sea like to happen as former Ages neuer knew. Yet the course of those times whereof I write gaue small probability of any such euent like to happen, for many reasons combining our minds together. First the happy amity that hath beene time out of mind between our Nations. Next the bond of loue on our part towards those we haue preserued from bondage (!), and the like bond of their thankefulnesse towards us, which howsoeuer ambition may neglect or despise, yet neuer any nation was more obliged to another in that kind, and so long as the memory thereof can liue, it must needs quench all malice betweene us. . . . In generall good men on both sides are to wish the continuance of peace betweene England and these Prouinces, by which both commonwealths haue long had and may still haue unspeakable benefit, and that the rather because we neuer yet had warre but perpetual amity together, neither can any war proue more bloudy or mischieuous to either part, then that betweene ourselues. To conclude, happie be the makers, cursed the breakers of our peace.

And Fynes Moryson, for all his English prejudices, knew what he was saying. He had been well over his ground, knew many who were serving in the Low Countries, and had stood shoulder to shoulder with the men of the splendid

Dutch battalions that fought in Ireland under Mountjoy in Tyrone's rebellion. But soon enough there arose heads on which Moryson's curse could fall. Wars inevitably came. Three, of the most desperate and sanguinary character, fell within the space of twenty years. They were more or less deliberately provoked by the English whose piracy on the seas and impossible navigation claims had long irritated the Dutch, and the Dutch had much more to lose through a war than their rivals.

The English were, it seems, proud of their restored monarch, Charles II, and their contempt for the mere republic across the Channel knew no bounds. They would stop at nothing until their bellicose duke of York had beaten the Dutch, while at home the mob broke windows at the embassies and hated the Dutch as cordially as they despised the French, both of whom they were imitating in so many respects. Even into the Far East and West the conflict reverberated. The American colonies were captured from the Dutch by a ruse, the Amboyna incident embittered relations for generations; indeed, the struggle between Dutch and English abroad was as important as that of the principals at home, and in a sense is still lingering in South Africa to-day. It certainly appears as if the main points of contact were of the most painful and unfortunate kind. The wars left a literature of vituperation, in which Dryden, amongst many others, played an ignominiously conspicuous part, Mrs Aphra Behn seconding his efforts at the expense of her husband's people. Of course, this trick of abuse had been cultivated even before the wars. The Dutch were far too successful to escape the gibe of caricature, and literature was soon affected. Gascoigne, Marston, Glapthorne, William Haughton, Cyril Tourneur, Belchier, are among those who sharpened their wits' teeth on the Dutchman. As a picture of unredeemed boorishness, simple and often mischievous, he was made familiar to guffawing theatre-goers. The very word Dutch carried a reproach. "All the qualities which the Englishman's philosophy of life made him despise, he called Dutch," Professor

Huisinga has said. The extraordinary virulence of this satire is indicated by its tenacity. In the mid-eighteenth century we find Goldsmith still continuing the tradition even in the very words which he was adroitly plagiarizing from a Dutchman, and epithets coined centuries ago have persisted up to the present day. That he was often brought in with the German under the sobriquet *Hans* did not tend to rehabilitate the Dutchman's reputation. Was it not common belief that the demesne of dulness and of necromancy was Germany? Germanic culture had not yet become self-assertive, or impressive as a harmonious unity. Germans, Dutch and English alike looked to France and each was suspicious or contemptuous of the other's pretensions to refinement. Cousinship merely helped to sap mutual confidence in this matter. "The Englishman saw in us, really his nearest relations, all the traits he hated to see in himself," observes Professor Huisinga. Yet, besides the lower masses, equally barbarous, both nations were strongly marked out by their strong, freedom-loving bourgeoisie, with a cream of aristocratic families; each had a healthy love for adventure abroad, and a special turn for commerce and navigation. In religion the sterner aspects appealed to both nations; in art, especially in literature in England, and in both literature and painting in Holland, solid strength, daring imagination and originality rather than Gallic refinement and neatness were equally characteristic of both; this one might expect from the racial, linguistic and cultural affinity. It is not strange, then, that a sense of deeper unity was at various periods freshly realized.

Even wars often seem to resemble the quarrels of lovers, and are often a prelude to periods of closer understanding. They seem to act, indeed, as the most telling advertisements nations have at their disposal. Few periods in English literature are more French than the age of Marlborough. In vain Addison makes fun of the fashion-doll from Paris when his country is at war with France. Similarly, at no period did Anglomania run higher in France than when, in the latter half of the eighteenth century, she and England were at each other's throats.

The Anglo-Dutch wars of the seventeenth century seem, at this distance, to have been much on the surface of things. Beneath the surface there were better and more permanent forces at work. Each country became magnified in the other's sight, was more closely scrutinized, and when the animosities of the wars passed, place was made for a fresher appreciation of each other's values. That British emulation flowed over into the sense of "Carthago delenda est" was, to say the least, unfortunate; but imitation was, in this case too, a sincere tribute paid by England to the genius of the Dutch.

In fact, "one of the greater achievements of seventeenth-century England was the effort to overtake the Dutch[1]."

It is not yet sufficiently well known or understood that one of the great periods of change and development in our history took its direction, in many most important respects, from the impulse given by the Dutch. The period is that which runs from about the accession of Queen Elizabeth to about the death of Queen Anne[2].

Within this period lies a record of brilliant achievement by Holland, in literature, learning, art, science, politics and economics, that will remain as amazing to the modern world as it dazzled the contemporaries of Milton. The distich in the first English history of the Low Countries quaintly expresses the impression created on the English mind,

> The muses, Neptune, Mars and Mercury,
> Haue sett their rests up in Low Germany[3].

It did not take long for a vigorous pamphlet literature to point out how far the Dutch were ahead and in how many desirable points they ought to be imitated.

Rayleigh was responsible for some of these writings. Histories and descriptions of the Netherlands grew increasingly numerous, all pointing the inevitable moral. Fynes Moryson tries to explain the problem of Dutch success,

---

[1] G. N. Clarke, *N. Gids*, Oct. 1923.   [2] *Ibid.*   [3] *Ibid.*

but gives it up, to speak of less strenuous matters, such as plays and players.

As there be in my opinion more Playes in London than in all partes of the Worlde I haue seene, so doe theese players or Comedians excell all other in the worlde. Whereof I haue seene some stragling broken companyes that passed into Netherland & Germany, followed by the people from one towne to another though they understoode not their wordes only to see theire action, yea marchants at Fayres bragged more to haue seene them, then of the good marketts they made[1].

Dutch acting he considered very poor:

But for Comedians they little practise that arte, and are the poorest actours that can be imagined as my selfe did see when the Citty of Getrudenberg being taken by them from the Span-yards they made bonsfyers and publikely at Leyden represented that action in a play, so rudely as the poore artizans of England would haue bothe pened and acted it much better. So as at the same tyme when some Cast Players of England came into those partes, the people not understanding what they sayd, only for their action followed them with wonderfull concourse, yea many young virgins fell in loue with some of the players, and followed them from Citty to Citty till the magistrates were forced to forbid them to play any more[2].

It would indeed have been strange if the tremendous energy of English drama had not overflowed to the continent. It did, and acted as a powerful educative force in the domain of the theatre[3]. Nor was its influence slow to penetrate through to Dutch literary drama. The new romantic school of dramatists in England was represented in Holland by a figure like Theodore Rodenburgh, who wrote some twenty-seven plays "in imitation of foreigners other than the Classical writers[4]." He was an emissary of the Dutch govern-ment to London and probably came into personal contact with Shakespeare and the English school. He introduced English scenes and characters into his plays, revealed

---

[1] *Itinerary*, chap. 2, "Of England," p. 476, ed. Chas. Hughes.
[2] *Op. cit.* p. 373.
[3] Cp., e.g., H. E. Moltzer, *Shakespeare's Invloed op het Nederlandsch Tooneel*.
[4] *Tijdschrift*, vol. XXIV, p. 4, 1905.

acquaintance with *Macbeth* and *Hamlet*[1], gave a free version of Sidney's *Apologie for Poetrie*, and translated Cyril Tourneur's *Revengers Tragedy*. With him and Coster, who wrote in similar vein, "a wholly new element enters our literary culture: the Spanish-English romanticism ...[2]." Voskuyl utilized Greene's *Pandosto* for a tragedy, and may have been influenced by *Antony and Cleopatra* in another work. In fact, "To utilize English sources at that time meant imitation of Rodenburgh," says W. Zuidema[3]. Unfortunately Rodenburgh has little real literary value and speedily reacted to the Spanish drama which was beginning to have great vogue in Holland. But there were other Dutch literary spirits who came into touch with Elizabethan literature and writers. Starter, who lived in England for a time, wrote a play on the same subject as that of *Much Ado About Nothing*, and his fine songs are frequently drawn from English sources[4]. There were plays such as the *Jood van Malta* (1645) by Silles, J. Bara's *Herstelde Vorst*, Brandt's *Veinzende Torquatus*, that may possibly reflect the influence of Marlowe and of *Hamlet*. But an undoubted imitation of *Titus Andronicus* is Jan Vos's *Aran en Titus*. It shocked and pleased the Dutch public immensely, acquired a European reputation and remained a popular play for over a century. On the whole it reflects the truth about English romantic drama in Holland, namely that it was a failure artistically. This play is more of a shambles than its original, and excels it in its stream of profanity. It illustrates, too, the important fact that English influences in Dutch literature still appeared sporadically and in isolated cases, so that we cannot speak of any continued pressure of new ideas from England in Dutch literature of this time. Nevertheless, the isolated cases were becoming increasingly common. Practically all the great literary figures of Holland's "Golden Age" visited England, or exhibit traces of acquaintance with English culture and literature. Jacob Cats, the great Dutch house-

---

[1] *Tijdschrift*, vol. XXI, p. 1, W. Zuidema.
[2] J. Prinsen, *Handboek Ned. Let. Geschied.* p. 288.
[3] *Tijdschrift*, vol. XIV, p. 75.
[4] *Vide Tijdschrift*, vol. XXI.

hold poet, visited England in 1600, going especially to Cambridge and Oxford. The brilliant Constantyn Huygens paid this country several visits. "He translated the now forgotten poems of a certain Dr Donne[1]" (*sic!*) whose influence has been detected in some of Huygens's similarly "metaphysical" poetry.

"I esteem it an honour," said Huygens, "thus to lisp the language of so great a man and it will afford me considerable gratification should my bold example prompt abler penmen to communicate to my countrymen an extensive participation in those numerous English literary riches which in reverential awe, I have not presumed to touch[2]."

This is a note more common to a later century, and Huygens is certainly an interesting forerunner of later Dutch admirers and imitators of English literature. With Huygens, as in the sphere of the drama, it is unfortunate that the kind of influence was as little salutary as the choice of models was discriminating, a fact which indicates, of course, that English literature was not properly appreciated. Vondel did not know English but manifested his interest in English history and affairs by a vigorous part in Anglo-Dutch polemics, and by works like *Maria Stuart*, which keeps as close to Camden, well known in Holland, as Shakespeare keeps to some of his sources. With the name of Vondel that of Milton has been associated. And indeed in the figure of Milton, Anglo-Dutch cultural relations of the mid-seventeenth century are crystallized. It will be sufficient here to recall his friendship with the learned Dutch scholar Franciscus Junius, editor of Caedmon, upon whom Milton probably drew; his acquaintance with and admiration for the great Grotius, admirer of Vondel; and his controversies with two professors in Holland which gave him a great European reputation. To this must be added Milton's knowledge of the Dutch language and of Dutch theology—a point which has apparently not been properly examined—his association with many Dutchmen in London privately, as well as in an

---

[1] N. J. van Kampen, *The influence of English literature upon Dutch literature*, Amsterdam, 1833.   [2] *Ibid.* p. 70.

official capacity, and his connections with the Dutch book-sellers. As to Vondel, it is highly improbable that Milton would have manifested no interest in the history and the work of that great man. Vondel was the most prominent literary man of his day in Holland, as troublesome to the State authorities there as Milton was to the party opposed to him in England. He had been publicly honoured as Holland's greatest poet, while the nature and the subject of his greatest work have such close correspondence with the subject Milton was contemplating, that only the most direct evidence to the contrary must be allowed to clear away the extreme likelihood that Milton was well acquainted with the *Lucifer* and the other biblical plays before he indited *Paradise Lost*. That the evidence provides any *proof* of this cannot be claimed, however, and the question of the indebtedness of the poet of *Paradise Lost* to that of *Lucifer* seems to belong rather to the realm of opinion[1], than to the sphere of scientific literary research. On the other hand, do not critics such as Moolhuizen[2], who, when he finds that "in generalities but not in particulars Milton and Vondel are in agreement," considers his case proved that no influence passed over from Vondel to Milton, expect too much? Surely Milton was not the type of man or artist to have descended to mere verbatim plagiarism at any length.

In religious and ecclesiastical matters there had, of course, been close sympathy for a long time, but the Restoration with its consolidation of Episcopalianism and the suppression of Presbyterianism marked a definite turning-point away from previous association with Dutch forms of worship, especially Anabaptism and Arminianism. But this was a period so "fruitful in religions," as Dryden said the Dutch were, that many of the different groups, such as the English and Scottish groups in Amsterdam, maintained correspondence with sympathetic Dutch groups.

[1] That of Sir Edmund Gosse, who believes that Milton duly used Vondel, being almost authoritative.
[2] Moolhuizen, J. J., *Vondels Lucifer en Miltons Verloren Paradijs* ('s Gravenhage, 1895).

An important field of cultural association was that of language. Hadrianus Junius, the lexicographer upon whom the mantle of Erasmus settled, long represented Dutch scholarship in England, and it was only fitting that Franciscus Junius should have been the man to give great impetus to English studies. After Richard Verstegan, the Anglo-Dutchman, had in his well-known *Restitution of Decayed Intelligence* made a spirited appeal to Englishmen to honour and study the origins of the language, some increased interest had been taken, especially at Cambridge. But Junius's edition of Caedmon and of the unique Gothic Silver Codex, *with a parallel in Old English,* inaugurated a new epoch for Germanic studies and comparative philology. It led for one thing to the Oxford school of Old English studies, of which George Hickes was the central figure. Also, Junius's important gift of types to the Oxford press is but one famous instance of the great moulding influence exerted by the Netherlands in the history of English typography. But not only were Dutchmen pioneers in the study of English philology and antiquities, but they also supplemented the spoken language, exchanges being numerous and useful. English borrowings from Dutch took place mainly up to the eighteenth century, while Dutch borrowings are more recent as a rule, the processes thus reflecting the general flow of other cultural relations.

The full contribution of Dutch[1] to the English language has yet to be assessed, but the most recent researches and especially the rich but necessarily scattered collection of the *Oxford Dictionary* bear out the conviction of older scholars that English has been enormously enriched from this source. In the language of the sea alone English would be rendered well-nigh impotent if robbed of its borrowings from Dutch;

[1] It is to be wished that Englishmen will abstain from the ambiguous nineteenth-century usage of Low German to mean New Dutch. To speak of English everywhere as Low German, denying it an autonomous name, would be as true but of as little practical value. If Low German, however, be used to denote ill-defined forms of Germanic speech, such as the supposed *lingua franca* of the North Sea in past centuries outside Frisian and Dutch— the educated speech of the Southern and Northern Netherlands—the term may serve some purpose in addition to its purely philological use to denote a category of languages.

furthermore, military terms, words relating to the textile trade, to engineering, building, art, science, cant words and more familiar words such as *boy* (probably) help to swell the debt of English to Dutch and give evidence of long and close intercourse, "as intimate as any we ever had with foreigners before the days of railways and steam navigation[1]."

In architecture, too, this is borne out. From the reign of Elizabeth onwards no foreign influence "is more persistent than the Dutch[2]." As in so many other things, "it was the fashion in England to adopt Dutch ideas and methods because it was seen that they invariably led to success[3]." In the literature as well as the practice of architecture Dutch ideas percolated into the most intimate domestic architecture. Dutch works on the subject, well produced as they were, were almost authoritative in England. From Dutch sources, Wren drew much of his versatility.

Politically, England and Holland, in spite of the wars, were in reality drawing closer together. We need only refer to the alliance of the houses of Orange and Stuart[4], which for over a century and a half had an incalculable effect in shaping the foreign policies of their countries to become at one time identical under William III. Cromwell himself had, according to the romancing *Boekzaal*, fought in Holland and studied at Leyden where "his quickness in the profound sciences brought him into the great respect of the professors," and where he was known as the "scholarly soldier"; therefore, also, "we Hollanders, renowned neighbours of the Britons, have a prior claim above all other nations on the face of the earth outside England, to have a good knowledge of Cromwell's life and deeds." Commonwealth days were, of course, not altogether happy for Anglo-Dutch associations, and neither was the régime of Charles II, although the Orange-Stuart alliance was once more cemented

---

[1] G. Clarke, *loc. cit.*

[2] A. Stratton, *Dutch influence on the architecture of Sir C. Wren*, Sir Christopher Wren Memorial Volume, 1923.

[3] *Ibid.*

[4] By the marriage of William II of Holland with Maria Stuart, eldest daughter of Charles I.

by the marriage of William III with Mary in 1676. But
William soon found occasion to complain of the "in
souffrable" conduct of his uncle-in-law. Still, the people of
Holland were on the whole strongly anti-French and pro-
English, and when later the revocation of the Edict of Nantes
brought clarity into the European atmosphere, there was once
more the old cleavage as in the days of the Spanish Terror,
and Protestant Europe realized that it was threatened with a
French Terror. William's plans against Louis received more
liberal support than before, and events in England moved
swiftly to their inevitable culmination. The liveliest interest
soon grew into enthusiasm in Holland, and the States,
giving way, supported William's adventure. The last decade
before 1688 had been anxious years for the Dutch with the
enemy battering at their doors and England deserting her,
and turning Catholic as it was feared; *England Exhausted
and her kings ruled by the Popes of Rome* runs the title of one
Dutch pamphlet[1]. Another deplores that she has given no
heed to the good counsel of her "blood-relations[2]." Pam-
phleteers became increasingly active and soon their strain
was: *The Salvation of Holland situated in her Union with England*[3] (1689), and *The Happy Union of England and Holland*[4].
In the words of the writer: "The English, weary'd with their
sufferings, privately call'd in the Prince of Orange; and that
Great Hero was received into the Island as their Tutelar
Angel, but with so much order and unanimity that the
sudden Commotion was taken rather for a public Rejoycing
than a Rebellious Insurrection." Near Newton, Huygens,
William's secretary, remarked the women and girls smoking
pipes, but shouting: "God bless you!" all along the way[5].
In Holland, says the *Historical Mercury* for 1688, it was
"impossible to express how greedy the People were after
news, and notwithstanding other considerable actions fall
out in other places which merit to be taken notice of,
all their curiosity runs after the news from England."

[1] 1688.
[2] *Engelants lang voorzeyde en tegenwoordig overkoomende Quaal* 1688.
[3] Amsterdam.   [4] London, May 1689.
[5] Journal.

The *Happy Union* writer saw only the greatest possible advantage in the "good correspondence" and "most strait alliance" of the two countries. "The Arts and Sciences," too, he said, "will flourish"; for the King and Queen "are so much the favourers of Learned Men."

Poets in each country acclaimed the happy consummation. Prominent among them were the best Dutch poet of the period, Rotgans, who evinced a lively interest in England, and "Mat" Prior, a well-known figure in social circles in Holland.

But however gladly the union may have been acclaimed, it did not turn out to be quite so "happy." There were Tory die-hards and other irreconcilables and grumblers, who invited well-merited castigation at the hands of Defoe[1], the confidant and enthusiastic supporter of King William. There were squabbles about place at Court and office in the government. William, incessantly busy planning to meet the opposition at home and abroad, fretted and was soon unpopular. The new constitution had still to justify its existence. The nation was disturbed and distraught by faction, and in the ceaseless spinning of petty intrigue there seemed little time or inclination for the cultivation of literary sympathies between the two nations.

Indeed, no time seems to have been more unfavourable to literature than those years of William III, if we except the scintillating coarse comedy of manners, for which this age was well suited. Temperamentally the period was delivered over to politicians, intellectuals and virtuosi. There is no other time when English culture flowered into so much science and philosophy and so little *belles lettres*. Now Hobbes was strenuously controverted, the darkness of Spinoza explored, and Descartes, before he was much known, superseded by the flourishing empirical English school. Now was the vogue of Cudworth and the English metaphysical and intellectual schools of philosophy whose bequest is prominent in the rationalism of the eighteenth century. It was the time that produced Locke, Shaftesbury and Mandeville, the three most representative writers of the epoch; but

[1] *True Born Englishman.*

it was above all the time of Boyle, Halley, Newton, Wren and the Royal Society. But if speculation dwarfed the fancy, the social atmosphere in upper circles gave the *coup de grâce*. Of this we have much testimony in the journal of Huygens, William's secretary and son of the great writer and brilliant young diplomat who had translated Donne. The remarkably full picture there given is not pleasing. Endless scandal, brutal infidelity, suspicion, slander, love and political intrigue appear to have been the order of the day, and altogether the Court atmosphere was well fitted to freeze out even the French dalliance of ode and sonnet.

Intellectual and artistic interests were cultivated, but hardly of the literary kind. Huygens does indeed go to the theatre to see "an old piece," *Love in a Tub*, and goes to the "comédie" in Covent Garden to see *Henry II*, but complains that he can neither hear nor understand the actors well—and the best seats cost a crown. Pictures and science are his *forte*. Readers of Evelyn and Pepys will know what a fashionable craze Dutch paintings had become in England. Huygens seems to have been for ever buying and arranging pictures, for William had made him chiefly responsible for hanging the walls at Kensington and Hampton Court. The picture of Anglo-Dutch society of the time is completed by the endless chocolate and sack drinkings, dinners and entertainments, the visits to picture sales and bookstalls; but Huygens, it seems, purchased the *Philosophical Transactions* mostly, the writings of le Clerc, or books on England, so that he appeared to be learning English geography and history at least. His great friend was Dr Stanley, chaplain to the Princess Maria. On one occasion he brings Huygens a copy of Boyle's *History of the Air*, which Huygens "instantly" orders to be bought in the "Citty." With Stanley he visits the Royal Society where he is "courteously entertained" and hears "Dr Hayley" read a paper. He has a "glass" made in Holland for the Society, and seems very proud of its size and finish. He entertained many society notables both in London and at the Hague, saw much of Burnet, and on one occasion records that he had a long conversation with Wren, a *persona grata* at Hampton Court. When in London he was visited several times by his brother Christiaan, the celebrated scientist with whom Newton was on very intimate terms and whom he rightly considered to be one of the "leading geometers of the age[1]." Huygens considered English roads abominable, English standards of cleanliness not high, but English scenery beautiful. He visited Vossius at Windsor, finding him in the library. The old scholar complained to him of the small civility and spitefulness of the English, with whom he mixed but little. Huygens and other members of the Dutch society had their sons educated at Leyden and not at Oxford or Cambridge; but he engaged a master to teach his son English.

The immediate literary associations resulting from the political association were, we may say, almost negligible. But there was a bustling intercourse in science and philosophy. The Royal Society had already acquired an international reputation, thanks chiefly to Harvey and Boyle. Sprat[2] says proudly that the Society put England at the "head of a philosophic league above all countries in Europe[3]." There was great benefit in its "universal correspondence and communications[4]," and in the Low Countries particularly "their interest and reputation had been established by the Friendship of some of their chief learned men and principally of Hugenius... and this learned correspondence is still continued even at this present time in the Breach between our Countries[5]." Amongst these Dutch correspondents was the famous Antonie van Leeuwenhoek, discoverer of the microscope, one of the most sensational discoveries of the century. In February 1692 the *Lettre Historique* records the death of Boyle, *célèbre physicien*, "Je vous avoue que tout ce qu'il a fait me charme," and in spite of the wretched style,

je ne saurois me lasser de lire ses Livres. Les personnes de ce caractère ne devroient jamais mourir....Vous savez qu'ordinairement les Physiciens non plus que les médecins n'ont pas

---

[1] *Principia.*　　　　　　　[2] *History of the Royal Society.*
[3] *Ibid.* p. 113.　　　　　　[4] *Ibid.* p. 424.
[5] *Ibid.* p. 127. Sprat wrote while the Dutch war was in progress.

beaucoup de Religion. Il sembloit qu'il n'avoit étudié la Nature, que pour admirer et adorer celui qui en est l'Auteur.

The writer of the report is a French correspondent from London. He was probably a refugee, for many of them meritoriously occupied themselves with writing, and it is largely through the literary activities of these men that English learning and literature were so widely advertised. Coming to England, they were surprised to find Descartes and Calvin ignored, and a new scientific movement flourishing, and long before Voltaire, as Sayous relates, "ils avaient entrepris de faire connaître sur le continent les travaux et le génie particulier des savants de la Grande-Bretagne[1]." Sayous appears to be writing of the year 1710; but what he says is equally true of the year 1690, and it is within these twenty years especially that continental culture became more and more infiltrated with English ideas, and that the basis was laid for a further burst of, one might almost say, propagandist activity during the time of Van Effen and after. We will not discuss here the inestimable benefits European civilization received from the refugees[2]. In trade, science, philosophy and rhetoric, their influence was to the highest degree stimulating. The names of Descartes, Bayle, le Clerc, Rapin de Thoryas, Abbadie, St-Evremont, and many others may be recalled. In Holland, "the great ark of the refugees," to use Bayle's *bon mot*, the exiles were elevated to high military, professional and other posts; people flocked to hear the eloquent Saurin preach, and "towns vied with each other in generosity[3]." In England, too, many found a new home and sphere of activities. M. Justel, "one of the best read men in Europe," became the royal librarian, and a large number of capable literary men applied themselves to literary work, and, what is of particular importance to our study, maintained a constant correspondence with their brethren in Holland, forming a double link between the already closely allied countries. The

---

[1] *Le Dix-Huitième Siècle à l'Étranger*, p. 14.
[2] *Vide* C. Weiss, *History of the French Protestant Refugees*; Sayous, *op. cit.*
[3] C. Weiss, *op. cit.*

age soon became one of newspapers and literary journals, and a stream of correspondence passed between London and Amsterdam, especially after Bayle had established his pioneer *Nouvelles de la République des Lettres*, which, with its significantly cosmopolitan title, inspired the imitation and policy of many subsequent journalists. "The Republic of Letters," said he, is "la plus libre et la plus indépendante de toutes les Sociétés[1]." He was inspired with the idea of the catholicity of art, knowledge and taste, and stimulated investigation by his example in demonstrating the need for revised judgments in many things. Coming to Holland he was surprised to find that although it was "signalée par la culture des beaux-arts aussi bien que par ses Victoires et par son commerce," it had not yet taken part in the new journalism, for certainly there were many "habiles gens," more booksellers than anywhere else in the world, and above all the Dutch press enjoyed an ,unparalleled freedom. "Assurément si Milton eût vécu dans ces Provinces, il ne se fût pas avisé de faire un Livre de *Typographia Liberanda*; car il n'eût point senti que les choses y fussent dans la servitude à cet égard[2]." In March 1684 appeared this "erste populär wissenschaftliche Zeitschrift," as Betz[3] terms it. It was received "avec un applaudissement universel.... Tout le monde s'empressoit à le lire," declared Desmaizeau[4]. Bayle soon acquired an extended European reputation. He was honoured perhaps above any other man in Europe[5]. His dictionary was a standard work up to late in the century. Addison, "sent abroad by King William and taken off from all other pursuits in order to be employed in his service[6]," found himself at Rotterdam in the early years of the century and wrote: "I have endeavoured to find out Mr Baile, but he is at present shut up in his study[7]." Tonson has told us that he seldom called upon Addison without finding Bayle's Dictionary open upon the table[8].

[1] *Œuvres Div.* II, p. 203. [2] Preface, *Nouv. de la Rép. des Let.*
[3] *Pierre Bayle und die Nouvelles de la Rép. des Let.* (Zürich 1896).
[4] Introduction, *Dictionnaire*. [5] *Vide* Life by Desmaizeau.
[6] Letter to Halifax, dated Oct. 17, 1714. Egerton, 1971-4, Brit. Mus.
[7] Add. MSS. 22908, Brit. Mus. [8] R. Phillips, *Addisoniana*.

"The *Nouvelle Lit.* procured Mr Bayle the esteem not only of particular persons but likewise of several illustrious societies.... The Royal Society in England wrote him a letter" wherein they expressed the desire of holding "a fixed and certain correspondence" with him from which "they might reap common advantages." Bayle was not a man of literary aesthetic tastes[1], so there is extremely little in his *Nouvelles* that has any relation to fine literature. But he was one of the first to direct the attention of the world to England, and give her that reputation for solid parts that made her so famous in the eighteenth century.

"Il est certain qu'il n'y a point de philosophes qui s'élèvent autant que les Anglois vers la Région de la vérité la plus abstracte.... Par cette profondeur de génie qui est ordinaire à leur nation, ils aiment les méthodes profondes, abstruses, recherchées," he said[2], agreeing with P. Rapin. Discussing a batch of English philosophical works which had then recently appeared, he expressed admiration for "cette profondeur & cette forte abstraction qui distingue les Écrivains d'Angleterre[3]." Cudworth is prominent among these. Boyle and Wallis of Oxford appeared frequently in the *Nouvelles*. "L'illustre M. Boile à qui l'on est obligé de tant de rares découvertes," wrote Bayle. Books of travel, such as Wood's description of England, are commended, Royal Society publications are not missed, and books of religious controversy in which, as he says[4], England had lately begun to abound, are regularly noticed.

After four years, the work was undertaken by Basnage de Beauval as *Histoire des Ouvrages des Scavants*. He, who formed with Bayle and le Clerc a "Triumvirat des werdenden internationalen Journalismus," as Betz has it, was "schöngeistig angelegt und hat Sinn für die Litteratur seiner eigenen Heimat und der fremden Länder, besonders Englands. Er bringt inhaltreiche Studien über Hobbes, Locke, etc. ebenso wie über Miltons letzte dichterische

---

[1] *Vide* also H. E. Smith, *The literary criticism of Pierre Bayle.*
[2] *Nouv. de la Rép. des Let.* Dec. 1685.
[3] *Ibid.* Dec. 1685.   [4] *Ibid.* Sept. 1686.

Werke von denen er mit Wärme spricht[1]." These men had a powerful influence in directing European thought and were at the same time important intermediaries between England and the continent. But besides them and their fellow-journalists, there were other famous intermediaries, among whom Sir William Temple, Burnet, John Locke, the Earl of Shaftesbury, Bernard Mandeville and William Sewell may be specially named.

The personality and writings of Sir William Temple appear to have had a peculiar charm for the Dutch, partly perhaps because they saw in him a friend and possible protector. It was he that urged and helped to arrange the match between William of Orange and Mary; it was he who cleverly manœuvred the States into entering upon the Triple Alliance in 1665. "It was impossible," wrote de Witt to the Earl of Arlington, "to send a minister of Greater capacity or more proper for the Temper or Genius of this Nation than Sir Wm Temple," while the States General wrote to Charles: "If your Majesty continues to make use of such Ministers the knot will grow too fast ever to be untyed[2]." The alliance, says Sir William, was "received with incredible joy and applause among them[3]." But he held that the Dutch had made a fatal mistake in making an alliance with England "without engaging a Confidence and Friendship" with her; so when the French war came, the Dutch made a poor stand; for "it was the name of England joining against them that broke their hearts[4]." Temple's little book on the Netherlands long remained a classic, and from its numerous editions on both sides of the Channel, and from the enthusiasm which, like the rest of his works, it excited amongst the reviewers, we gather that it was very widely read. "What we know of their Oeconomy and Constitution with any certainty has been chiefly owing to Sir William Temple," observed Mandeville[5]. Sixty years after Van Effen, the Addison of Holland, writing in the *Hollandsche Spectator*[6]

---

[1] *Op. cit.* p. 51.   [2] Introduction, *Works*, ed. Swift.
[3] *Observations on...the United Provinces of the Netherlands*, 1672.
[4] *Ibid.*   [5] *Fable of the Bees*, p. 168.   [6] No. 106.

of a recent book on the Netherlands, remarks: "The observations of the acute and statesmanlike Sir William Temple on the State of the United Dutch Provinces, have rightly made us and our countrymen eager for these sort of writings." Le Clerc remarked in the *Bibliothèque Choisie* that the *Observations* have been "deservedly received with an universal approbation[1]." As the book is one of the few literary products of this kind of geographical writing, and interpreted Holland and the Dutch to a wide audience at home and abroad, it is necessary to glance at it here.

He observes in the Preface, "how ignorant we were generally in the affairs and constitutions of a country so much in our eye, the common road of our travels as well as the subject of our talk; and which we have been of late not only curious, but concerned to know." The *Observations* are a mixture of high praises and severe censures, and altogether they represent many popular views, and at the same time the best he could do for the Dutch in the eyes of his violently prejudiced countrymen.

"The State of Holland in point both of riches and strength is the most prodigious growth that has been seen in the world," he begins. Amsterdam is "the most frequented Haven of the World" and its banks "the depository of Europe." "It is evident to those who have read the most and travel'd farthest, that no country can be found either in this present Age or upon Record of any Story, where so vast a Trade has been managed as in the narrow compass of the Four Maritime Provinces of this Commonwealth." The Dutch are "the common Carriers of the World." Such prosperity he ascribed to "the vast confluence of people" from abroad and the great influx of French refugees (and Temple wrote before the greater trek of 1685).

From all parts there had been a steady stream of exiles throughout the century. "It is not to be credited what numbers of disaffected persons come dayly out of England into this country. They have settled at Rotterdam an Independent Anabaptist and Quakers Church & doe hire

---

[1] Theobald's translation, 1718.

the best houses and have great bills of exchange come over from England to them," Sir George Downing had written to Clarendon[1].

As to relations with England, "the greatest [interest] they have in the world is to preserve and encrease their alliance with us." "The youth of the upper and educated classes travel chiefly into England and France" to complete their liberal education and "make them fit for the service of their country." One of the causes that influenced the Dutch to adopt the "Evangelical Religion" is given as "the great commerce and continual intercourse with England[2]." He extolled their tolerance. "In this Commonwealth no man having any reason to complain of oppression in Conscience...men live together like Citizens of the World associated by the common ties of Humanity."

This pleased Van Effen mightily, who writes a *Spectator* number[3] on this text[4].

Temple greatly admired the magnificence of their public works and hospitals, "that are in every man's curiosity & talk that travels their Countrey." "Charity seems to be very National among them," he observes, and tells of the old sea-dog at the home for disabled seamen at "Enchusyen" who enthralled him with his "plain stories of his Fifty Years' Voyages and Adventures."

He admired their government: "Though perhaps the Nation generally be not wise, yet the Government is, because it is composed of the wisest of the Nation," and although they have always had a Head, it has always been "a Head subordinate to their laws & customs and to the Sovereign Power of the State." And this statement had more significance before 1688 than it has to-day. In fact

---

[1] T. H. Lister, *Life of Clarendon*, vol. III, p. 139.
[2] Chap. 5, *Observations*.   [3] *Holl. Spect.* no. 79.
[4] "The renowned Knight, Temple, one of the wisest Britons of his century, praises nothing in the praiseworthy conduct of our Commonweal so much as the manner in which the Government deals with the Clergy to whom they show all possible honour and favour, though on the other hand they take care, with the greatest vigilance, that these remain within the pale of their duty....It is not possible that anyone...will not append his seal to this sentiment of that great statesman...."

there can be little doubt but that the example of the Dutch in this respect must have exerted a constant influence upon English constitutional experiments from Charles I to William III.

Sir Thomas Overbury, who had made his *Observations* in 1609, had expressed admiration for the Dutch form of government: "they still retaine that signe of a commonwealth yet uncorrupted...."

Temple admired their sobriety, being greatly struck with "the simplicity & modesty of the magistrates in their way of living," no one in public ever exceeding "the common frugal popular air." The Dutch are "the Great masters of the Indian Spices & of Persian silks; but they wear plain woollen"; "they furnish infinite luxury which they never practise," and are a standing refutation of the maxim "current in our modern politics" that "Encouragement of Excess and Luxury if employed in the consumption of Native commodities is of advantage to trade." This is a highly interesting remark which proves that the thesis Mandeville was to expound later was not so novel and advanced as is commonly thought.

In spite of all this praise, Temple can remark with conventional British prejudice: "These speculations may perhaps a little lessen the common wonder how we should meet with in one Nation so little show of Parts & Wit & so great evidence of Wisdom & Prudence." With naïve psychology he analyses the Dutch character. It is "cold & heavy" and not "ingenious enough to furnish a pleasant or agreeable Conversation." Their "plain downright sense" is as a "hatchet" to the "razor" of true wit. Their tempers are not "warm enough to Love." "This is talkt of sometimes among the younger men but as a thing they have heard of rather than felt." When the country people are too honest and independent to accept gratuities, it is because they are too "dull & slow of understanding." The honesty of the merchants, "the best dealers in the World," does not proceed from a "principle of Morality" but purely from "the necessity of Trade." Their "vaunted cleanliness" is simply a necessity proceeding from their situation in a boggy country and murky climate. Even the spleen "is a disease too refined for this Countrey and people." But Temple also saw the real weakness of their culture:

They strive to imitate the French in their mien, their clothes, their way of Talk, of Eating, of Gallantry or Debauchery, and are in my opinion, something worse than they would be by affecting to be better than they need; making sometimes but ill Copies whereas they might be good Originals by refining or improving the Customs & Virtues proper to their own Countrey & Climate.

The Dutch had evidently not changed in this respect since Fynes Moryson wrote[1]:

The French toung which most of the inhabitants by education learne to speak as naturally as the vulgar, besydes that many of them speake the English, Italyn & other languages of nations with whome they traffique as there is almost no place in the world where they trade not....The Netherlanders so much assert the sweetness and alacrity of the French toung, as they prefer it before their owne vulgar language....and by reason of the Flemings generall skill in strang languages, strangers may passe & trade among them though they cannot speake a worde of the vulgar toung.

The essay *Of Poetry* and other writings of Temple were well known and soon translated and must at least have helped to introduce the continental public to the great names of English poetry[2].

The labours of Burnet as an intermediary were as conspicuous and effective as those of Temple. Burnet must be held to have had great influence in promoting the invasion of England by William, whose close confidant and adviser

---

[1] *Itinerary*, p. 377.

[2] Temple's condemnation of the "French Wits or Pretenders" and their fuss about rules was refreshing, if not provocative: "The Truth is there is something in the Genius of Poetry too libertine to be confined to so many Rules, and whoever goes about to subject it to such Constraint loses both its Spirit and Grace which are ever Native and never learnt even of the best masters." It must have seemed an astounding claim that English dramatic poetry has "excelled both the modern and the antient" owing to its quality of humour, "Shakespeare being the first that opened this Vein upon our Stage." Continental readers must have wondered who this personage was at whose tragedies Sir William was not surprised to see so many cry, "and with downright Tears" too.

he was in those critical months of 1688. He had married a Dutch wife and so further became a typical figure of the Anglo-Dutch society of the time. The effect and influence of his works on the minds of contemporaries were tremendous and no name was more conspicuous in the European reviews. It must be emphasized, too, that in the writings of Burnet and Temple the continental public were getting a fair sample of first-rate English prose before the *Spectator*. Locke and the Shaftesburys are perhaps even more illustrious figures in Anglo-Dutch intercourse. When Locke died, his friend le Clerc wrote a moving *Éloge Historique*[1] which was soon translated into English. With Lord Shaftesbury (Dryden's Achitophel) he had taken refuge in Amsterdam. "C'est un honneur pour cette Province & pour la ville d'Amsterdam...d'avoir reçué & d'avoir protégé un si illustre Refugié," said le Clerc in reference to Shaftesbury.

Les descendans de ce Seigneur en conservent une mémoire pleine de reconnaissance. Comme Mr le Comte de Shaftesbury, son petit fils[2], me l'a témoigné plus d'une fois. Puisse cette ville être l'asyle assuré de l'innocence autant que le monde durera, & s'attirer par une si généreuse conduite, les louanges et la bénédiction de tous ceux qui aiment la vertu.

There le Clerc had "l'honneur d'avoir quelque part dans l'amitié de feu Mr Locke," and profited "beaucoup dans sa conversation pendant qu'il a été en Hollande"; and this is an important statement in the mouth of an influential thinker like le Clerc. But Locke received as well as exerted influence. At Amsterdam he visited Guénélon whose lectures on anatomy he had heard in Paris. In Holland he met Limborch and "lia une amitié qui a duré jusqu'à sa mort & qu'il a entretenue avec soin, dès qu'il a été en Angleterre." As for le Clerc, he passed "bien des heures utilement & agréablement avec lui." Locke showed him the first chapters of his great *Essay*, and himself made a summary of them which le Clerc turned into French and proudly published in the *Bibliothèque Universelle*. At the end of a sixty-nine page

---

[1] *Bibliothèque Choisie*, vol. VI, 1705.
[2] Pupil of Locke and author of the *Characteristics*.

éloge le Clerc wrote: "C'est ainsi que mourut l'un des plus excellens Philosophes de nos jours....Je voudrois qu'il fût en mon pouvoir non seulement de rendre sa mémoire immortelle, mais encore de faire vivre éternellement son esprit en portant les gens de Lettres à rechercher la Vérité, à l'aimer & à la défendre comme il l'a fait." Le Clerc devoted a long journalistic life to effect what he has here expressed. Every new edition or translation of Locke was sure to find an appreciative review from le Clerc's pen, and he must have contributed considerably to the great fame and vogue which Locke had from the beginning to the end of the eighteenth century in Holland. The *Nouvelles de la République des Lettres*[1] published a loving memoir written from London by Coste who had lived with Locke during his last years. He sketched the human side of "l'illustre Mr Locke, un des premieres Philosophes du Siècle"—"C'est une perte générale," he lamented.

With Shaftesbury too le Clerc had formed a fast friendship.

"Since you honoured our nation," wrote Shaftesbury to him[2], "in learning our language, I shall continue to write thus to you in English, for I think it not to be esteemed a compliment merely to say that by having won so great a man as yourself to an esteem of our sense and writings we have gained as much honour in letters as lately in the field of arms."

Shaftesbury recalled Holland with gratitude, affection and admiration. He was also a true *cosmopolite*, well suited in his tastes to the growing internationalism of literature. He wrote for people "who delight in the open and free commerce of the world, and are rejoiced to gather views and receive light from every quarter." As a thinker he was to take a position not far below Locke. Le Clerc reviewed his *Characteristics* at length in the *Bibliothèque Choisie*[3], saying that the dialogues are "more clear, more concise and likewise quite otherwise animated" than those of Plato. Of the *Advice to an Author* he said, "this little Book is full of excellent advice....The turn of the whole is singular and the style

---

[1] Dec. 10, 1704. [2] Jan. 1705, edit. J. M. Robertson.
[3] Vols. XIX, XXI, XXIII.

full of Spirit and Wit. The Morality is nice and curious.... His whole work shows that he has thoroughly studied the Heart of man." Van Effen translated him in 1711, the *Spectator* popularized his philosophy, the *Essay on Man* epitomized it and so Shaftesbury's teachings were reinforced as Herder said to "influence the best heads of the eighteenth century[1]."

Of Mandeville, Shaftesbury's antithesis in culture, style and thought, we will only say that he was a Dutchman born, who came over to London at the end of King William's reign, and seemed to be content to become an Englishman, and an English author. He strongly reminds us of Richard Verstegan who a century before had tried to rouse scholars of the day into taking up Old English studies, and written some poems in imitation of Spenser. But Mandeville made verses in the style of *Hudibras* and formulated philosophical theories which considerably agitated the eighteenth century. Van Effen translated him in 1722. So for him, too, Holland became the ready exchange for ideas that issued from England. Mandeville, of course, reveals that he is a Dutchman, by the many references to Holland in support of his various arguments. He appears to have become a confirmed Anglophile, however[2]. From his analysis and comparison of the two countries and their inhabitants he must have assisted considerably in improving the acquaintance of each with the other. In the *Female Dialogues* (no. 7) he thus criticizes Sir William Temple:

"We had a man that has left us very valuable remarks made of a neighbouring country: he is generally very exact in the Description of their Governments; yet though he was a great statesman, a light of his age that was an ambassador there... I can show you in his writings what could not be there unless he had been misinformed. The Seven United Provinces are very near; there is a strict Alliance between them and us, and both actually show at this present time such an unparalleled Confidence in one another as never was seen before between two such powerful Neighbours of so different[3] an interest in Trade, and

---

[1] *Vide* J. M. Robertson, introd. to *Characteristics*, vol. I.
[2] *Vide* the excellent edition of *The Fable of the Bees*, by F. B. Kaye.
[3] Likely to give rise to difference.

yet though we have so great a commerce with them, how few people have we here that exactly understand their Government." In fact, "I know some Persons of Good sense & even of Quality that have no clearer notion of 'em tho' they are next Door to us, than they have of the mandarins in China; and what is worse, think themselves no more obliged to know the one than the other...."

In the pungent flavour of his style Mandeville is always illuminating. In the eighth dialogue there is a very interesting comparison of Dutch, French and English culture, important and significant for the time. It is noticeable that when the discussion turns to literature, the Dutch are allowed to drop quietly out of it. Mandeville's praise of England is noteworthy. In the *Free Thoughts* he had claimed that "England is blessed above other nations." He admired the English character and physique, and considered that "the most substantial blessing & the peculiar happiness we enjoy above all other countries are the Laws & Liberties of England." But in spite of this, "our discontent and grumblings are publickly known & all Europe hear us murmur in the midst of so much Ease....Should any State Physician behold our goodly Countenance & having felt our low dispirited Pulse examine into the real cause of all our grievances, he must infallibly pronounce the nation hypp'd." Mandeville, it will be seen, was a shrewd observer of the British character, and, apart from his striking position in the field of moral and economic theory, is well worthy of consideration in a study of the literary and cultural relations of England and Holland[1].

William Sewell is another Anglo-Dutch personality whom we have selected for discussion. His grandfather was an English Brownist; his mother was Dutch. He spent only ten months in England, but had an extended circle of English acquaintances and correspondents that included Thomas Elwood, Theodore Eccleston, William Penn, Burnet and others. He was in fact accused of being an "Engelsagtig Batavier" and was at great pains to defend himself as

[1] *Vide* "Studies in Philology," *Journal of English and German Philology*, vol. xx, no. 1, Jan. 1922.

a true Dutchman[1]. His great work, a *History of the Quakers*, was written *in English and in Dutch*. It still remains a classic. His translations include Burnet's *Short History of the Reformation*, Sherlock's *Immortality of the Soul* ("in consideration of the glorious nature of the matter")[2], Matthew Prior's *Ode on King William's Arrival in Holland*, Dampier's *New Voyage round the World*, and the account of the terrible adventures of Dickenson and his party on their way to Pennsylvania[3]. Perhaps his English-Dutch *Dictionary*, which superseded Hexam's, was the most useful contribution to Anglo-Dutch relations. It is full of all manner of interesting comments on the pronunciation, etc., of the two languages and merits the attention of students of language to-day. Finally he conducted for some time that important Dutch review the *Boekzaal*[4], begun by P. Rabus, another worker in the Anglo-Dutch literary field. The *Boekzaal* commenced its long run in 1692, soon established itself in the public estimation[5], and by its attention to English studies must have been one of the most influential mediums in the early eighteenth-century cultural intercourse of Holland with England. It is clear that increased interest was being taken in English studies, but how far it went is difficult to say. Le Clerc, much occupied with English thought and applying himself assiduously to the paraphrasing and interpreting of English writers, says: "J'ai de la peine à croire qu'il se trouve jamais personne, qui puisse, ou qui veuille faire une semblable entreprise[6]." Le Clerc is not boasting. "Mr le Clerc I'm creditably informed among his other attainments is too great a master of the English Tongue not to be able to give a just account of any of our authors[7]," testifies an English writer. His attainments in English were clearly regarded as unusual. Even the great Bayle did not know

[1] *Vide Boekzaal*, 1707–1708. [2] *Boekzaal*, July–Aug. 1708.
[3] *Vide* P. van der Aa, *Travels*. [4] Or, *Tweemaandelyke Uittreksels*.
[5] "It is known to the world with what great pleasure and no less benefit these extracts have been received and read"—*Tweemaandelyke Uittreksels*, Jan.–Feb. 1702.
[6] *Biblioth. Ch.* vol. ii, Avertissem. 1703.
[7] Le Clerc's account of Clarendon's *History*, London, 1710.

English. Speaking of Cudworth, le Clerc said, "peu de gens pouvant avoir recours à l'Original Anglois[1]." He welcomed a history of England and Holland by Vanel, because "il y a peu d'étrangers qui sachent les Langues Angloise & Hollandaise, et qui soient bien instruits de leurs Loix & de leur Gouvernement[2]." But he regarded the international position of French as unassailable. Reviewing s' Gravesande's work on perspective (Hague, 1711), he wrote: "L'Auteur a très bien fait de se servir de la Langue Françoise, qu'il possède fort bien & qui deviendra avec le tems la Langue de la Philosophie, aussi bien que celle des Cours & des personnes polies." This was still the common attitude. "Aussi," continues he, "est elle plus propre pour s'exprimer nettement que la Latine[3]." "He who does not understand French nowadays is scarcely half a human being," declared the *Boekzaal*[4]. The cultivation of the English language and literature, on the other hand, seemed to be regarded as properly confined to the enterprise of a few daring spirits. The disgruntled Rymer had exclaimed in 1694: "Had our tongue been as generally known, and those who felt our blows, understood our Language, they would confess that our Poets had likewise done their part; and that our Pens had been as successful as our Swords[5]." Dennis's *Advancement of Modern Poetrie* was really written with a view to the advancement of English poetry, to make "our Neighbours and with them all Europe sensible of the advantage which we have by nature[6]," an object which Nash had cherished a century before. But Dennis would have remained unknown equally with his subject had not the *Nouvelles de la République des Lettres* come to his assistance. In September 1701 the book was noticed and again in January 1703, when the reviewer said that it "est pourtant très peu connu en deçà de la mer & nous sommes assurés que ce que nous en allons dire dans cet Extrait sera nouveau pour bien des Lecteurs." Paraphrasing from Dennis, and in full agreement with his

---

[1] *Biblioth. Ch.* vol. II, Avertissem. 1703.   [2] *Ibid.*
[3] *Ibid.* vol. XXII, 1711.   [4] March–April 1693.
[5] Translation of René Rapin's *Reflections on Aristotle's Treatise of Poesie*, preface, 1694.   [6] Epistle Dedicatory.

views, we fear, the writer observes, that French is heard and cultivated everywhere, but

les Anglois s'étant opiniatrément attachés à leurs manières Gothiques & Barbares on peut faire bien du Chemin au delà de leurs Isles sans trouver trois personnes[1] qui ayent une médiocre connoissance de la Langue Angloise.... Il est bien sûr, comme le remarque Mr Dennis, que Molière, Corneille, Racine & Boileau, sont connus dans toute l'Europe, mais qui est-ce hors de l'Angleterre qui ait ouï parler de Spencer, de Milton, de Ben Johnson?

and in a footnote this remark is made: "On doit entendre cela par raport à leurs Poësies." Bayle does not appear to have been aware of the existence of Shakespeare, but had noticed Milton in his celebrated *Dictionary* as the "fameux apologiste du supplice de Charles I"; "un de ces esprits satyriques" whose "réponse au livre de Mr Saumaise fit parler de lui par tout le monde"; but who also "se mêloit de poésie." Upon second thoughts he changed this sentence to "Il aimoit la poésie" in the second edition and devoted some more space to a consideration of Milton's poetry. Still, he will not take the responsibility of the views expressed and makes Toland and Dryden speak.

Toland's *Life* was duly reviewed by the *Histoire des Ouvrages des Scavants*[2], but the ten pages devoted to it are mostly occupied with Milton's life and controversial writings. The review is by no means unsympathetic.

In July 1699 the *Boekzaal* announced the book, and referred to Milton as "the extremely learned and notorious Englishman." In 1695[3], discussing Blount's *De Re Poetica*, the paper had gravely informed readers that Milton was an Englishman. But in the same review occurs a blunt avowal of indifference that speaks volumes. "The renowned English poet Mr Dryden" is quoted; several names, mentioned in Blount's book, are discussed, and then the reviewer says: "but my zeal for further transcription has been somewhat dulled" as there are still "a number of English poets that do not interest us Dutchmen, such as W. d'Avenant, J. Denham,

---

[1] Buckle, *Hist. of European Civilization*, has generously increased the number to *five*! For France cp. the testimony of Montesquieu, *Notes sur l'Angleterre* (*Œuvres Compl.* 1839, vol. II, p. 484).

[2] Feb. 1699, p. 78.   [3] May–June.

J. Donne, B. Johnson, J. Milton, J. Oldham, W. Shakespeare, Ph. Sidney, E. Spencer, J. Suckling, E. Waller."

Sewell, in fact, was greatly amused at English poetry: "I am well aware that it is an inborn characteristic of the English to be unwilling to learn from foreigners." He quotes a triplet from Dryden as an example of "English embellishments" and adds ironically: "this example, which our writer[1] finds so pretty, is taken from the chief of English poets, Dryden, and would it not therefore be good?" In his *Dictionary* he returns to the point on which he has had an exchange of letters with a "learned and ingenious Englishman." He calls upon Englishmen to bestir themselves to "civilize their Spelling and banish the supernumerary letters as the French and the Dutch have done." Yet later[2] he felt constrained to say: "and whatever some Dutchmen may say of English it is certain that this language has been so polished and civilized during the last century that it far excels in beauty of words and expression what it was a century ago." The English language was, in fact, attracting a great deal of attention in Holland. "Les Anglois sont beaucoup plus hardis que de nous. Ils ne font point de difficulté de forger des mots nouveaux toutes les fois qu'ils en ont besoin," said one reviewer[3]. Le Clerc, never tired of discussing the point, seems to have been much influenced by Chamberlaine's articles on *Le Génie & la Force de la Langue Angloise* which he reviewed in 1709[4]. But Sewell had not done with English poetry. For English edification he put his arguments in verse at the back of his *Dictionary*, where he considers the great advantage that would have accrued to English poetry if the "famous Dryden who was indeed a transcendent wit and who was pleased to call the Dutch heavy and gross-witted fellows" had only imitated the practice of Vondel. "Nevertheless," he admits[5], "one must say in praise of the English that there have been poets among them who have penned the most sublime,

---

[1] E. Bysshe, *The Art of English Poetry*, reviewed *Boekzaal*, March–April 1705.

[2] *Boekzaal*, July–Aug. 1708. [3] *Nouv. de la Rép. des Let.*

[4] *Biblioth. Ch.* vol. xvii. [5] *Boekzaal*, March–April 1705.

meaningful and fine thoughts in elevated, powerful and beautiful expressions, and who, if they would only learn something from the Dutch, would greatly improve their poetry." These discussions and occasional reviews of English critical works, as well as of better literary products, must unquestionably have played a great part in overcoming the indifference of a public generally ignorant of English fine literature. The news column which "n'est pas là l'endroit du Journal qui soit lu le dernier, ou qui fasse le moins de plaisir," contained many notices of new books or editions, sometimes with interesting comments. So notices of Tonson's publications of the "fameux Shakespeare," Cowley, Dryden, Prior, Congreve "un de nos meilleurs auteurs pour la Poësie et les Pièces de Théâtre," etc. appeared. Or again, "Mr Swift nous a donné une troisième Partie des mémoires du Chev. Temple[1]." The *Holy War* is noticed as "un livre assez curieux[2]." The *Boekzaal*[3], in a notice of the writings of "the author of the *True Born Englishman*," says: "The author of these writings is the well-known Daniel Defoe who stood in the pillory three times last year in London for the writing of a little book entitled the *Shortest Way with the Dissenters*." It is advertised as on sale at Amsterdam. So at intervals the *Utopia*[4], Oldham[5], Swift[6] and Addison[7] received some notice. The *Tale of a Tub* is described as "une Allégorie perpétuelle, mais d'un stile badin & enjoüé. La Diction en est extrêmement pure & l'on y trouve beaucoup de feu & d'esprit." Swift is defended against Wotton's slur on *A Tale of a Tub* that it is "plein d'impiété & de profanation."

Tout le Monde n'est pas de son sentiment en cela. On doit pardonner quelques expressions libres dans des Ouvrages de cette nature....Il y a apparence que le *Tale of a Tub* a été fait sur le modèle de Rabelais, comme *la Bataille des Livres*...qu'on y a ajoutée, est une imitation de *la Guerre Poétique des Auteurs* & du *Parnasse Réformée* de Gueret.

[1] *Nouv. de la Rép. des Let.* (Nov.–March 1707, etc.).
[2] *Ibid.* July 1700.   [3] May–June 1704.
[4] *Nouv. de la Rép. des Let.* 1703. *Boekzaal*, May–June 1701.
[5] *Boekzaal*, Jan.–Feb. 1695.
[6] *Nouv. de la Rép. des Let.* Aug. 1704, Sept. 1705.   [7] *Ibid.* Sept. 1706.

In fact, as Coste said, London was a "Ville féconde en Nouvelles Littéraires[1]." Desmaizeau, the good friend of Steele and Addison, writes from London to Bernard, the editor of the *Nouvelles de la République des Lettres*[2]: "Il n'est personne, par exemple, qui connoissant un peu l'Angleterre n'avoüe que c'est peut-être le lieu du Monde le mieux fourni d'habiles gens & où il paroît le plus de bons Livres." But the words of Dennis about the appreciation of English poetry by foreigners still held, and are perhaps as true in respect of the best English prose literature. "When Gentlemen begin to study the Poetry of any Language the first thing they understand is the reasonable part of it. For the fineness of the Imaginative part which depends in Great measure upon force of words & upon beauty of Expression, must lye concealed from them in a good degree till they are perfect in the Language[3]." He continues to remark that English is more readily acquired by the "peuples du Nord," and instances the "plusieurs Ecclésiastiques qui en ont assez appris en très peu de tems pour faire leur profit des livres de Théologie écrits en Anglois[4]." This was indeed the truth. The vogue of English religious writers seems to have been very great. Simon, Bishop of Ely, Richard, Bishop of Bath, Dodwell, Samuels, Wells, Jeremy Taylor, Tillotson, Ussher, Chillingworth, and especially Sherlock, are praised, reviewed and translated until the *Boekzaal* by 1696 feels it necessary to protest: "Let us no more envy England her divines, translate no more books from that land," as we have our own.

The protest passed unheeded. "Tous ceux qui ont quelque connoissance de l'Angleterre & de la Langue Angloise les connoissent assez & on a même traduit une grande partie en Flamand," said le Clerc in a lengthy review[5] of Tillotson's *Sermons*. But English philosophical speculation and scientific research were becoming at least equally popular. The letters of Antonie van Leeuwenhoek to the "widely-

---

[1] *Nouv. de la Rép. des Let.* Dec. 10, 1704.   [2] *Ibid.* Sept. 1701, p. 258.
[3] *Advancement of Mod. Poetry*, Epistle Dedicatory.
[4] *Nouv. de la Rép. des Let.* Jan. 1703.   [5] *Biblioth. Ch.* vol. VII, 1705.

renowned[1]" Royal Society attracted much attention and were copiously treated in the *Boekzaal.* Sewell had translated something from Boyle in 1688. In 1705, the *Nouvelles de la République des Lettres* referred to Newton as "cet incomparable Mathématicien[2]," but it was only at a later date that the Newtonian philosophy was appreciated. Many medical treatises were reviewed, the quarrel between Bidloo, the Dutch physician, and Cowper, who had apparently plagiarized Bidloo, receiving considerable space. In the various departments no names were more advertised than Cudworth, Locke, Shaftesbury, Clarendon, Sir William Temple, Tillotson, and in a lesser degree Toland and Wotton.

Toland's *Christianity not Mysterious* was already "notorious[3]" in 1701. Le Clerc grew warm over Cudworth in many a long review. Clarendon's *History of the Rebellion* is given no less than 145 pages in one number of the *Bibliothèque Choisie,* and the account is continued at length in another. Indeed, there seemed to be an insatiable demand for any sort of English history. The writings of Edward Ludlow and Buchanan were popular. Rabus regaled his readers with stories of the English kings and queens and was asked to continue. There are strong indications that England and the English had captured the Dutch imagination. Locke occupied much space in five of le Clerc's volumes. English scholarship was held up by le Clerc for admiration. The undertaking of the Cambridge press in editing classical texts is lauded. "La République des Lettres est donc très-obligée à ceux qui ont conçu ce dessein....Il faut avouër qu'il n'y a guère qu'en Angleterre que l'on puisse exécuter à présent un semblable dessein, parce-qu'on y aime plus qu'en aucun lieu, les Belles Lettres." Cambridge turns out better work than the Louvre press itself, in spite of the Jesuits who wish to persuade the world that everything good from Britain is printed in Scotland, and "que l'on ne fait rien en Angleterre que quelques petits Livres de Politique." In every way it is clear

---

[1] *Boekzaal,* Jan. 1702. [2] Sept. 1705.
[3] *Boekzaal,* Sept.–Oct. 1701.

that under the stimulus of enthusiasts like le Clerc the continental public were becoming conscious of new spiritual forces in the air that could be traced back to England. A new element was entering into Dutch culture, whence, as well as through more direct channels, it spread out in all directions over Europe. Often there was opposition.

On sait confusément en France & en Hollande qu'il y a en Angleterre des Esprits pénétrans & hardis qui parlent & qui écrivent avec beaucoup de liberté contre les opinions le plus généralement établies. Ils passent dès là pour de vrais Pyrrhoniens. On leur donne ce titre fort communément: & bien loin de s'en choquer, ils commencent à s'en faire honneur. Comme ils attaquent tout le Monde, on les attaque aussi de tous côtez en chaire, en conversation & dans la plûpart des Livres qu'on écrit sur des Points de Théologie ou de métaphysique. C'est à eux aussi que l'on en veut proprement dans cet Ouvrage; mais notre auteur fait voir en passant que ces messieurs ne sont pas si Pyrrhoniens qu'on pourroit bien croire; & que s'ils font profession d'un parfait Pyrrhonisme, ce n'est apparemment qu'un tour dont ils se sont avisez pour mieux disposer les Esprits à entendre revoquer en doute des Doctrines respectées, qu'ils croyent effectivement contraires aux véritables intérêts du Genre-humain[1].

In these words we have a clear statement of what the English philosophy stood for. They occur in a preface to the first translation of Shaftesbury into French and are the first public utterance of a young *littérateur* named Van Effen, who was to become a leading apologist and interpreter of English literary culture and form. New standards were being set up in thought. Quick to perceive this, he showed that he was reacting to the newly felt pressure of the English contribution to this process, by translating Shaftesbury. It was only a question of time before England was to assist greatly in the establishment of new standards and ideals in literature in place of the old fetishes for which France stood.

[1] J. v. Effen, *Essai sur la Raillerie* (Shaftesbury), 1710, preface.

CHAPTER II

JUSTUS VAN EFFEN

It will have been seen that the intellectual and literary atmosphere in Holland was electric with the new impulses emanating from Britain. The time indeed was ripe for a more idiomatic translation of them than Bayle, le Clerc or Sewell and their journals had afforded. At least, certain English writings had been recorded and reviewed with increasing assiduity, and English thought occupied the minds of a few enthusiasts; but English *belles lettres* had received only the scantiest attention.

In this atmosphere appeared the personality of Justus van Effen than who none could have been more fitted for the rôle of intermediary which he was destined to play. He was the son of a Dutch cavalry officer, was born in 1684 and died in 1735. His life[1] therefore covers the greater part of that period in which the cosmopolitanism of modern European literature may be said to have been established as a general formative principle, putting each national literature in a much more vital connection with the rest than ever before. The novel discovery of the time was, of course, that England had a great literature, and it was at first the brilliant group of Augustans that made the literary conquest of Europe.

This indeed is an aspect of their achievement which has not been adequately recognized. The Augustan Age, far from being peaceful, was one of restless activity. It was a time of war and rebellion, of fierce antagonisms and partisanships when the new party system was painfully but strenuously fighting its way into acceptance as a regular political institution. It was a time of great political progress, of rapid expansion of trade, and determined intervention, if not

---

[1] *Vide* Appendix i.

leadership, in European affairs. The age applied itself with determination to the deeper study and appreciation of man and of nature with ever-deepening self-consciousness. "Study Man", and "follow Nature" were no idle maxims. Acquiescence and authority were swept away to make room for doubt, pessimism, sentimentality or Swiftian irony. The *Essay on Man*, e.g., fluctuates between all these moods in a distraught endeavour to cling to the theory of "whatever is, is right."

In the changing attitude to nature the Augustans were pioneers. The topiary gardening of King William's day was too methodized for this age with its crazy landscape gardening, in wretched taste; but it was an attempt to bring nature closer and tie it up to the doorpost. Pope's Twickenham grotto was but premonitory of the Gothicism of Strawberry Hill. The great vogue of the pastoral, the popularity of the *Seasons* and of *Robinson Crusoe* as an alluring picture of the simple life are premonitions of the conscious *fin de siècle* nursing of nature. The *Tatler* and the *Spectator* contain freshly felt remarks on nature and the simple and fundamental in life, neither must their revival of Shakespeare, of Milton and of the ballad be forgotten.

There was a great awakening of the social consciousness. Reform societies and charitable organizations sprang into being. In business, too, it was a time of "projects." The age was prosperous and lavish. Even to-day the rambler through London churches is impressed by the numerous records of charitable bequests made in the early eighteenth century. In science, in philosophy, in literature, the age was brilliant and alert. It displayed an energy and efficiency which naturally made it an age of conquest politically, economically and culturally. From that time England never looked back. The foundations of her later magnificence were being well and truly laid.

What is usually said of the age of Pope is true only in a relative sense. Seen from the modern point of view, the age may appear coarse, brutal, less strenuous, with a culture of tinsel and a cold heart. Yet the fact is that it was less coarse, less brutal, more strenuous, if perhaps less hectic, and more genuinely cultivated than, say, the period of King Charles II.

An impassable gulf seems to divide the conscious, eye-on-the-object, deliberate "nature work" of, say, Wordsworth, from the spontaneity of Shakespeare's painting. The change was inevitable with the growing sophistication of civilization, and it was the early eighteenth century which, by its vigorous intellectual effort, made possible the new harmony of the intellectual and the spiritual elements in the later literature of nature and of man. Empirical emphasis on the major tones dulled their sense of the overtones of life; but it gave to the Pleasures of the Imagination that consciously rational colour, which is inseparable from the modern outlook.

If the great work of the age of Pope is not given its due by a graceless posterity, contemporary Europe, at least, was more appreciative. The age itself furnishes abundant testimony of the profound impression England was making on the minds of men on the continent. "Ce tems si fécond en beaux esprits Anglois" is a characteristic bit of applause. It was not in the first instance the more glorious age of Shakespeare that impressed all Europe, but the age of Newton, Locke, Congreve, Defoe, Swift, Addison, Pope and Thomson, to name but a few. It was this age which, by sheer brilliance of achievement accompanied by an insistence on its claims to attention, first wrested from contemporary Europe a reluctant approval, and finally enthusiastic applause, not only for its own performance, but for the English achievement as a whole.

There were, however, other important mediators, and of these Van Effen was one of the foremost.

The character, education and reading of Van Effen were well suited to his career as journalist, moralist and periodical essayist. From the very first he enjoyed the careful training of his father, who guided him in the principles of tolerance, humanity and right thinking, and who, like Addison's father[1], seemed to be both wise and sympathetic in the treatment

[1] *Vide Tatler*, no. 235.

of children. Unfortunately, Melchior van Effen died when his son was still in early adolescence and needed his guidance most; but from numerous loving and admiring references[1], Van Effen shows that the tender and sensible training he had received had left ineffaceable memories and had not been wasted. "All my upbringing and good qualities I have to thank him for. Hardly had Reason illumined my understanding with its first rays when the man attracted all my love and admiration. He showed me the greatest possible fatherly affection and I could hardly say now whether I loved his virtues for his sake or him for his virtues."

As the affectionate, generous nature of Steele has endeared him as man and writer to generations of readers, so the filial devotion and tenderness of Van Effen win the affection of his readers. The writer of the *Éloge Historique* has rightly praised him for the dutiful and manly way in which he assumed the care of his mother and sister. Verwer has testified to the great love he bore his wife and children, and altogether his domestic experience was such as must have ennobled and mellowed him in advance of his years. Van Effen's character is further embellished by a generous capacity for friendship. His school and college friendships were kept up throughout his life, and it was a characteristic act when in 1730, at the age of 46, he defended an old school friend, Dr Maty, minister of the Walloon Church *à la Haye*, from an unfair attack, and appealed for fair dealing in the *Essai sur la manière de traiter les Controverses*[2]. After that, he defended his good friend Dr Pingré, a physician, against the attacks of a "cabale envieuse." His circle of friends was wide and distinguished. In particular, the grateful friendship of the young nobleman Van Welderen, who had been his pupil, is a significant index to the character of the tutor. It was through the young Van Welderen that Van

[1] *Holl. Spect.* nos. 133, 40, 332, etc.; *La Bagatelle*, no. i, p. 29; *Le Misantrope*, no. i, pp. 3, 4, no. ii, pp. 90, 91, 212; *Le Nouveau Spectateur Français*, pp. 8 ff. Cp. *Tatler*, no. 181—Steele on his parents.

[2] *Vide* W. Bisschop, *J. van Effen geschetst in zijn leven* (1859), chap. 15; also Verwer, pp. lxviii–lxix and *Éloge Hist.*

Effen could visit England as secretary to the embassy extraordinary; in his home Van Effen began his last and greatest work, and it was through him that Van Effen received the post of "Kommies" which brought competency and domestic dreams within his grasp. Whatever Van Effen gained from his conversation with the great was the result of their esteem and his merit. Mean solicitation had no place in the sturdy independence of his character.

To return to his early training, it seems that he was a clever youth and made rapid progress in his studies[1]. "His inclination seemed, at an early age already, to have been that of gaining an honest sustenance by his learning or in any other office for which literary cultivation was necessary or useful," says Verwer[2]. But at the outset his father had other plans and intended that his boy should follow a military, not a literary, career[3]. This object was followed so far that Van Effen did actually serve as a Cadet for some time[4]; thus, like his forerunner Steele, Van Effen could boast some experience of the sterner craft of war, an experience that must have enriched the minds of both in the knowledge of men and practical affairs. But Van Effen also had the keen and intimate knowledge of the classics which nourished and moulded the mind of Addison[5]. At Utrecht he passed through the Latin school where the curriculum was of the classical type approved in his days, and by assiduous reading he improved upon it until the classical literatures, particularly the Roman, became to him an abiding source of knowledge and pleasure. "Nourri des préceptes d'Horace," he says of himself[6], and throughout his works the classical bias of his mind is evident. Nevertheless he belongs to the new school. Although he had drunk deeply of classical humanistic culture, his admiration for it did not mislead him into the

[1] "Je vis bientôt tous mes compagnons ne me suivre que de loin dans la carrière des Sciences"—*Nouv. Sp. Fr.* no. i.

[2] *Leven*, p. xi.   [3] *Vide Holl. Spect.* nos. 16, 22, 172, 292, 343.

[4] *Leven*, p. viii.

[5] *Vide*, e.g., Caroline Goad, *Horace in the English Literature of the Eighteenth Century.*

[6] *Misant.* (1726 ed.), no. xxxviii. Cp. Addison—"To Horace he is most akin in spirit" (Caroline Goad, *op. cit.*).

pedantic depreciation of the moderns, affected by the school of Boileau and smaller savants. He was a modern who believed in the European culture of his day, without being "entêté des manières de leur siècle[1]," but who loved whatever there was in the classics that answered to his standards of taste and gave him pleasure. Similarly, with modern literature he approved nothing but what satisfied his rational, critical mind, and, on the whole, Van Effen's outlook, though by no means free from the prejudices of his day, was fundamentally sound[2]. His knowledge of French literature was wide and intimate[3]. "From the first his desire to understand the French writers had induced him to apply himself with uncommon industry to the thorough mastery of this language, in which he progressed in the most astounding manner[4]," says Verwer, who also mentions the surprise of Frenchmen "that a Dutchman born could have penetrated so deeply into the spirit of French writing[5]," as he proved by his *Misantrope* and other papers. M. Potin, the writer of the letter to the elogist, likewise expresses his admiration, and to spice it, invents or uses a tale to the effect that Van Effen had commenced learning French as late as at the age of seventeen[6]. We may, with Zuydam, take this for an agreeable fiction; but the admiration excited by Conrad's mastery over a foreign language in our own time, will help us to understand the feeling of our genial Rotterdam Consul, M. Potin, who wrote in the eighteenth century. The effectiveness with which Van Effen's assiduity was rewarded is evident from his French writings, both in their style and volume; and however much it has become a sort of tradition among French historians of literature to depreciate him as a French writer, there does

[1] *Misant.* no. LV.
[2] Cp. Bisschop, chap. 2; Zuydam, pp. 20–23.
[3] *Vide* Bisschop, pp. 14–15; P. Valkhoff, *De Gids*, Nov. 1917; R. Oomkens, *Revue de Hollande*, nos. 4, 5, 6, 8, 10.
[4] P. viii; cp. *Éloge Hist.*: "Il s'attacha par goût à la Langue Françoise & à la belle Littérature."
[5] P. vi.
[6] M. Potin also cites in proof of Van Effen's mastery of French his earliest work, the *Parallèle*, which was long attributed to Fontenelle.

not seem to be any reason to disagree with Valkhoff's view that his French is correct and "most noteworthy for a Dutchman who had never been to France[1]." The verdict of Valkhoff's correspondent is in the same strain[2], and Bruys, a Frenchman who knew Van Effen, says: "M. Van Effen connaît toutes les délicatesses de notre langue[3]." Except, perhaps, for Horace himself, Boileau[4], Molière and La Bruyère were his favourite authors, and they exerted a considerable influence over his mind and practice as a writer. As an essayist, he was more directly than Addison and Steele a lineal descendant of the pictorial French character-writer, and it was only in imitation of the novel methods of these English writers that Van Effen managed to give a new direction to the character-genre as practised by his great French predecessor. Even more than the age of Pope in England, the age of Van Effen crystallized in Holland the pseudo-classical French spirit, and Addison, who went to Blois and buried himself in French studies for a year, was scarcely nearer the fountain-source of this spirit than Van Effen, who had grown up in the French society and atmosphere of early eighteenth-century Holland. It is just possible that Van Effen visited France in his early youth[5]. In 1719, when he had suffered a disappointment and his tutorship in Paris was to be arranged, "Il souhaitoit s'éloigner pour quelque tems de ce pays et que Paris étoit l'endroit qui lui convenoit le mieux[6]." But there were rumours, the Paris plans were abandoned, and Bruys in his *Mémoires*[7] can say with truth: "Il est fâcheux qu'il n'ait pas voyagé en France."

In addition to having an intimate knowledge of the classical and the French literatures, Van Effen was well read

---

[1] Valkhoff, *De Gids, u.c.* p. 346.

[2] *Ibid.* p. 347: "Le style de v. Effen est très, très honorable, parfois même d'une énergie personnelle."

[3] *Mémoires*, cit. Valkhoff.

[4] Not on account of his classicism, however. *Vide Misant.* no. LV, p. 125, 2nd ed.

[5] *Vide Holl. Spect.* nos. 30, 341.

[6] *Lettre de Mr P. à l'auteur de l'éloge.*

[7] Cit. Valkhoff, *De Gids, u.c.* p. 351.

in philosophy and, as his writings show, took a lively interest in the moral, theological and political speculation of his day. His translation of Shaftesbury and Mandeville was plainly the outcome of his reading, while his avowed stand as a Lockeist shows him to have made the Lockeian philosophy a part of his thinking. In addition to this, Van Effen was abreast of the scientific movement of his day and was indeed something of a "virtuoso" in his way. It was on the strength of some of his scientific reviewings in the *Journal Littéraire* that he was admitted to the membership of the celebrated circle of Newton and Wren in London[1]. His scientific and philosophical studies brought him into touch with English culture, which attracted him, and soon he was acquainted with English life, language and literature, as well as speculation.

We do not know when Van Effen first began to read and speak English, but it is certain that ample opportunity for it offered in the Holland of his day. Each of the larger towns had its English colony. English traders and sailormen came and went, and English soldiers then more than ever filled the land. His father, a lieutenant of horse, was probably familiar with the language of his English fellow-soldiers and, without doubt, would have passed it on to his son. In view of the fact that Van Effen translated an English philosopher in 1710, we must date his first acquaintance with English language and literature considerably before that time, while the readiness with which he transplanted the new type of literature that had risen to eminence in England, under the hand of Steele and Addison, must mean that his interest in English letters was maintained and steadily growing towards an appreciation of English *belles lettres*. Van Effen's first reference to his knowledge of English occurs in the *Bagatelle*, no. LIX, Nov. 1718, "Dans le langage d'un peuple voisin que *j'ai practiqué pendant assez longtems* j'ai remarqué un tour de phrase...," etc. In the *Parallèle*,

---

[1] *Vide* letter to Camusat appended to *Je ne sais quoi. Cartier de St. Philip* 1723.

which had been written as early as 1707, perhaps, he ridicules Barnes's foolish theory, a point to which he returns in the *Misantrope*[1].

In this paper references to English writings are scanty, but sufficient to show that Van Effen was keeping in touch with them. He mentions "comment Mr Locke renverse les idées innées[2]," and in his paper on vogues[3] occurs a significant remark on English philosophy: "Aristote a été longtems en vogue," but "Descartes a chassé cet illustre Grec du Trône de la Philosophie, pour l'occuper lui-même...." Again, "Descartes pourroit bien tomber à son tour" and

les Philosophes Anglois se mettent sur les rangs; & quoique la mode de les suivre ne soit pas encore entiérement établie, il y a de l'apparence, que la nouveauté de leurs raisonnemens, jointe à leur véritable mérite, leur donnera de l'accès dans l'esprit de tous ceux qui veulent se tirer du commun

—we may be sure that Van Effen was among these.

In his comparison[4] of the English and the French which places Van Effen well in advance of the movement of his time in the direction of English culture, he betrays, however, that his acquaintance with English *bel esprit* stopped short of *belles lettres*. English writers, he says, have indefatigable application, learning and penetration, but "peu attachez d'ordinaire à polir leur stile & à le rendre aisé & fleuri, ils trouvent ces minuties au dessous de la solidité de leur esprit. *Ils sont plûtot grands Esprits que beaux Esprits, et leurs écrits sont plus propres à instruire qu'à plaire.*" Van Effen, we feel, was thinking of the Locke under his pillow when he wrote these words. But the very periodical in which this verdict occurred was undertaken by him in imitation of English *beaux esprits* and reveals familiarity with their work, the *Tatler* and the *Spectator*.

Between the *Misantrope* and the *Journal Littéraire* lay a period which gave him ample opportunity of extending

---

[1] No. i, p. 23: "C'est Barnes qui le dit; bon, Barnes est un sot," and a footnote explains: "un Anglais qui prétend faire voir qu'Homère était Solomon." The reference is to Joshua Barnes, Regius Professor of Greek at Cambridge.
[2] *Misant.* ii, p. 84. [3] *Misant.* ii, no. xxiii. [4] *Misant.* Dec. 19, 1712.

his acquaintance with English letters. By his work on the *Journal Littéraire* a further opportunity came. Numerous English works were reviewed in it and read before reviewed. "Nouvelles littéraires" came regularly from London, Oxford, Cambridge, Edinburgh, etc., so that, everything considered, it is safe to conclude that Van Effen had advanced far beyond the attitude of the *Misantrope* with respect to the qualities of English *bel esprit*, which even there, as in the preface to the second volume, is highly appreciated.

The probability that Van Effen undertook a translation of *A Tale of a Tub* in 1715, in challenge to the vanity of the English who considered it untranslatable, indicates the trend of his literary interest as well as his sense of command of English.

The two visits Van Effen paid to England are events of considerable importance in his literary development. We cannot say of him as Condorcet does of Voltaire, that he went to England a man of letters and returned a *philosophe*, mainly because he was already a *philosophe*. The first visit not only clarified his notions and consolidated what must necessarily have been a somewhat uncertain and shifting knowledge of the real literature of the English, but also contributed to impress him with a new sense of literary and cultural values which were to spread over Europe from the direction of England and of which he was a pioneer, in the same way as he was one of the earliest of a number of famous literary personalities of this period to visit the El Dorado of the eighteenth century—England. It is true that Holberg had been to Oxford fifteen years before, but, except for "a remarkable chapter on England and the English[1]" in his history of 1711, his writings on this, perhaps the most absorbing topic of the mid-eighteenth century, come comparatively late, when many were doing the same kind of thing. Holberg's celebrated *Niels Klim* imitates Gulliver, and there are many scattered references to England and its people in his works, but he seems to have

[1] S. Hamer, lecture on "Holberg...."

been almost exclusively an intermediary between England and the Scandinavian countries[1]. Van Effen stood directly in the main current, had been formed as a *littérateur* in the school of Bayle and in international Holland, the very fountain-head of the "cosmopolitisme littéraire" of the eighteenth century, and, if it is true that "France has been the intermediary between England and mankind" as Macaulay has said, Van Effen is one of the most important go-betweens in the process. He went to England at the age of thirty-one as an essayist of distinction[2], a journalist of repute, a man of extensive reading, especially of English thinkers, with a mind well stored, but alert and guided by *la raison* in a philosophic, but not pedantic, sense. He arrived in the spring of 1715, more than ten years before Voltaire, Montesquieu and Prévost, who fled before the *lettre de cachet* of 1728. He has left us no record of his feelings and experiences, but the visit must have been a memorable event to him. Van Effen was of too rationalistic and phlegmatic a temperament for us to say that England was "the fairyland of his westward dreams[3]" as it was to Holberg, but anticipation as well as distance could not but have lent enchantment. London, where throbbed the life of English thought and culture, where in succession to Locke and Shaftesbury the brilliant Queen Anne group of men were winning immortality, London, the home of the *Tatler* and the *Spectator* whose spell had already fallen on him, the home of Newton and the celebrated circle of scientists round him, must have appeared to Van Effen in nothing but the brightest colours and attracted him as it attracted Conti from Venice in the same year. England had already come to mean even more to him than it would to Voltaire a decade later, who honoured it as the land that "produced a Newton, a Lock, a Tillotson, a Milton, a Boyle and many

---

[1] Holberg learnt much from the French too, especially Molière. *Vide*, e.g., *Autobiography*.

[2] Though at that time, generally unknown as a writer. Cp. Verwer, *Leven*, p. xvii: "Hoewel zyn naem, in hoedanigheit van Schryver veelal onbekent was."

[3] S. Hamer, *op. cit.*

other great men either dead or alive, whose glory in war, in state affairs or in letters, will not be confined to the bounds of this island[1]"; nor, we may be sure, was the English language to Van Effen one which he "cannot pronounce at all and which he hardly understands in conversation[2]" as it was to Voltaire.

In March the embassy extraordinary entered London. The great 's Gravesande was secretary, Van Effen undersecretary, and the man who headed the embassy the patrician Wassenaer van Duivenvoorde, Van Effen's patron and employer. The object of the embassy was to congratulate George I, on behalf of the States, on his accession to the English throne[3]. In the words of the historian Wagenaar: "The ambassadors made their public entry into London on the 20th March 1715 and had an audience with the king and the prince and princess of Wales on the same day. They remained in England for a considerable length of time and had the opportunity of observing the beginnings of a dangerous revolt....[4]"

Van Effen had come at a rather unfortunate time; turbulence and agitation reigned and party strife ran high. Swift sat in sullen retirement in Ireland. Addison, there too on his secretarial duties, returned in mid-winter to enter the political field with his *Freeholder*, and Steele had been busily pamphleteering all the year. Gone were the days of the *Spectator* and the social atmosphere that had produced it. The taste of the Town was no more for the good fun of the *Tatler* and *Spectator*[5], but for the sterner and harsher things of violent and now really dangerous faction.

The share Van Effen had in it all was probably confined to his secretarial work and connected with the feverish negotiations with the Netherlands for support, which was, as usual, liberally granted, especially after Walpole's personal

---

[1] Voltaire, Preface to *On the Civil Wars of France*, 1727.   [2] *Ibid.*
[3] The coronation had taken place on October 20, 1714.
[4] The rebellion of 1715.
[5] E.g. Chas. Lillie, in *Unpublished Letters to the "Spectator*," speaks of "the happiness we enjoyed while you presided at the head of wit, pleasure, politeness and good manners."

visit to the Hague. The Dutch, after all England's perfidy, were still staunch to the old Anglo-Dutch political traditions of the maintenance of the Protestant succession and the natural alliance of the chief maritime powers. Early in 1716, Van Effen's chief negotiated an important agreement between Holland and England, and it must have been an experience of some value to the clever young under-secretary to see something of the inner workings of international politics. At the same time his personal connection with Anglo-Dutch political intimacies could not have failed to score deeper the impressions already made on his mind by English men and books, and thus to contribute towards making him the representative and interpreter of English thought and literature in Holland.

We have little knowledge of how Van Effen spent his time in England. Verwer says: "He saw and conversed with many famous scholars in London, amongst others the knight Isaac Newton, that great light of modern philosophy[1]." That Newton had become a beacon-light of philosophy on the continent in 1755, when Verwer wrote, was mainly due to the activities of the first secretary of that very embassy. "In the company of a gentleman in the first rank of scholars, who was well versed in the philosophy of the English, although he deviated somewhat from it, Van Effen could have found no greater enjoyment for his inquisitive mind," says Verwer. 's Gravesande had been at the University of Leyden with the sons of the famous bishop Burnet, one of the most active intermediaries between England and Holland. The friendship made at Leyden with these two young men is renewed in London. 's Gravesande arrives unfortunately only just in time to attend their father's funeral. Through them and others he naturally gains admission to the best circles of English culture and learning. Prosper Marchand[2], one of the circle of Van Effen and 's Gravesande, tells enthusiastically

---

[1] *Leven*, p. xvi.
[2] *Dictionnaire historique* (1758), Vol. II, p. 221: "il retrouva à Londres ses anciens amis," etc.

how the latter delighted in the conversation of learned
men in England, of his meeting with Newton and the cordial
affection which the great man conceived for him[1]. Their
friendship became such as Clarke's unmannerly attack on
's Gravesande as an anti-Newtonian could not shake. The
Dutch scholar now made himself thoroughly familiar with
Newton's *modus operandi* and conceptions, acquiring even his
distaste of metaphysics, as Voltaire has said. He was indefatigable; he studied in his room in spite of the racket the young
men, who had made his quarters a rendezvous, raised about
his ears; he maintained a scientific correspondence with the
continent, and attended the meetings of the Royal Society.
Van Effen, though quite capable of having a good time
and indulging his animal spirits, would not have spent, and
in fact did not spend, his time in boisterousness for which
he had but little taste[2]. Instead, he attended the weekly
meetings of the Royal Society with 's Gravesande. The latter
was elected on the 9th of June 1715 and admitted a member
on the 16th. Van Effen's election took place at a meeting on
November 30, and his admission on December 8[3].

At this meeting the business was of the usual nature.
Dr Halley read letters, one of which was on "the late great
eclipse of the sun." Then Mr Desaguliers performed an experiment on specific gravity. Finally "Mr Justus Van Effen
of the Hague, having been chosen on St Andrew's Day last,
was admitted a Fellow of the Society by the President[4]."

[1] "...conçut pour lui beaucoup d'amitié et d'estime," etc.
[2] *Vide*, e.g., *Voyage en Suède*, Let. xi.
[3] *Vide Archives of the Royal Society*. The minute in the Journal Book of
the Society reads:
"The President in the Chair.

Mr Justus Van Effen and Mons. Chevalier Fleury having been approved
by the council were proposed by the President and being severally balloted
for were chosen fellows of the Society."

As this was St Andrew's day, on which no business was usually transacted
except the annual election of Council and officers, it is strange that the
names of Van Effen and Fleury should have been passed for election on that
day. As Van Effen was admitted on Dec. 8 his name would appear on the
list of members for the next ensuing official year, 1716, as it actually does,
while 's Gravesande is on the list for 1715. (*Vide* "A list of the Fellows of
the Royal Society," British Museum.)
[4] Journal Book.

The ceremony involved a subscription to the "Obligation" by signing the Charter Book[1], upon which the president shook hands with the new member. On the same day were admitted several other members of whom no mention is made in the Journal Book. On February 2, 1715/16, the minutes record: "Mr 's Gravesande told the President he was going into Holland the beginning of the next week and desired to know if he could do the Society any service there. He was thanked by the Society for his civillity...."

This entry therefore fixes exactly the time of departure of 's Gravesande and probably also of the rest of the embassy. Van Effen's name appears regularly on the list up to 1738 (three years after his death) and it is some evidence of how he valued his membership that he regularly paid up to the last the quarterly subscription of 13s. after an entrance fee of 40s. The members for 1715/16 included Sherlock, Halley, Burnet, Sir Hans Sloane, Arbuthnot and Sir Christopher Wren, Sir Isaac Newton presiding. When 's Gravesande returned to Holland he carried with him the fiery cross of Newtonian philosophy which was quite unknown on the continent, Mr 's Gravesande being "le premier hors de l'Angleterre qui entreprit de l'enseigner[2]." Wassenaer van Duivenvoorde, Van Effen's employer and patron, helped 's Gravesande to a professorship at Leyden and there he taught with "tout l'applaudissement possible[3]." His clever inventions in scientific apparatus were universally admired, his lectures in geometry, algebra, astronomy and physics, etc., were very popular, he received royal invitations, was consulted in practical matters, e.g., it was greatly due to him that Dutch windmills were improved, the very kind of thing that was required to impress the sceptical multitude with the practical benefit, if not the dignity, of science. That this scientific movement was felt to be emanating from England left an impression which considerably magnified England's new greatness in the minds of the continental peoples. 's Gravesande was resorted to from all parts.

---

[1] Van Effen signed in a very plain, legible hand: "Justus van Effen."
[2] Prosper Marchand, *Dict.*   [3] *Ibid.*

Voltaire, that great disseminator of English learning and literature and culture, became his pupil and got the information necessary for the writing of the chapters on Newton in his *Lettres sur les Anglois,* Voltaire himself not having been able to meet Newton. Van Effen must have met Voltaire at that time, and probably saw something of him in England during 1728.

Bentinck, another historic example of the Anglo-Dutch family alliances of those times, son of William III's trusted adviser, living the life of an English nobleman, though officially a Dutch patrician, showed the keenest interest in English science and thinking then circulating in Holland. He met 's Gravesande probably at the home of his (Bentinck's) brother-in-law Wassenaer van Duivenvoorde, if not at the University and felt for the enterprising 's Gravesande "beaucoup d'estime et d'amitié[1]." But we are anticipating. We left Van Effen and 's Gravesande in England making the best of their opportunities, and the year is only 1715. The results were to come some decades later and were due in no small measure to the pioneer work of our two sojourners in London. Van Effen seemed also to have at that time a settled predilection for the life of the *salon* and society. His wise words in *Bagatelle,* no. XXXVIII, come from one who had done his *devoirs* to the English ladies, whom he seems to have admired and studied pretty closely. On his second visit, Verwer says that "through his former visit he was known and not unregarded at the English Court." At the Swedish Court it is the same. Van Effen loves to spend some of his time with the ladies[2]. But his gallantry was as genuinely gallant as Steele's. Wherever he can he speaks with candid admiration and respect for women, of whom like his forerunner Steele he was a persistent champion. In the *Spectateur François*[3] he says: "Une femme de mérite dit un Auteur Anglois a de commun avec la véritable Religion qu'on l'aime & qu'on l'estime à mesure

---

[1] Marchand, *op. cit.*   [2] *Voy. en Suède,* Let. IX.
[3] P. 136, 2nd ed. *Vide Holl. Spect.* nos. 148, 83, etc.; *Misant.* I, no. IV; II, no. XLIX.

qu'on raisonne"; a typical half-true eighteenth-century aphorism. But there was much else to do, besides, which Van Effen did not neglect to do.

In the circles of the talented wits in London a work of the famous Dr Swift, that in the original has the title of *Tale of a Tub*, later known to us by that of "Vertelsel van de Ton", was at that time much discussed. That work, as acutely as it was attractively satirical, was regarded by the English as not only inimitable in respect of the original treatment of the subject, but also as being untranslatable into any other language without losing the characteristic wit that animated the English work....It seemed, then, to annoy him that other languages were considered so despicable, as if they were quite incapable of giving an idea of the spirit contained in the Fable of a Tub. He knew of the great prejudice that the English always felt for the works of their own writers and was aware that the sentiment of being inimitable was pretty general amongst them with respect to everything that was undertaken in a foreign language out of their mother-tongue[1].

Van Effen embarked on the translation, of which he showed some parts to his acquaintances, who applauded his efforts. Van Effen, then, was clearly enjoying the company of literary circles in London, and in all likelihood frequented Steele's new quarters in Villiers Street, in the Strand, whence emanated a brisk succession of papers attempted in the famous style which even Bickerstaff seems to have lost. But armed with his new patent Steele was pushing an extensive *répertoire* at the Theatre Royal. Drury Lane never gave better seasons than when Steele was in command. The plays Van Effen could have seen included the following: *The Tender Husband, Volpone, The Country Wife, Henry VIII, The Tempest, Hamlet*; the last on May 27, Wilks appearing in the title-rôle, Booth playing the Ghost and Mrs Mountfort Ophelia. He would also have attended the performance on April 19 of the *Beaux' Stratagem* played for "Bickerstaffe's Benefit." At Lincoln's Inn Fields where young John

---

[1] Verwer, *Leven*. Cp. also Preface, *Le Conte du Tonneau*, vol. i. Verwer is uncertain whether this happened during the first or the second visit to London. It must however have been during the first visit as the translation eventually appeared in 1721, six years before Van Effen's second visit.

Rich was proving an enterprising manager, *Henry IV*, *The Jew of Venice*, *Sophonisba*, etc., were duly performed.

In October 1715, the *Daily Courant* announced the opening of the Drury Lane winter season after extensive alterations and decorations had been completed. On October 13 the opening took place with *The Country Wife* followed on the 14th by the *Old Batchelor*, properly expurgated we hope by the Society for the Reformation of Manners. Then came *Richard III* (Cibber), *The Distressed Mother*, *The Tempest*, *King Lear*, *Timon of Athens*, *Othello*, *Macbeth*, *Venice Preserved*, etc., in fact a galaxy of famous plays such as London rarely sees nowadays. Van Effen probably never saw *The Drummer*[1] unless, perchance, he saw it produced somewhere in the provinces or at the Universities. *The Drummer* was played on March 10, 1716, at Drury Lane, but Van Effen was back in Holland by that time. *Cato* was first produced at Drury Lane in 1713 and Van Effen may possibly have seen one of the performances given in 1715.

The chief literary event during Van Effen's stay was the publication of Pope's *Iliad* in June 1715. The scale on which it was done and the interesting introduction impressed Van Effen even more than the execution[2]. No doubt, too, he heard all the discussion on the Tickell-Pope controversy. The publication of Steele's *Lady's Library* also excited his notice, as did that of Addison's *Freeholder*, but otherwise the period of his visit was barren of important events in the world of literature.

Meanwhile, our two visitors were still active members of the *Journal Littéraire* Club, but their absence from the Hague must account for the reduction of the paper to four (instead of six) issues in 1715. Two of the numbers contain at the end a long news-item from London, probably from the pen of Van Effen, and the volume for 1716 opens with a forty-page account of Pope's *Iliad*, the projected appearance of which had been discussed in the London news-column of the previous year.

---

[1] He could have seen it, however, during his second visit.
[2] *Journal Littéraire* 1716.

Early in 1716 Wassenaer van Duivenvoorde hastened back, probably on account of the illness of his son, Van Effen's pupil. The young man died soon after, and in March 1716 Van Effen proceeded to the University of Leyden with a new pupil, the son of Baron van Welderen.

It was with this pupil that Van Effen made his second trip to England twelve years later as chief secretary to the embassy of which the young Van Welderen was a member. In the interval Van Effen had added six years' university study to his store of learning, had written freely and done several important translations from English literature. His *Bagatelle* (1718), which was the first to appear after the *Misantrope*, shows naturally a much greater familiarity with English writing and life than he had before. In 1719 he made his voyage to Sweden, where, from several references in his *Voyage en Suède*, we see that he was also in the society of Englishmen and was probably reading English works.

When he reached London in October 1727, for the second time, he was better read in English literature and acquainted with the English outlook than the great majority of his contemporaries on the continent. In marked contrast to Voltaire, who was being initiated into the novel mysteries of English life, language and literature at that very moment, and whom the Dutchman probably met in England, Van Effen could now correct his former impressions and extend his already comparatively extensive knowledge of things English. In 1720, five years after his first visit and seven before this second, Van Effen could remark in his preface to *Le Conte du Tonneau*, "Pour moi, *qui suis au fait, & qui ai lu avec attention ce qu'ils ont produit de plus estimé....*"

Of this trip Verwer says that the young Van Welderen, "mindful of the good qualities of his teacher," wrote to him, and Van Effen made no delay in accepting the secretaryship:

In London he found every means of enjoyment and could enrich his spirit and knowledge in the conversation of the fine wits of that time, and delight in the Court life of which, when it was not inconsistent with reason, he was particularly fond[1].

[1] *Vide* also *Voy. en Suède*, esp. Let. ix.

Of the company he may have kept with the Great and the Learned of that Kingdom, I have not been able to unearth the particulars. He returned laden with honour and regard, having been presented with the royal gift of a gold medal.

Van Effen also composed a panegyric on the occasion of the crowning of George II and his spouse[1], an event which he had attended with the other members of the delegation on October 22, 1727. There is little in this account, and it is strange that Van Effen has left us no record of his experiences, as he had of his travels to Sweden. Perhaps England was *terra cognita*. There had been much change since 1715. Thomson was now the giant of the moment, and the town was buzzing over his remarkable instalments of nature poetry. Van Effen must have felt deeply interested, but this kind of poetry was not so novel to a Dutchman whose native literature preserved a more noticeable continuity of nature writing than English literature. In the *Journal Littéraire* of 1717, the reviewer (Van Effen) had been enthusiastic over Poot's *Mengeldichten*. "Un Paisan, véritable Paisan dont les occupations ordinaires sont de traire des vaches et de labourer la terre et qui employe son loisir à faire des vers qui sont bien au-dessus du médiocre," he has "beaucoup de pureté, de force et de précision,...une imagination heureuse et assez correcte." It sounds like a verdict that might have been passed on Thomson, and the writer of it would, a decade afterwards, have welcomed the Scotsman's work as openly and fully, no doubt, as he had welcomed that of his own countryman. Thomson duly had his admirers and imitators in the Netherlands.

Another sensational literary event was the appearance and phenomenal run of *The Beggar's Opera* at Lincoln's Inn Fields from January 29 to June 19, 1728. At the same theatre Van Effen could have seen *Othello*, *King Lear*, *Oronooko*, *The Drummer*, etc., and at Drury Lane, *The Way of the World*, *The Tempest*, *The Alchemist*, *Macbeth*, *Richard III*, *Henry VIII*, with Booth creating a sensation in the title-rôle. Of the old school, Addison was no more, Steele a

[1] Cp. Addison's poem on William III.

benign old man in his retreat at Carmarthen, and Swift, whom Van Effen never saw, back in Ireland before the Dutch embassy arrived in London. Pope was about to launch his *Dunciad*, which appeared soon after Van Effen's departure. But of all the happenings in the world of literature we may be sure that none interested Van Effen more than the appearance of *Gulliver's Travels* in the year previous to his visit. Many editions were called for and the book was one of the most discussed of the time.

Although Van Effen has left only the briefest sketches and no set and sustained description or panegyric of English life and letters like his more famous younger contemporaries, Prévost, Montesquieu, Voltaire and others, he had learnt more from his island neighbours and, by virtue of his very priority in respect of time, has, at least, equality in respect of place as an active and able participator in the great movement of the eighteenth century which spread literature, and especially English literature, beyond national boundaries. For the significance of Van Effen's presence in England, his remarks on, and laudable imitation of, English literature, the words of Voltaire[1] might be quoted:

Our European travellers for the most part are satyrical upon their neighbouring countries and bestow large praises upon the Persians and Chineses, it being too natural to revile those who stand in competition with us and to extol those who being far remote from us are out of the reach of Envy.... We should be busied chiefly in giving faithful accounts of all the useful things and of the extra-ordinary persons whom to know and to imitate would be a benefit to our countrymen.

A traveller who writes in that spirit is "a merchant of a nobler kind who imports into his native country the arts and virtues of other nations."

The last years of Van Effen's life are notable chiefly for the production of the *Hollandsche Spectator*. Having already acclimatized the famous English genre on the continent twenty years previously in his *Misantrope*, he now worthily utilized the form Steele had discovered for him and produced a national classic.

[1] Preface, *On the Civil Wars of France*.

It will have been seen from the foregoing that Van Effen's career was remarkably well adapted for the rôle he played in literature, and often curiously similar to that of his English predecessors, especially to Addison's. Van Effen held four official appointments, enjoyed without snobbishness or sacrifice of poise the favour of the great, travelled, had Addison's interest in medals, and in view of their prominence as reformers, both were worried on their death-beds as to their final opinions on the Christian religion! Addison took pupils and lost a tutorship; so did Van Effen who, however, held three such appointments covering altogether some seven years. But his duties were not onerous, and these years allowed him not only to publish writings and translations, but also to study assiduously. He graduated Doctor of Laws at Leyden, so that he has not unjustly been referred to as a "savant[1]," a man who was altogether *au fait* with respect to the science and philosophy of his day and their previous development[2]. His knowledge of classical, French, Dutch and English literatures need not again be stressed. But with it all Van Effen was essentially a man of spirit. The earliest incident recorded of him tells of a witticism for which his father reproved him. Again when he sought a first tutorial appointment at Madame Bazin de Luneville's, he met her objection to his youth with: "C'est un défaut, dont je me corrige tous les jours," a reply which appeared so apt to the noble Wassenaer van Duivenvoorde, says Verwer, that, attracted by the young man, he became employer, friend and patron to the aspirant *homme de lettres*[3].

His first original work was something in the burlesque style, the *Dissertation sur Homère et sur Chapelain*[4], in which a ridiculous *parallèle* is sustained between two things that are too far apart for comparison without laughable absurdity. To complete the impression of wrongheaded, mal-

---

[1] E. Hatin, *Les Gazettes de Hollande* (1865), p. 217.
[2] Cp. also C. G. Jöcher, *Gelehrten Lexicon* (1726): "Ein Philosophus und Criticus." [3] *Leven*, p. xv.
[4] One of "the most impertinent poets that ever scribbled"—Voltaire, preface, *Civil Wars of France*.

adroit criticism, Van Effen finally casts in favour of Chapelain, and delivers a bludgeon blow to the foolishness of commentators upon whose impertinences the fate of authors appears to rest. The work is juvenile stuff, written at the age of about twenty-three, but shows Van Effen's predilection for wit, irony and burlesque applied to absurdities that should be laughed out of countenance. In 1714 it was printed with the famous *Chef d'œuvre d'un Inconnu*, in which Van Effen had some slight share and which indeed was in all probability suggested by his earlier work. It would be most unlikely that Van Effen's club friends would be ignorant that he already had an essay in his cabinet on the same subject as the later *pièce de résistance* of St Hycinthe who received hints from his *fratres journalistes*. Van Effen may thus be said to have inspired the *Chef d'œuvre*[1], and both on this account and on that of his *Parallèle*, which J. P. de Crousaz[2] considers "a porté de plus grands coups aux Partizans outrés des anciens que les Dissertations les plus sérieuses," was a creditable participator in the battle of the books, which Perrault had unchained some two decades before by his paper read in the French Academy.

In 1710 Van Effen had translated Shaftesbury's *Essay on the Freedom of Wit and Humour*, and he retained a bias for Shaftesbury's views on this question ever afterwards. "D'ailleurs, le moien de raisonner sérieusement avec des gens qui n'admettent pas le bonsens comme juge naturel de leurs sentiments, et qui trouvent du crime à y avoir recours? S'il y a quelque chose qui puisse reveiller leur raison de la Léthargie où ils la jettent de propos délibéré, c'est le sel piquant de la Raillerie[3]." This view Van Effen had learnt from Shaftesbury who wished to establish *raillerie* as the great test of truth[4]. Van Effen, after Addison's essays on false wit in the *Spectator*, discusses at length the subject of

---

[1] Sayous is therefore mistaken in saying of the *Parallèle*: "n'est guère qu'un reste bien refroidi du *Chef d'œuvre d'un Inconnu*."

[2] *De l'Éducation des Enfans* (1722), vol. II.

[3] Preface, *Conte du Tonneau* (1732), vol. I.

[4] Though, with characteristic caution, Van Effen held: "La raillerie par elle-même ne prouve jamais rien"—*Misant.* no. XXXVIII, 2nd ed.

bons mots in *Misantrope*, no. xxx, etc. The *Bagatelle* of course set out with the idea of being ironical in everything that was said. *Discours Ironiques* Van Effen called his essays, and in fact the term describes most of his writings. What object had he in view? it might be asked. His object was the same as that of Addison and Steele and many other eighteenth-century writers. It is well expressed many times over in their writings, in Swift, in Pope, in Voltaire, but Van Effen's defence of Swift's *Tale of a Tub* may be quoted in part for its statement of what these writers, and Swift in particular, were aiming at:

> ...il tourne en ridicule cet Esprit d'Enthousiasme et de Fanatisme, qui rend la Piété incompatible avec le Sens commun. Je m'imagine que toutes les personnes sensées en seront obligées à l'auteur. On ne sauroit rendre véritablement un plus grand service à la seule religion raisonnable et digne de la majesté de Dieu et de l'Excellence de la nature humaine, que de la débarrasser de la superstition, et de la Chimère, qui non seulement l'avilissent mais la détruissent de fond en comble en l'arrachant de sa base unique et solide la Raison et le Bon-Sens. La Piété est pour ainsi dire la santé de l'âme: les superstitieux, et les Fanatiques en font une Fièvre chaude; et quiconque s'efforce à y remédier efficacement mérite les plus grands éloges[1].

This illustrates Van Effen's settled philosophy of life as applied to religion, and this is the spirit which animates almost all his work. The correspondence of Van Effen with what may be called the time-spirit, from the moment at least that Bayle wrote, has led Dr Sybil Goulding[2] to suggest a parallel between him and Swift in the essentials of their spirit and taste: "il est vraiment étonnant que pas un seul des critiques modernes de Van Effen, à notre connaissance, ne semble avoir remarqué que son choix de ce sujet de traduction peut servir comme illustration excellente de plusieurs de ses traits de caractère les plus intéressants." This writer urges that, both in the *amour du badinage* and their detestation of anything unreasonable and false in life, they were temperamentally akin. We have indicated how in a general way the

---

[1] Preface, *Le Conte du Tonneau* (La Haye, 1721).
[2] *Swift en France* (1924), chap. 2.

minds of the men were not dissimilar, but particulars prove that the parallel can readily become forced. Van Effen had nothing in his constitution of the "ribald priest." His main reason for undertaking the translation of *A Tale of a Tub* is expressed by the paragraph I have quoted, but he is the first to regret that the author had permitted himself so many liberties. It would have been wiser if he had omitted from his ironies "certains tours gaillards, qui révoltent une Imagination un peu délicate." "A mon avis l'Auteur auroit agi sagement, en écartant toujours de ses Badinages tout Passage formel de l'Écriture Sainte," etc. Van Effen has thus "adouci ces endroits autant qu'il m'a été possible; et j'ose espérer que la Pudeur du Public François ne se gendarmera jamais contre mes Expressions"(!). His defence of the book is obviously special pleading, which was probably evoked both as a palliative to his own conscience and as the possible censure of the public that read and was expected to buy. In the spirit of badinage many men share, but few share alike. Swift's is, of course, distinguished by being *outré* and bizarre far beyond what Van Effen would have allowed himself. "I hate and detest that animal called man, although I heartily love John, Peter, Thomas and so forth[1]" is a sentiment Van Effen could never have brought himself to utter, although he would have subscribed to the concession as heartily as he would have repudiated the impiety of the postulate. No creed of Van Effen's is more insisted on than that of the dignity of human nature; he is as enthusiastic over it as are Addison and Shaftesbury, to whom he was partly indebted for it. Van Effen was too devoted a lover of wit not to recognize and admire it in Swift, but his selection of Swift for translation does not illustrate anything in his character which is not elsewhere fully expressed. Nor must we dismiss Verwer's story that Van Effen had undertaken the translation purely out of a spirit of challenge to English excessive *amour propre*, although we may readily agree that Van Effen would have been attracted by the general aim as well as by the intellectual brilliancy of Swift.

[1] Letter to Pope, Sept. 1725.

Van Effen, with all his cleverness, was a simple, natural man; so far from trading on mere weight of learning, he believed that learning was useless unless it could be passed over into everyday life[1], to beautify and improve it. Dullness and pedantry he abhorred as much as flippancy or stupidity. Plain humanity was the essential—all the rest accessory. A New Year *Misantrope* number[2] opens:

Bon jour et bon An, Ami Lecteur. Le compliment est un peu trivial, et vous avez attendu apparemment de moi quelque chose de plus singulier. Vous vous êtes trompé comme vous voyez; j'aime autant à me confondre avec le Vulgaire pour les bagatelles innocentes de la cérémonie, que je serois ravi de m'en distinguer du côté de la réfléxion et du raisonnement.

There is, of course, a little sarcasm in this at the expense of dull people who would appear clever at all costs no matter how forced their wit is. The circumstances of Van Effen's early life made him well acquainted and sympathetic with the middle and lower classes, while his later education and social intercourse brought him into close touch with the intellectual and fashionable society of Holland, Sweden and England. Not only were aristocratic and Court circles open to him, but he associated with the best wits and finest intellects of many countries. He had, therefore, an unrivalled opportunity for gaining a wide, catholic and thorough knowledge of life, not through books, but by actual intercourse with men of all classes. And we know that he loved nothing better than making use of his opportunities in this regard. He was an observer of men and a lover of the *genre humain*. He would have endorsed Pope's dictum as to the proper study of mankind. There are social pictures in his pages that are superior as pen pictures to anything I know in English literature of Van Effen's time; papers like nos. 294, 68, and the Kobus and Angietje numbers[3], prove him to have had the essential qualities of a Dutch painter, combining sympathetic and minute observation with a genius

[1] *Vide*, e.g., *Nouv. Sp. Fr.* no. v; *Misant.* i, p. 15, ii, xi, xiii, xxvii, etc.
[2] 1712.
[3] *Holl. Spect.*

for the selection of detail. In a convivial age such as the eighteenth century, with its acutely developed social sense, Van Effen naturally played his part. Speaking quite *à propos* of the subject of pedantry, Van Effen says:

> Ce qu'on appelle dans le monde un Honnête-homme, songe de bonne heure à se mettre en état de goûter les agrémens de la société, & d'y contribuer de sa part... il n'a pas le ridicule orgueil de se croire au-dessus des sujets de conversation les plus triviaux. ...Quand on entre dans le commerce de la Vie Civile on n'y entre ni en qualité de Poëte, ni en qualité d'Orateur, ni en qualité d'Ecclésiastique; on y entre en qualité d'Homme, il n'y faut porter que le bon-sens. Si l'on peut y ajouter de la vivacité de l'esprit, du feu, c'est bien fait; mais il faut modérer ces agrémens & les mettre au niveau des lumières de ceux qu'on fréquente; il faut se munir surtout de complaisance & de douceur, & renoncer à la sotte vanité de primer & d'usurper la domination sur l'esprit des autres. (*Bagat.* no. LXIX.)

We have already quoted Verwer to the effect that Van Effen was enamoured of Court life, but he was also smart in appearance and gifted in conversation. "His stature was well formed, though not of the tallest nor thickset; his bearing and step brisk, firm and lively, with a turn for gentility and civility in keeping with which he arranged his dress which was neat and well kept, and outwardly one would have said that he was of French descent and not averse to imitating the beaux[1]." Indeed, there were not wanting those who accused him of affectation, of which I, too, think him guilty at times in his writings. If so, it was his chief weakness. Still, no one would disagree with Van Effen's views on dress:

> Mais un véritable Philosophe peut-il sans démentir son caractère, aimer la propreté, s'habiller de bon goût, mettre à profit la juste proportion que la Nature a donné à son corps, & se ménager un air prévenant & agréable? Il le peut sans doute, et même je crois qu'il y est obligé.... Est-ce agir raisonnablement, que de rendre nos lumières et nos vertues inutiles à la Société, faute d'une complaisance innocente pour les bizarreries de la mode? Mais le vrai Philosophe ne prodigue pas son tems et son

---

[1] *Leven*, p. cxxxvii.

attention aux vêtilles de l'ajustement...il n'augmente pas son
estime pour lui-même, quand il se voit couvert d'un habit
brillant; il s'habille et il n'y pense plus.

His talents for company have been so well described by
Verwer that the whole description ought to be quoted:

"Friendly and communicative he would always have
wished to be, especially in any conversation that might be
profitable, but he was continually as if sunk in deep meditation and his thoughts were frequently withdrawn to the
subject with which his mind was occupied." This tense
abstraction "sometimes lasted until the evening"; but then,
when he had come into congenial company,

one might gradually see his expression becoming unclouded and
a fire shine in his eyes that loosened the tongue charmingly, and
one might hear him discuss with the greatest sportiveness,
though with politeness, exactness and perspicacity. These were
the most enjoyable hours of companionship for his friends, and
as it seldom bored him, it also bored nobody else that those hours
were prolonged[1].

The next morning he would surprise his friends by another
fit of the blues, which, however despondent he was, never
allowed him to be bearish, "for that his civility would not
permit." Nevertheless, "his presence was always profitable
and he had uncommon address in making himself understood." But Verwer is speaking of Van Effen's last years
when an internal malady had already gripped him. The love
of conviviality and company is marked in his writings, and it
is clear too that he was not always prepared to indulge this
passion indiscriminately, but, like a true social connoisseur,
wanted the choice spirits, the select circle for real conversation[2]. The light badinage of the *salon* would hardly have
been his forte, while the foppish frivolity of modish young
gallants was beneath him.

We see how striking, in this respect, too, is the resemblance between him and Addison. There is that desire for a
"little senate" for the best kind of conversation to flow, that
initial reserve which, when overcome, leaves each the most

[1] *Leven.*   [2] E.g. *Holl. Spec.* nos. 88, 329, 94.

delightful of talkers. How can "the sweetness of a witty conversation be relished[1] in a boisterous, ill-sorted dinner party"? Remarks such as these clearly reveal the typical conversational connoisseur of the eighteenth century. Van Effen had the advantage in a comparison with Addison, that he did not resort to a stimulant to loosen his tongue. "Convivial excesses," to use Macaulay's euphemism, were not among Van Effen's failings. In an age of heavy drinking, Van Effen had the merit of being "un très petit buveur," as he admits when he tells of how the English captain tried to make him drunk[2].

But the quality that most wins our admiration for him is that of gentlemanliness and sincerity. The elogist who does not seem to understand Van Effen's character quite rightly in many respects has done well to insist on his reputation as "honnête homme." "Il est vrai que la qualité d'honnête homme que vous lui donnez, est une justice que ceux qui l'ont le moins aimé ne peuvent lui réfuser, sans déroger eux-mêmes à ce titre," is the striking remark made by the Consul Potin in his letter to the writer of the *Éloge Historique*. As a critic of books and men, as a friend, Van Effen has made it abundantly clear that he had taken a firm stand for truth, Christian tolerance and fairplay. Van Effen's treatment of La Motte, the French writer, is a good example of his desire to be fair in his criticisms. La Motte expressed himself in appreciative terms over this review, the whole passage being "d'honneur à l'un & à l'autre" as the elogist has said.

"Upright and generous was his character," says Verwer, who proceeds to tell of a significant incident in illustration[3]. From an earnest, reflective nature like Van Effen's one must expect much self-revelation. He lacked the lyrical enthusiasm of J.-J. Rousseau, or the headlong openness of Steele, who contributed his actual personal love letters to himself in the *Spectator*[4], but the sincerity of Van Effen inevitably made his writings a kind of confession. What he gave to the

---

[1] *Holl. Spect.* no. 94.
[2] *Voy. en Suède*, Let. xi.
[3] *Leven*, pp. cxlv–cxlvii.
[4] E.g. no. 142.

public was, as La Bruyère says of his own work, taken from the public, but Van Effen returned it always as something personal, something enriched by the mature meditation of a fine and acute spirit, something that had become a part of his life. He could analyse and psychologize men because, like Shaftesbury, he had long subjected himself to such examination. "He gives an illustrated self-criticism, as a test for his people," says J. Koopmans[1]. "By the continuous maintaining of his own nature, by testing all his actions and impulses, his circumstances and his spiritual experiences by the standards of the best moments of his steadily deepening consciousness[2]," he gained that inner equilibrium which comes only after inward moral struggle and victory. And it is as original moralist and *Aufklärer* that W. Zuydam wishes us primarily to consider him a figure of importance[3]. The same writer has made a careful study[4] of Van Effen's character, and rightly warns readers against accepting the "Lettre d'un Homme d'âge[5]" as a piece of autobiography. On the other hand, Van Effen was not tracing figures in the air; most of that sketch is the living experience of the author enhanced by the fictitious addition permitted to artistic freedom[6]. This character sketch, then, can be regarded as something in the nature of *confessions*, as long as we do not look for facts in it; for these, as in most confessions, are either untrue or distorted out of all proportion. On the whole, the impression it gives of the profound moral struggle of a man who has lived intensely is not false to what we know of Van Effen, although some aspects of the character must be regarded as quite beneath him, as, e.g., the weak sentimentality and criminally erotic nature of the hero. But these things are a part of that other life of most human beings which they suppress with all their power and, if they are fortunate, prefer to forget. Van Effen is amusing himself by picturing the conduct of a man who is a slave to the

[1] *De Nieuwe Taalgids*, no. i. [2] *Ibid.*
[3] *Justus van Effen*, p. 173. [4] *Ibid.* pp. 39–65.
[5] *Nouv. Sp. Fr.* (1725).
[6] E.g. the story of his marriage. Van Effen married seven years after the *Nouv. Sp. Fr.* appeared.

strong emotions everyone feels, and few, Van Effen pre-eminent amongst them, learn to control. In the "homme d'âge" we see the kind of man that would be produced if he carried to their logical fruition the sexual instincts of our purely animal consciousness and applied in swift reaction the self-criticism of a highly-developed moral sense.

The moral constitution of such a man is ever in a state of unstable equilibrium. We see then that the "homme d'âge" is not Van Effen in the sense in which men judge one another, but is a projection of what he might have been as he saw himself in his most atrabilious moods, for although Sir William Temple had naïvely discovered that a Dutchman was not "delicate or idle enough" to suffer from the "spleen," and Steele repeats the notion[1], Van Effen was a proof that this fashionable malady was not confined to the British Isles. Perhaps the best comment one can make on this question is to cite the case of Steele's gentleman[2], "a very eminent lingerer and something splenetick," who, besides his other excesses, received a thousand affronts during the North-Easterly winds, and in short run through more misery and expence than the most meritorious bravo could boast of......

During this lethargy he had some intervals of application to books which rather aggravated than suspended the painful thoughts of a misspent life.

Like the damn'd in Milton:

> "He felt by turns the bitter change
> Of fierce extreams...."

Thus did he *pass the noon of his life in the solitude of a monk and the guilt of a libertine.*

Van Effen had only a few years previously translated the *Guardian,* and his character sketch might well have been suggested by such a paper, and done in *romanesque* style. Indeed, it does seem as if the significance of the "Lettre" has not been fully understood. It is, more clearly than anything else in literature, the prelude to the psychological, sentimental novel of the mid and late eighteenth century. It is to be regretted that Van Effen did not work out his sketch more fully. Yet it is not an unworthy *morceau* and

---

[1] *Guardian,* no. 131. [2] *Ibid.*

runs into sixty-four pages. Its interest lies chiefly in the consideration of character from the inside. As a personality the
hero is unattractive, but his case from the moral point of
view is really interesting and sketched with a closeness to
the probabilities of life that is quite unusual for the time.
Nor is action lacking. There is a drunken attempt on the
honour of his mistress, a public quarrel, a duel, a romantic
marriage that is not a success, and so on. Then there are re-
criminations, mortifying reflections, tears—plenty of them—
honourable resolves often broken, but the end is calm and,
"all passion spent," the hero has attained serenity of soul.
We must not dismiss the sketch as a mere bilious figment;
it is a piece of work that is on all fours with life—indeed,
Van Effen has not, after all, gone very far from his own
inner life experiences. The professed writer is a Dutchman
who flings himself into the society of Frenchmen and has a
craving for winning their applause as a man of spirit.

Par une seconde imprudence, je résolus de me défaire de ma
douleur chez un peuple où la gayeté inconsidérée est dans son
centre, et où *vivre & se dissiper* est la même chose. Le Torrent de
la joie Nationale m'entraîna en moins de rien, je *vécus* plus dans
un mois que je n'avois fait dans tout le reste de ma vie. Ma vanité
rompit sa digue...les maximes de la mode usurpèrent chez moi
les droits des principes de la Raison. La Réputation *d'avoir bien
de l'esprit pour un Étranger me parut la plus belle chose du monde*[1].

We inevitably recall Van Effen the Dutchman who had
more French than Dutch friends, who had seemed bent on
carving out a niche for himself in French journalism and
literature, and who at the same time seriously warned his
countrymen against the inordinate gallicizing which Dutch
national life was suffering. None had experienced it more
than the writer himself, so none knew its dangers better. In
the afternoon of his life the "homme d'âge" followed the
advice of a friend "de consacrer pendant toute ma vie quelques heures du jour à l'examen de moi-même, à la méditation,
à de bonnes lectures, & surtout à la prière." As a result,

La tendresse ridiculement délicate que j'ai sentie autrefois pour
le Beau-Sexe est devenue une sensibilité vive & générale pour tout

[1] Lettre 4, *Nouv. Sp. Fr.* no. xxviii.

le Genre Humain, & surtout pour mes amis.....Je sens pourtant avec une souveraine satisfaction, que de jour en jour mon amour propre se subordonne avec docilité à la Raison & la Vertu.

The character of Van Effen has inextricably entered into all this[1]. For my part, therefore, I would, with the qualifications made above, regard the "Lettre d'un Homme d'âge" much in the same light as the *Boekzaal* reviewer for January 1745, who says: "This narrative is not only a picture of the *writer's*[2] life, but also an exact exposure of his heart, of his inmost thoughts and emotions." Le Clerc, the translator, considered it a noteworthy piece, and the *Boekzaal* believes that, despite its length, it cannot bore anyone. It was even then appreciated for what it primarily is, a psychological character sketch. It is not impossible that Steele's *Christian Hero* may have suggested the Sunday school ending to Van Effen, although the "Lettre" is on a higher level, artistically. Van Effen was a writer of distinction as well as an international literary figure of importance. It remains to discuss him more closely in his rôle of journalist, translator and original writer in both French and Dutch.

---

[1] We must compare with the "Lettre," the *Nouv.Sp.Fr.* no.1, e.g., "abandonné à moi-même dans l'âge où les passions exercent sur l'âme l'empire le plus tirannique, elles causèrent dans mes sentiments les révolutions les plus funestes, un vif penchant vers la tendresse, et un désir outré de plaire. Heureusement je ne me rendois jamais sans combattre"—quite so! otherwise we should not have had the "Lettre d'un Homme d'âge."

Also *Misant.* II, XI: "Quand je songe quelquefois à ma jeunesse, le souvenir d'un tendre commerce vient souvent se présenter à mon imagination, avec tout ce qu'il a de plus flatteur pour la vanité: l'imagination remplie de ces idées riantes émeut bien-tôt les ressorts le plus cachez de mon cœur; elle y cause un desordre délicieux, un mouvement tendre & vif, dont j'ai de la peine à me défendre, & auquel je me fais un plaisir de m'abandonner: mais ma Raison soûtenue par mon âge ne laisse pas long-tems mon cœur en proye à cette dangereuse agitation, je m'efforce bien-tôt à rappeler dans mon esprit les chagrins que traîne après elle la passion la plus heureuse même; la bassesse qu'il y a dans la conduite d'un amant & l'extravagance de ces sentiments délicats dont il s'applaudit le plus. Ces images me ramenent bientôt du Plaisir à la Raison & revenue à ma première tranquillité, je me félicite de n'avoir pas attendu le secours de la vieillesse, pour sauver mon cœur d'un trouble si cruel, & mon esprit d'un déréglement si funeste. Ma Raison est alors contente d'elle-même, & cette satisfaction de la Raison est une volupté, qu'on ne sauroit comprendre à moins d'en avoir goûté toute la douceur.

[2] My italics.

CHAPTER III

THE *MISANTROPE*

In the eastward spread of English literary influences, no personality was more conspicuous than that of Addison. As we look back on the history of international literary contact, it becomes clear that from the mediaeval Age of Romance, at least, there was on the whole a steadily growing *rapprochement* between France and England in literature of which the ages of Chaucer, Spenser and Dryden may be said to mark the crests. But it was still a most one-sided affair, the English learning and imitating actively from their neighbours who remained indifferent to, if not ignorant of, the literary culture of the islanders. It was the age of Addison that finally nationalized French classical culture in England to form a *point d'appui* whence English originality could be more readily appreciated in countries where French taste ruled. English and French literature had almost reached a point of fusion, and it was this fact which, as it was more and more realized by the eighteenth century itself, profoundly affected contemporary and subsequent literary development in Europe. Addison himself is an admirable example of the process that was going on. Formed in the classical and French classical schools of taste, his literary outlook was international, and his close application to French language and literature, especially Boileau, La Bruyère, and the tragic dramatists, made him a typically Anglo-French literary figure, so that we are not surprised to find that it was largely through the medium of his writings and reputation that English literature overflowed far and wide over the continent.

As Milton had created no small impression on the continent in favour of English scholarship by his command of a vigorous latinity, so Addison, who did so much to convince his age that Milton was also a great poet, carried the fame of English culture abroad. As Tickell has well expressed it[1]:

> Our country owes it to him that the famous Monsieur Boileau first conceived an opinion of the English genius for Poetry by perusing the present he had made him of the *Musae Anglicanae* which he said gave him " a very new Idea of the English politeness and that he did not question but there were excellent compositions in the native language of a country that possessed the Roman genius in so eminent a degree."

Boileau's commendation of the Latin verses in Addison's volume, and his conjecture as to the existence of English literature, coming as it does at the meeting-point of the seventeenth and the eighteenth centuries, is very interesting. It sums up the average ignorance of the past and suggests the curiosity which overcame Europe with respect to English literature not long after. And in the process of discovery Addison was one of the first and most cherished finds. His continental tour had, of course, opened the way for this. His *Remarks on Italy* and his *Letter* excited interest. The news from London for November 1705[2] contained a notice of the prospective publication of the *Remarks*. " Mr Addison nous donnera bientôt un voyage d'Italie, où il nous parlera de tous les monumens qui nous restent de l'Ancienne Italie dont il est parlé dans les meilleurs auteurs. Ce sera un excellent morceau." Appetites thus whetted, the relish of a twenty-nine-page review for September 1706 was probably all the keener.

"Ce Livre," says the reviewer, "a tout ce qu'il faut pour se faire lire avec plaisir. Il est parfaitement bien imprimé, & c'est pourtant là le moindre de ses avantages. Ceux qui se piquent de savoir la délicatesse de la Langue Angloise disent qu'il est très-bien écrit & que les vers Anglois qui servent de Traduction à divers passages des Anciens Poëtes Latins, citez par Mr Addison, auteur de ce livre, répondent à la réputation qu'il s'est acquise d'être un des meilleurs Poëtes qu'ait aujourd'hui l'Angleterre."

And a footnote explains: " Il a fait un Poème sur la Bataille d'Hochstet, & quelques autres Pièces très-estimées. Il y a

---

[1] Preface, *Works of Addison* (1721).   [2] *Nouv. de la Rép. des Let.*

aussi de ses pièces Latines dans les recueils qu'on a imprimé en Angleterre."

By his personal association with the Italians, the French and the Dutch, he was indeed, in respect of English literature, Voltaire's "merchant of a nobler kind." We do not know much of his early stay in Holland, but have noted his admiration for Bayle, whom he looked up at Rotterdam. There it was that Tonson found him with the first four acts of his revised *Cato* all ready[1], and there probably he met le Clerc, who became one of his warmest admirers. The subject of the *Campaign* was thoroughly congenial to the Anglo-Dutch feeling of the time. Le Clerc hailed him as "one of the greatest Poets which England at this time boasts," and "one of the first poets in Europe." The poem was soon translated, other translations followed, and so it came about that Addison was admired as Tickell says[2] as "one of the best authors since the Augustan age in the two universities, and the greatest part of Europe before he was talked of as a poet in Town." But this happened considerably later. Addison's widespread popularity had not yet come. Beyond the remarks of 1706 in the *Nouvelles de la République des Lettres*, a careful scanning of the Dutch reviews has revealed nothing to show that the writings of Addison were not speedily forgotten on the continent until he came into the literary limelight again when the *Spectator* was already well under way. And the first man on the continent to resuscitate the literary reputation of Addison was Van Effen, while the works which stimulated this revival of interest were principally *Cato* and the *Spectator*. These gave him a blaze of world-wide literary fame quite unprecedented in the history of English *belles lettres*, and in the wake of this exhalation, other English writers, both greater and lesser, readily followed.

The history of the *Spectator* and the *Tatler* is too well known to be retold here, but certain aspects may be noted. It is certain that the *Tatler* was a composite genre, novel in its composition of elements that had long been developed and lay ready to hand. Of the best work in the *Tatler* and

---

[1] According to J. Spence, *Anecdotes....* (1820).
[2] Preface, *Works of Addison* (1721).

the *Spectator* it is customary to name Bacon, Cowley, Sir William Temple and others as predecessors, but the best numbers in the Queen Anne papers are more than pure essays. The Sir Roger papers alone are sufficient to remind us of what Steele and Addison had learnt from the character writers from Theophrastus to La Bruyère. As Steele is careful to say with intent to disarm criticism:

at the same time I shall take all the privileges I may as an Englishman and will lay hold of the late Act of naturalization to introduce what I shall think fit from France. The use of that law may I hope be extended to people the polite world with new characters as well as the kingdom itself with new subjects. Therefore an author of that nation called Le Bruyère [*sic*] I shall make bold with.

The *Spectator*, speculating on his fame in future ages[1], thinks that he will live because of "the diversions and *characters* of the *English* nation in his time" which he has depicted. But the novelty of the *Tatler* lay neither in its essays nor its characters, nor indeed in its moralist aims, nor in the manner of its appearance, but in the quality of the work turned out and the spirit in which it addressed its audience. It in fact combined the familiar essay and *caractère*, with the spirit of the current gazettes somewhat refined, and the addition of some features of the literary review. But even in this form the *Tatler* was not new, at any rate at its first appearance. The two previous decades alone had produced a batch of predecessors with whom the practice of the *Tatler* shows Steele to have been acquainted, but to Defoe belongs the merit of being the direct forerunner of the *Tatler*. When Defoe commenced periodicalist in the more polite vein, he certainly had the example and experience of at least a dozen similar papers to guide him. But Defoe was nothing if not original. Publications such as Motteux's *Gentleman's Journal*, Dunton's *Athenian Mercury* and the rest of them, can scarcely be said to have handed on any ideas to Defoe in so far as he suggests the later periodical essay. Their purpose was different, and their tone, as a little honest examination will show anyone, does not suggest the Spectatorial style of

[1] *Spec.* no. 101.

Defoe's *Review*. He it was who for the first time combined the newspaper and the essay in a sort of social periodical in such a way that between his work and the early *Tatler* numbers there is little difference in essentials. Ordinary news with comments is the main item in each, both writers attempting at the same time to foist some original lucubration upon the public through the medium of the newscolumn[1]. Steele's position as gazetteer ensured his access to the most authentic views and the latest news, giving him a standing above his brother "novelists." He could therefore afford to trifle with and amuse (ostensibly at least, for his purpose went deeper than the title of *Tatler* indicated) his public as Defoe had attempted five years before.

On February 19, 1704, Defoe issued a full sheet called *The Weekly Review*. It appeared every Saturday, but was soon reduced to a half sheet (the form Steele adopted) published every Tuesday and Saturday. Like the *Tatler* and the *Spectator*, it had its advertisement section, upon which the financial success of most of these papers depended. In the introduction Defoe said: "After our Serious Matters are over we shall at the end of every Paper, present you with a little Diversion as anything occurs to make the World Merry...," and in the general preface, written later, occurs a remarkable passage that shows an almost awed sense of the birth of a new genre in literature.

"When I first found the Design of this paper which had its Birth in Tenebris, I considered it would be a thing very historical, very long..." but "this age has such a Natural Aversion to a solemn and tedious affair that however profitable, it would never be diverting and the World would never read it. To get over this Difficulty *that secret Hand I make no doubt that directed this Birth into the World* dictated to make some sort of Entertainment or Amuzement at the end of every Paper... which innocent Diversion would hand on the more Weighty and Serious Part of the Design into the Heads and Thought of those to whom it might be useful."

[1] *Vide* also dedication to Mr Maynwaring, *Tatler*, vol. i: "To make this generally read it seemed the most proper method to form it by way of a letter of intelligence." Also "the addition of the ordinary occurrences of common Journals of News brought in a multitude of other readers."

This "diversion" was to consist ostensibly of social tittle-tattle, but actually of original and amusing observations on the social life of the time served up in semi-dramatic form as judgments pronounced by a proper court deliberating on the scandals of the age. The item ran under the super-scription of "Mercure Scandale or Advice from the Scan-dalous Club." Over this title he had to fight a prolonged duel which is also significant. In no. 38, he says:

We have been so often on the Defence of our Title that the world begins to think Our Society wants Employment.... If scandalous must signify nothing but Personal Scandal... we desire those gentlemen to answer for us how Post-Man or Post-Boy can signify a News-Paper...? From hence our Club thinks they have not fair Play in being deny'd the Privilege of making an Allegory as well as other People.

Defoe had paved the way for the use of titles like *Tatler*, etc. When Van Effen set up as a *Misantrope*, or wrote his *Bagatelle*, no predecessor had attempted anything of the kind in Holland, and literal-minded folk gave him no rest over his titles. Steele did not seem to have had any trouble about his.

We need not trace here the changes Defoe made in his paper, because it is clear how he proposed to entertain his readers. Now Steele is justly praised not so much for having taken up this sort of thing where Defoe had left it, but rather for the new direction which he gave to it. Before the first hundred numbers had been reached, the division "from my own apartment" had so encroached on the others that it filled nearly the whole paper, while the news-column from Saint James's Coffee House had dwindled into nothing, Addison had come in, and the too accommodating motto "quicquid agunt homines... nostri est farrago libelli" had changed to "celebrare domestica facta" and other appro-priate signboards. The true periodical essay had gradually evolved and been enlarged in scope by Steele and his co-adjutors only.

But the influence of Defoe persisted and cannot be said to have given Steele only the first initial hints. The first striking correspondence is the desire to expose the popular newswriters. Defoe's paper was advertised as "purged from the Errors and Partiality of newswriters and Petty Statesmen of all sides." He wished to set "the affairs of Europe in a clearer light and to prevent the various uncertain accounts and the partial reflections of our Street scribblers who daily and monthly amuse mankind with stories of great victories when we are beaten, miracles when we conquer." He made game of these brethren of the quill. One of them was arraigned for saying that "he had killed the Duke of Bavaria" and the "Scandalous Club," before which he appeared, voted that it was "a scandalous Thing, that newswriters shou'd kill Kings and Princes and bring them to life again at pleasure."

"The Club," he continues, "has had a great deal of trouble about the News-Writers who have been continually brought before them for their ridiculous stories...."

This fight was taken up by Steele and Addison. Addison's first contribution to the *Tatler*[1], indeed, rallied those gentlemen in inimitable fashion. "Where Prince Eugene has slain his thousands, Boyer has slain his ten thousands" is the strain of this pleasing satire. Numbers 19 and 42 return to the same topic, and as the Grub Street fry continued to be stung, the *Spectator* eventually found that he had roused a veritable wasp's nest of "paltry scribblers" about his ears, from which he was only rescued by the deadly stamp act of August 1, 1712. Defoe had vowed that he would tell the whole truth about the progress of the war and the state of the enemy. France, he insisted again and again, far from being decimated, is a great and vigorous country, and a formidable enemy whom it is foolish to underrate. Steele, in the second *Tatler*, wishes to "contradict what has been so assuredly reported by the newswriters of England, that France is in a most deplorable condition, etc...."

But Defoe's purpose with his "innocent diversion" was not so "innocent" as it looked. His society "resolve to treat vice and villainous actions with the utmost severity,"

[1] No. 18.

and he declares in the preface, "my firm resolution in all I write to exalt Virtue, expose vice, promote truth and help men to serious reflection is my first moving cause and last directed end." He speaks of the "endeavours" of his society "against the follies of the times." Indeed, it is to be feared that Defoe had, like his imitator Steele, later on, fallen to the lure of the "Society for the Reformation of Manners." Steele as a reformer was famous also for his fight against duelling, carried on at no small personal risk from bullies and gamesters whom he had provoked. In this matter again Steele was following the lead of Defoe whose society found that "duelling and challenging to duel are scandalous practices unchristian and unlawful." The paper for Saturday, April 29, 1704, is devoted to duelling and so are many others. "Indeed Gentlemen," he is provoked to say to objectors, "if whoring, Duelling and Blasphemy are but misfortunes, I am in the wrong and so are all our reformers, but if they are flagitious crimes that wise men ought to abhor & the Guilty be hanged for, then we are in the right." Such a sentence cannot be distinguished in tone from many similar ones in the *Tatlers* and *Spectators*. Defoe, like his successors, made much of his correspondents, and although he complained once that he was "letter baited by Querists," the correspondence column was not relinquished.

Defoe's determination to "censure the actions of men not of parties," "not to expose persons but things," and "to offend no party," coincides with the much-emphasized impersonal and impartial attitude of the later writers. Steele even makes use of Defoe's "Pasquin of Rome," the "Patron" of the *Society scandale* and Rome correspondent. Steele makes this correspondent write to Isaac Bickerstaff in *Tatler*, no. 129: "your reputation has passed the Alps," "you are looked upon here as a Northern droll," a sentence which suggests a conception popularized a century later by Madame de Staël, i.e. that of the *génie du Nord* invading the classically formed South.

In Defoe's *Scandal Court* we may be allowed to see the genesis of Steele's *Court of Honour* of *Tatler*, no. 250 and other numbers. As to the manner of publishing, Steele could not claim like Defoe: "*'Tis a new thing for an author to lay down his thoughts piecemeal,*" but Addison expands this idea in *Spectator,* no. 124. We who can be wise after the event are apt to forget how even the smallest innovations now hardly noticed, or accepted without question, were obliged, when they were still novelties, to win their way into public acceptance. So the whimsical and pleasantly ironical title characteristic of this new literature was not accepted by the public without protest, and Defoe and Van Effen, both pioneers, had difficulty over it, the half-sheet essay had to be defended by its innovators. In *Misantrope,* no. XII an objector is made to ask: "Why publish a paper which will be confounded with a Gazette and yet professes to be a literary work? "Oh," answers the author, "all you have to do is to save the sheets and make them up into a volume." Van Effen is clearly trying to win his readers over to what is felt to be a new departure in literature. These points suggest how Defoe and others helped to pave the way for the *Tatler,* but, as we have shown, he may fairly be held to have influenced Steele in a more vital way. Defoe's policy of recommending trade to the fastidious or ignorant public as the fitting occupation of a gentleman and of supreme importance is also fundamental to the later writers. In this respect Defoe, Steele and Addison did a first-rate national service at a time when England was making a determined bid for commercial supremacy. Defoe as an economist seems to have been rather neglected, but undeservedly. In his *Review* he makes a special feature of trade topics. "The matter of our English trade appears to be a thing of such consequence and so little understood that nothing could be more profitable to the readers & more advantageous to the public interest" than to make it a thing of general interest and esteem. No sentiment is more pronounced in the *Spectator* than this. We need hardly recall the many papers, allegories and other references to this topic. Sir Andrew Freeport (commerce), as member of the Spectator Club, was a standing challenge to Sir Roger (agriculture), and we might recall the expression in no. 69, that there are "not more useful members of a commonwealth than merchants."

It is an oft-told story how the excellent Steele and his coadjutors formed practically the whole of reading and cultured London, and finally England, into one ever-widening reading circle whom they diverted and entertained with drolleries and all manner of whimsical pretensions, combined with what can on the whole be described as sturdy good sense and simple right-minded humanity. With the assistance of Swift, Steele made an excellent start by sustaining the joke against Partridge and by using the pseudonym of Isaac Bickerstaff, Esq., of which mere name he proceeded at once to make a personality: "it happened very luckily that a little before I had resolved upon this design, a gentleman had written predictions and two or three other pieces in my name *which rendered it famous through all parts of Europe (sic)*....By this good fortune the name of Isaac Bickerstaff gained an audience of all who had any taste of wit[1]." With his usual reckless generosity he added that it was Swift and Bickerstaff to whom he owed "the sudden acceptance which my labours met with in the world." Indeed, the proper humorous atmosphere and sympathy had been created by Swift, and care had to be taken not to dissipate it. But Steele so completely established himself in the confidence of his readers that he soon ventured upon open reproof and reform. Gay is perhaps our best witness[2]:

Bickerstaff ventured to tell the town that they were a parcel of fops, fools and vain coquets, but in such a manner as even pleased them and made them more than half inclined to believe that he spoke Truth. Instead of complying with the false sentiments of Vicious Tasts of the Age either in Morality, Criticism or Good Breeding, he has boldly assured them that they were altogether in the wrong and commanded them with an authority which became him well, to surrender themselves to his arguments for vertue and good sense.

[1] Dedication to Mr Maynwaring, vol. i.
[2] *The Present State of Wit* (May 3, 1711).

In fact, the genial Bickerstaff soon acquired a real authority, and people allowed themselves to be taught, advised and admonished by him. "'Tis incredible to conceive the effect his writings have had on the Town" exclaims Gay, "how many thousand follies they have either quite banished or given a very great check to, how much countenance they have added to vertue and Religion." The extra *Tatler* number to be found at the end of the collection in the British Museum avers that the "Lucubrations perhaps have done more good than all the moral discourses that were ever written in our tongue." In the politest drawing-rooms he was allowed to direct the conversation: "All the town are full of the *Tatler*, which I hope you have, to prepare you for discourse, for no visit is made that I hear of but Mr Bickerstaff is mentioned," writes Lady Marow to her daughter Lady Kaye on January 5, 1709/10.

By amusing animadversion on little follies, thinly veiled accounts of social happenings, by the correspondence column, by social satire, not always kindly it must be said[1], on men, women and events, curiosity was effectively stimulated until few spoke before they knew Mr Bickerstaff's opinion on the question. Hughes told Steele that Nicolini, the Neapolitan operatic actor (who, by the way, was an excellent customer of the advertisement columns of the *Spectator* and the *Tatler* and was constantly puffed in these papers), had expressed "beaucoup d'inclination à étudier l'Anglais pour avoir seulement le plaisir de lire le Tatler," a compliment which Steele found "fort galant," writes Hughes to Nicolini. The esquire was cheered at the theatre, where a performance was given for his benefit[2]; his lucubrations, says Gay, "brought the coffee-houses more customers than all their other newspapers put together." "Everyone read him with pleasure and goodwill." But morality, entertainment and social improvement did not absorb all Bicker-

---

[1] Indeed, Bickerstaff frequently indulged in what would now be judged unpleasant personalities, e.g. the caustic remarks on Mary Astell in no. 32 by Swift, and elsewhere; the somewhat ill-natured characterizing of Dr John Radcliffe as Aesculapius, no. 44.

[2] Monday, January 16, 1709/10.

staff's attention. The *Tatler* educated and formed the taste even of the *beaux esprits*. The really fine critical comments on the stage and literature, especially on Shakespeare and Milton, which came mostly from the pen of Steele, the noble and poetic passages of Addison on things of deeper significance in life, the beautiful mellow sentimentality of Steele in numbers like 181, where he easily equals the best of Addison, could not but have the happiest results in cultivating sounder cultural feeling. But they descended some way to meet the popular intelligence of the time. Gay testifies:

How intirely they have convinced our fops and young fellows of the value and advantage of learning. He has indeed rescued it out of the hands of pedants and fools and discovered the true method of making it amiable and lovely to all mankind. In the dress he gives it 'tis a most welcome guest at Tea-Tables & assemblies & is relished & caressed by the merchants on the Change; accordingly there is not a Lady at Court nor a Banker in Lombard St who is not verily persuaded that Captain Steele is the greatest scholar and the best casuist of any man in England.

But for all this popularity Steele, with a sure journalistic instinct that Pacolet, The Table of Fame, The Court of Honour and the like would become wearisome and that even Bickerstaff himself had gone near the limit of the general liberty of censure allowed him, abruptly closed the paper. "His disappearance seemed to be bewailed as some general calamity, everyone wanted so agreeable an amusement," and even Swift grumbled at Steele's laziness[1]. But "the expiration of Bickerstaff's lucubrations was attended with much the same consequences as the Death of Melibeus's Ox in Virgil; as the latter engendered swarms of Bees, the former immediately produced whole swarms of little satirical scribblers." One of these authors called himself the "Growler," another gentleman with more modesty called his paper the *Whisperer*, and a third to please the ladies christened his *The Tell-Tale*. But there were later swarms more worth the hiving, and among these were the *Spectator* in London and

---

[1] *Journal to Stella*, Jan. 2, 1711.

the *Misantrope* at the Hague. In London the imitations became "wholly invisible & quite swallowed up in the Blaze of the Spectator...," and "they despaired ever to equal him in wit, humour or learning." The *Spectator* worthily took over the entertainment of the great and admiring audience that the *Tatler* had created. It

is in everyones hand and a constant topick for our morning conversation at Tea-tables and coffee-houses. We had at first indeed no manner of Notion how a diurnal paper could be continued in the spirit & stile of our present Spectators; but to our no small surprise we find them still rising upon us and can only wonder from whence so prodigious a run of wit & learning can proceed, since some of our best judges seem to think that they have hitherto in general outshone even the esquires first Tatlers.

Old Isaac the diviner now gave place to an observer, in itself a sign that the authors were getting closer up to life and the realism of the domestic novel. But still the rôle of whimsical eccentricity was deliberately maintained to make pardonable what in the ordinary direct address and intention would have been considered impertinent. And even then the Spectator, by his pose of something between a harmless drudge (to borrow the self-description of his descendant the Rambler in a different capacity) and a public mentor, did not quite escape or disarm the sort of criticism which no. 165 of September 8 evoked[1]. "That old tatling fool," snaps the poor outraged critic at Mr Spectator, and, with a vehemence which now sounds strangely discordant and futile, he thumps out:

"What can be a greater usurpation...than for a fantastical, splenetick discontented wretch to assume to himself the authority of a censor." "What can be a greater Tyranny upon the subject, than to have a constant spy upon their actions, to publish in a false light family conversations, harmless mirth & other trivial incidents which would never be thought faults if they were not by his talent improved into such."

And the Spectator is anxious to disarm such criticism by admitting some guilt on both counts. In no. 101 he is careful to admit that a future tercentenary estimate would find

[1] *Vide The Spectator Inspected.*

that "Allowance must be made for the Mirth and Humour
of the Author who has doubtless strained many Represen-
tations of Things beyond the Truth," and with an arch
smile Addison points out to his public that all the extravagances in the papers must not be taken literally, but as
"remote Hints and Allusions aimed at certain Follies...in
vogue."

Nevertheless, this does not remove the feeling that the
papers include a vast store of oddities, extravagant cru-
dities, and offences against refined literary taste. We can
understand that, by posing as invincible humorists, whose
eccentricities entitled them to free animadversion, both
the Spectator and his hero, Sir Roger, endeavoured to seek
indulgence of a very mixed audience—superficially refined,
and morally vitiated, on the one extreme, and of commonplace bourgeois tastes and narrow outlook on the other.
They assumed no sort of superiority; the Spectator allows
himself to be called "musty sir" by a confirmed coquette
and so scores his point that singularity of behaviour is
merely deviation from a standard which is often false.
But even in these charming characters there are needless
extravagances. Sir Roger is reported to have "frequently
offended in point of chastity with Beggars and Gypsies[1],"
while his benevolence is exaggerated to a degree, e.g., in
no. 107, that is stupid. The exaggerated silence of the Spectator and his special visit to Grand Cairo "on purpose to
take the measure of a Pyramid[2]" may be recalled. The
"Ugly Club," etc., the "Trunkmaker" at the theatre[3], and
much other broad humour, is often clumsy and hardly less
blunt than that of the grinning match[4] which Addison
caused to be abandoned by his disapproval. Neither subject nor expression in the *Spectator* can always be commended
for the pure essay. There is some coarseness, such as Will
Honeycomb's pleasantry in no. 2, the proposed mating
of Hecatissa of the long face with the Spectator of
"short face[5]." Steele's "Thoughts on the Present State of

---

[1] No. 1. [2] No. 2. [3] No. 235.
[4] No. 173. [5] No. 52.

Fornication[1]" which were well rebuked for indelicacy[2], the jest of the woman enceinte[3], the somewhat prurient theme of no. 154, etc., doubtless gave little offence when manners were coarser, but cannot be said to please to-day. But however unrefined the Spectator may have been, he was generally robust, human and eminently social, remaining everywhere close to the more or less obvious things in each department of life, and manifesting a wonderful ubiquity of interest. He advised people what to eat and drink and wear, urged them to take physical exercise, gave hints for getting rich, and recommended the best firm for wines (probably because that firm advertised freely in the *Spectator*), gave advice as to the plays one should see and the books one should read, not forgetting to puff himself and his friends. Charles Lillie made his fortune by enjoying the Spectator's patronage for his perfumes and nick-nacks. The Spectator disapproved of chocolate and romances for women as "inflamers," advised mothers to suckle their children, interested himself in ladies' dress, fashions and deportment, became a "courier of love" and "censor of small wares[4]," and generally set up as medical as well as moral, mental and social adviser. Paltry superstitions, popular prejudices, social improprieties, all passed under his scrutiny, and nearly everything was allegorized, dramatized, or presented in concrete form; stories were made up to teach the moral, and morals were given human shape and interpreted in terms of human conduct. Everything was made as simple, easy and pleasant as possible; there was no tax on the most ordinary intelligence, no subtleties beyond the popular reach. Added to all this were the advertisements with their Wanteds, To lets, Articles lost, stolen, or strayed, notices of books and plays, lengthy recommendations of preposterous quack medicines for the *toothake, stomachake, vapours* or any other *ake* and ailment. Advertisements were inserted of meetings, liaisons, duels, etc., and contribute to make of the papers what seems an odd, if not bizarre farrago. Philo-

---

[1] No. 274.   [2] No. 276.   [3] No. 7.
[4] *Vide Spect.* no. 16.

sophy had indeed been made to jostle among men. It was the Spectator's laudable and proud boast that he aspired to the fame of having brought Philosophy "out of closets and libraries, schools and colleges to dwell in Clubs and Assemblies, at Tea-Tables and in Coffee-houses[1]." There is no doubt that he effected a great reform in this matter. The coffee-house atmosphere at that time was scarcely congenial to deep spiritual earnestness and refinement.

Wills's "is very much altered since Mr Dryden frequented it," sighs Steele. "Where you used to see Songs, Epigrams and Satires, in the hands of every man you met, you have now only a pack of cards; and instead of the cavils about the turn of the expression, the elegance of the stile and the like, the learned now dispute only about the truth of the game[2]."

When we reflect that by the middle of the century the better club-talk, such as that of Dr Johnson, had become definitely philosophical in character, there is no doubt that the growing tendency to rationalize conduct and to theorize, must have been given a powerful impetus by the Spectator, although he writes as a moralist and but seldom as a philosopher. To counter deism, philosophy came to mean popular middle-class prejudice, and generally the Spectator paid the penalty for boldly attempting to bring philosophy from the clouds or the cloister to *inhabit* among men who were not philosophers. Platonic Reason was now indeed brought down to earth and set up as an idol in the market place, nay, given the attributes of all her Platonic glory in theory, but used as a handy drudge by reformers, atheists, religious apologists and other theorists alike. Nor was this inevitable levelling of philosophy unapprehended by either the Spectator or some of his audience, who took care to remind him that he had "prostituted Learning to the Embraces of the Vulgar and made her...a common Strumpet[3]," an exaggerated censure which Addison countered by a homily on the proper public spirit and intelligibility of writings.

It is clear that the Spectator had, as unobtrusively as

---

[1] *Spect.* no. 10. [2] *Tatler*, no. 1. [3] *Spect.* no. 379.

possible, to descend to the level of the general intelligence. He would not sacrifice a general hearing by rendering his style tumid with the speculation of a Shaftesbury, profound with the intellectualism of a La Rochefoucauld, brilliant with the subtlety of a La Bruyère, close-packed with the apothegms of a Bacon.

On the whole, he reflects very faithfully the civilization and temperament of honest bourgeois England, whose virtues he preached in manners, in the same spirit as he urged her to stick to the tradition of beef and beer in diet. But considering the didactic spirit which animated him and the large and ill-assorted audience he addressed, it is surprising how much sound thinking, scholarship, extensive reading, artistic sense and good taste which the happy authors managed to convey to their readers. It constitutes indeed the distinction and charm of the Spectator that within the narrowed horizon of the moralist, with the sacrifice of the highest artistic refinement to popular range of subject and style, he achieved a distinctiveness of artistic effect that was the despair of later didacticians (as Young significantly found it) and essayists that would be popular. As he had reached Reason from her empyrean throne, so he boldly raised the humblest domestic topics to the sphere of literature. Naturally, ordinary people were delighted and cultivated people amazed. The Spectator had achieved the bourgeois domesticity of Richardson, without the frequent jumbled familiarity of his expression, and the middle-class comedy of Fielding, without his coarseness, rising in what are generally the best-known essays into the nobility of sentiment and expression which characterizes all art in the highest sense purposive. I will not speak of the excellent literary and aesthetic education the *Spectator* provided for an early eighteenth-century audience, because any average educated reader will to-day still admit that he has read the *Spectator* with advantage to his general information and critical taste. Modern taste has been offended by the dumb gentleman's disapproval of everything Gothic, but the word had come to have a merely verbal use and by no means carried the logical content it now does. At the same time most readers would rightly consider inexcusable his condemnation of "Gothick" architecture for its "meanness[1]."

When Addison in *Spectator*, no. 10, computed the extent of his audience, he left out of reckoning his readers overseas. It would be curious if a paper of the novelty, excellence and popularity of the *Tatler*, which had started exactly one year and eleven months before Addison wrote no. 10 of the *Spectator*, had remained unread and unnoticed abroad all that time. Yet I have not been able to discover any reference to the sale or the knowledge of the existence of these papers until more than two years after the *Tatler* had first appeared on April 12, 1709. It is an illuminating instance of how, in spite of the growing knowledge of English philosophy and controversy, English *belles lettres* was still for the most part a closed book. When we consider how continental publishers kept their fingers on the pulse of the English book market not many decades after the *Spectator*, we shall realize that it is the period up to about 1730, and the men who worked then, that merit the closest attention of historians of later international literary relationships. Of these early workers, Van Effen is one of the first in the field and one of the most important. In spite of the general silence as to the popularity of the new periodicals in England, there must have proceeded a subterranean exchange, as Van Effen soon proved by publishing either at his own or at Johnson's initiative, the first moralist periodical on the continent—*Le Misantrope*. Johnson, a bookseller of English descent at the Hague, was an indefatigable salesman of English books; there were more like him and much of the spread of English literature across the Channel must be attributed to their enterprise and sagacity. In the *Misantrope* we find advertised: "Toutes sortes de livres nouveaux tant François, que Anglais, & particulièrement toutes les Pièces curieuses qui regardent les affaires présentes d'Angleterre, & les autres affaires du tems." Was the bookseller stimulating or meeting a

---

[1] *Spect.* no. 415.

demand for English books? He was, in fact, doing both, although it does not seem as if he had much more to offer than controversial, topical, and incidental literature of the period. But in the paper for September 1711, T. Johnson advertises: "toutes sortes de livres nouveaux tant d'Angleterre, que de ce pais, et un beau Recueil de toutes les meilleurs Comédies Angloises, très proprement imprimées en petit volume." Pocket editions were soon advertised, an encouraging sign. We know that among the "meilleurs Comédies" was a pirated edition of Congreve. In the weekly parcels which this bookseller received from London would surely have been some copies of the papers then creating so remarkable an impression in London[1]. Perhaps it is best here to quote from the preface of the *libraire* to the first volume of the *Misantrope*.

After a highly interesting sketch[2] of the history of the *Tatler* and the *Spectator*, the bookseller continues:

> *Je ne sais si une chose de cette nature sera aussi-bien reçûë ailleurs qu'en Angleterre; non pas qu'il y ait moins de vices & de folies en un autre Pais pour en fournir la matiére; mais parce qu'il s'en faut bien que les Ouvrages d'esprit soient si généralement goûtez ailleurs qu'en Angleterre. J'ai eu pourtant envie depuis quelque tems d'essayer ce qui en serait, & par bonheur il se rencontre un Auteur qui a dessein sans se faire connaître, de sonder le goût du Public dans un pareil Ouvrage. On continuëra donc à donner une demi-feuille tous les Lundis, jusqu'à ce qu'on voye comment ce Misantrope sera reçû.*

It is quite clear, then, that it was the example of Bicker-staff and the *Spectator* that prompted the joint experiment of Johnson and Van Effen. This has been questioned by Valkhoff on the ground that the *Misantrope* takes nothing from the English papers; but apart from the very strong *a priori* grounds of closer cultural contact between England and Holland, and the extreme improbability of Van Effen's independent happening upon a literary genre which although

---

[1] In *Tatler*, no. 129, Feb. 4, 1710, Steele acknowledges the receipt, among other "honours" "from the learned world abroad," of a complimentary letter, and a present of some paintings from "a burgher of Amsterdam."

[2] Quoted below.

it had been half a century evolving in Europe, had required the combined wits of the greatest Queen Anne writers to develop it to harmonious maturity in the later *Tatlers* only—apart from these *a priori* reasonings, there is much else to support the view that the idea of the *Misantrope* was an importation from England.

In his preface Johnson has also given an appreciation of the English papers, which is the earliest public expression on the continent of the praise that was soon to swell into a chorus. It is therefore an exceedingly interesting little piece of criticism, as valuable at least as Gay's, by which it may, however, have been influenced.

C'est ici un *nouvel amusement* pour le Public, & qui pourra lui être utile, s'il y prend goût. On voit s'introduire tous les jours parmi les hommes grand nombre de mauvaises coûtumes, & de maniéres sottes & ridicules, qui ne sont pas justement punissables par les Loix d'aucun Païs & qui cependant ne laissent pas d'être très nuisibles à la Société. Le meilleur moyen de faire revenir le monde de ces folies, c'est d'en faire si bien voir le ridicule qu'on aye honte de s'y laisser tomber. C'est ce que La *Bruyére, Moliére* & d'autres habiles Gens ont tâché de faire, mais de différentes maniéres, chacun selon son génie, & selon les occasions qu'il a euës. Un des plus beaux Génies de notre tems voulant faire quelque chose de cette nature en Angleterre, pour réformer les mœurs de ses Compatriotes, s'avisa il y a deux ans de publier trois fois la semaine, en forme de Gazette, une demifeuille volante, qu'il nomma *The Tatler*, le *Jaseur*, ou *Babillard*, où il a dépeint les vices, les déréglemens & les mauvaises coûtumes de son Pais, avec des couleurs si vives, & en a fait voir le ridicule & la laideur avec tant d'adresse & d'habileté, que tout le monde en est charmé. La Lecture en est aisée...., & il n'est presque point de Famille à Londres où l'on ne prenne le *Tatler* toutes les fois qu'il paroît, afin de le lire le matin en bûvant le Thé, pour l'instruction tant des jeunes gens que des vieux; de sorte qu'on en a débité, à ce qu'on assure, entre douze & quinze mille à chaque fois. Si cet habile Auteur a sujet d'être content de ce que son écrit est si recherché, il ne le doit pas être moins du succès qu'il a eu; car on dit qu'il a plus fait pour la réformation des mœurs de toutes sortes de personnes en un an, que tous les Prédicateurs du Royaume n'avoient fait en vingt. Il a trouvé à propos depuis peu d'interrompre cet Ouvrage, & d'en com-

mencer un autre dans le même goût, mais sous un autre tître:
& on en donne tous les jours une demi-feuille avec le même
succès qu'auparavant.

From these appreciative words it is clear that the scope,
aim and method of the English writers were thoroughly
understood and that Van Effen set out with a good idea of
what was required of him. Moreover, Van Effen had a
literary secret to keep. The preface was written some months
after the first number of the *Misantrope* appeared, and we
may well believe that the young aspirant to literary
honours was keen to get the full advantage out of his own
or his publisher's discovery before all the world was let
into it. It does not require much knowledge of human
nature to realize why Van Effen himself makes no
mention in the *Misantrope* of his English predecessors
or why he was careful to avoid direct imitation. But
when once the fame of the *Spectator* became common
knowledge, then it was the best possible advertisement
to avow imitation openly. Thus in later papers Van Effen
is as profuse in allusions to his predecessors as, in very
emulation of Mr Spectator himself, he had preserved a stiff
silence as to their existence in his first imitative venture.
Although Johnson in the preface gives him away afterwards, it is still insisted that the whole thing is "un
nouvel amusement." It is of importance to remember,
too, that amongst later contemporaries there was little
doubt as to the origin of the *Misantrope*. Scarcely a single
chronicler of literature of the eighteenth century looks upon
the *Misantrope* as anything else than a work "dans le même
goût" as the famous English periodicals. The elogist will
allow a dispute only as to whether it was the *Tatler* or the
Spectator that fathered the *Misantrope*:

Le désir de la gloire qui étoit en lui la passion dominante,
l'engagea à essayer le goût du Public par un Ouvrage périodique,
à peu près dans le goût du fameux Spectateur Anglois, qui com-
mençoit alors à faire beaucoup de bruit. Il y avoit de la témérité à un Jeune-homme de vingt-six à vingt-sept ans, d'entre-
prendre de lutter seul contre deux des plus Beaux-Esprits de

l'Angleterre; mais cette témérité devenoit d'autant plus grande & on diroit presque plus impardonnable si elle n'avoit été justifiée par le succès que le jeune Van Effen donnoit son coup d'essai dans une Langue qui lui étoit étrangère. Son Ouvrage en François sous le titre Le Misantrope, commença le 19 Mai 1711, en une demi-feuille en 8 & continua sans interruption à paroître tous les Lundis jusqu'au 26 Décembre 1712.

A footnote then develops the point of "un ami de Mr Van Effen" that the *Tatler* inspired the *Misantrope*, since the *Spectator* was "peu connu alors dans ce Pays." But, answers the elogist, many numbers of the *Spectator* had already appeared when the *Misantrope* began, and, besides, "le Babillard & le Misantrope ne sont point dans le même goût, & il y a beaucoup plus de rapport entre le Misantrope & le Spectateur"—a somewhat strange remark, unless the writer is referring to the earliest *Tatlers*.

Verwer seems to be translating from the *Éloge* when he says that the *Misantrope* was written as nearly as possible in the style of the English *Spectator* which had then begun to make its fame[1]. In the paper *L'Europe Savante* (A La Haye, 1718), in which Van Effen had some share, occurs a review of vol. III of the French translation of the *Spectator*, in which the writer gives an appreciatory sketch:

La Variété de sujets, & la quantité de matières dont cette sorte de Livres est susceptible a déjà produit en Angleterre un grand nombre d'ouvrages semblables à celui-ci.... *On a voulu imiter en Hollande ces sortes de Feuilles volantes. Il en a paru une en* 1711, *sous le Nom de Misantrope, qui finit à la fin de* 1712. Une autre sous le Titre de *Censeur* qui a paru pendant tout le Cours de l'année 1714. Une Troisième sous celui de *l'Observateur*, qui n'a duré que deux ou trois mois. *Et un quatrième, qui a commencé avec le mois de mai de cette Année & qui continue, sous le Titre de La Bagatelle,*

and of this paper Van Effen again is the author.

An examination of the contents of the *Misantrope* leaves a similar impression of its inspiration. In the excellent author's preface the author states his aims. "La principale

---

[1] "Ten naesten by in den smaek van den Engelschen spectator geschreven, die toen gerucht begon te maken."

raison qui m'a engagé à faire cette petite Piéce, c'est le désir de tâter le goût du Public, & de voir s'il recevroit avec plaisir d'autres Ouvrages dont mon amour-propre le menace depuis longtems." The public, therefore, must also be propitiated:

Vous voyez, Lecteur, que mon premier but n'est pas tant de corriger le Public, que d'essayer si je suis capable de lui plaire. Cependant je n'ai pas été fâché de lui dessiller les yeux, sur la bisarrerie de ses maximes & sur le ridicule de ses maniéres. Quoi que les sujets que j'ai traitez soient assez variez, [ils montrent] aux hommes le mauvais usage qu'ils font de leur raison, en l'asservissant aux opinions vulgaires; qui, quoique fort oposées au bonsens, en ont pourtant occupé la place par une espéce de prescription. Ce dessein n'a rien que d'innocent, & même c'est peutêtre ce qu'il y a de plus louable dans mon Ouvrage. Je m'y suis toûjours attaché à donner des idées avantageuses d'une vertu éclairée, je n'y ai jamais attaqué que le vice, & rien n'y a été l'objet de mes railleries que le ridicule & le mauvais sens.

Peut-être me serois-je acquis plus de gloire si j'avois suivi une route oposée, & si par une lâche complaisance pour certains Lecteurs, j'avois favorisé le libertinage contre la Religion.

Bien des gens charmez de trouver chez moi des Armes pour combattre les sentimens que la Nature a gravez dans tous les cœurs auroient sans doute aplaudi à ces subtilitez dangereuses: il y a de l'aparence que le nouveau, tenant dans leur esprit la place du vrai, m'eût procuré parmi eux la réputation d'un génie du premier ordre.

Mais je méprise trop un honneur si criminel et je préférerai toûjours la honte de passer pour un homme de probité sans génie, à la gloire d'être estimé le plus habile d'entre les Libertins.

Observe the "parson in a tyewig" (as Mandeville, the ironic philosopher, laughingly described Addison), the confirmed reformer, the type of writer who in his youth might have produced *The Christian Hero*.

In the passage quoted, which serves also as an illustration of Van Effen's manner and style, there are a trick of style, a pitch and a general tone and sentiment which will be readily recognized by readers of the *Tatler* and the *Spectator*. Of the innumerable expressions suggestive of the English original, we might refer to no. 262 of the *Spectator*[1]. It

[1] Also, e.g., *Tatler*, nos. 71, 74, 76.

is indeed so much *à propos* that quotation, unless it be
of the whole, will only spoil the full effect of the parallelism
which one feels upon reading the preface and such an essay
side by side. Steele speaks of the high tone of his paper
which has not availed itself of "the popular topics of
Ridicule," etc., in order to extend its sale and says:
"...I broke loose from that great Body of Writers
who have employed their Wit and Parts in propagating
Vice & Irreligion." He vindicates himself on the charge
of "Defamation of particular Persons" and argues at
length that his portraits are composite ones and not of
individuals. He has taken as "much care" to avoid obscenity as to obviate the possibility of invidious inter-
pretation of his characterizations.

So Van Effen:

Quelque précaution cependant que j'aye prise, pour ne rien
écrire de contraire aux bonnes mœurs, il ne m'a pas été possible
d'éviter le tître de médisant, que bien des personnes me donnent
trop libéralement. Je crois avoir déjà dit une autre fois que je ne
fais pas mes portraits en l'air, & que je tâche d'y copier fidellement
certains Originaux: mais je puis protester que je fais tous mes
efforts pour cacher les personnes dont je dévelope le ridicule.

The point is then further developed, the author asking the
public finally "de n'être plus si clairvoyant" and to desist
from making false interpretations of his sketches. This
part of the preface is a fuller exposition, in the spirit of
Steele, of the point raised in *Misantrope*, no. 12, where
Van Effen pleads that he is as little liable to the charge of
defamation of persons as any "Prédicateur pieux & zélé."
In this number, as well as in the opening one, he justifies his
title and very *raison d'être*. No writer, not even Molière or
La Bruyère can exhaust the richness of such material. "Le
vice & le Ridicule sont des sources intarissables de critique"
—"Sur la Sottise encore je puis longtems briller."

That Van Effen elects to create a definite personality, a
character through whose spectacles readers will regard the
world around them, suggests the most obvious correspondence with the creation of a genial Isaac Bickerstaff, Esq.

and a sober but indefatigable Mr Spectator of happy memory. The Misantrope was no mere name, he was a man who moved among his fellow men, a personality with a philosophy of life. The title is, of course, taken from Molière, but Alceste hates human vices more "par fantaisie que par principe," while our Misantrope's convictions will stand square with reason and consistency. Indeed, in a spirit of pleasantry Van Effen had made a philanthrope of his Misantrope, who is so prompted by "l'amour qu'il a pour le genre-humain qu'il s'efforce à développer toute l'extravagance de leur ridicule & toute la noirceur de leurs crimes." To the thoughtless, pleasure-seeking *beau monde*, he would appear to be an atrabilious anchorite, so that his choice of title is, of course, an ironic and apparent concession to the disparaging epithets with which they would try to dismiss him. He would, like Mr Spectator, be a "musty sir" or, like Bicker-staff, merely a Tatler, to people who could appreciate neither reason nor morality. Such is the sense expressed or implied in the title *Misantrope*. The character is strongly reminiscent of Mr Spectator. He is a man who

dès son enfance s'est fait une habitude de raisonner juste, & un devoir de suivre dans sa conduite l'austére exactitude de ses raisonnemens; libre des erreurs du Peuple, dégagé de l'opinion, débarassé du joug de l'autorité, il proportione l'estime qu'il accorde aux choses à leur juste valeur; il n'atache la honte qu'au crime, & ne rougit jamais d'être plus raisonnable que les autres: opulence, dignitez, rang, tîtres, vous ne lui arrachâtes jamais le moindre désir; appliqué à la recherche de la vérité, amoureux de l'évidence, il ne connoit pas vos charmes. Le bonheur où il aspire c'est la souveraine liberté de sa Raison, qu'accompagne une médiocrité aisée,

Like the Spectator, again, he loves "le doux commerce d'un petit nombre d'Amis vertueux." Rather than be intolerant and for ever impertinently setting people right, he would keep his peace, but if he speaks, he "n'a que la vérité pour but." He is fearless of criticism; for it is love of mankind that has determined him to wage "une guerre mortelle au vice & à la sottise." Wit, he says[1], should

---

[1] *Misant.* no. XIV.

be a quality "qui rend la vertu plus agréable & le vice plus hideux," and on this principle he will meet criticisms. But Van Effen could not satisfy the small wits in that age of "correctness" as to his title or the form he adopted[1], for, as suggested above, he had no Dutch Defoe to clear the way for him. At a single bound this young scholar placed himself on the same literary platform that had been slowly constructed in England by a succession of clever writers. Single-handed he bravely tried to sustain a paper of the same kind as several score of the best wits in England had produced by co-operation. Needless to say, he had attempted an impossibility. Even the pure essay genre had been so neglected in Holland that there is not a single name one could place by those of Bacon, Cowley and Temple, distinguished forerunners without whose prose the *Spectator* essays, though incorporating novel elements, could scarcely have sprung into life by the year 1711. Van Effen therefore is an innovator of the highest possible significance for Dutch literature and particularly, in his *Hollandsche Spectator*, for Dutch prose. The *Misantrope* is, in a sense, a contribution to Dutch literature, for not only was it written by a Dutchman in Holland, but it was written at a time when the use of the French language did not prevent any such new development from being readily assimilated into Dutch artistic life and expression. Van Effen, then, is scarcely to be blamed if he does not succeed, at least when judged by the standards applied to his English contemporaries. He plainly has an imperfect idea of the essay, whether of the periodical kind or not. He is generally vigorous and entertaining; but in the excess of his youthful powers he tries to give too much and loses control over his medium, with the result that his numbers grow too long and the subject too extended. There is not that crisp manner in which Addison manages his work and thought, the sense of craftsmanship with which he steers an essay to its inevitable conclusion in good time. The half-sheet restriction may have exercised wholesome

Vide, e.g., *Misant.* nos. XII, XIV.

disciplinary action on the tail-end of the essay, but a glance at original *Spectators* will reveal that by no means all the available space was used, and that by the insertion or omission of a few advertisements a certain amount of elasticity of space was ensured. Yet there are few examples of the advertisements being crowded out by the final periods of a long-winded essayist. Van Effen frequently exceeds the proper artistic length and introduces too large a variety of points for any one essay, although he seldom treats his public to left-over scraps, of which not a few of the *Spectator* numbers appear to have been hurriedly made up.

Van Effen seems to have learnt all the tricks of the periodicalist trade from the amiable Bickerstaff and his worthy successor[1]. He talks frequently of himself, of the stir he is creating[2], and makes criticisms with the sole object of following them up by commendations of his paper in the form of letters. He goes to the coffee-houses and book-shops where he overhears what men say of him in the manner of the *Spectator*. There is a familiar trick in the public warning Van Effen appends to *Misantrope*, no. XIII: "On avertit le Public que ce n'est que pour les petites Folies que le Misantrope veut recevoir des Contributions; car pour les grosses il ne prétend pas les souffrir en aucune manière. Ainsi tous ceux qui en sont atteints sont priez de s'en corriger incessamment sous peine d'être traitez selon leur mérite." In *Tatler*, no. 148, Addison registered his disapproval of the French *ragoût* in the dietary economy of the day, and in *Misantrope*, no. IX, Van Effen likewise appears as "Censeur des Ragoûts." *Misantrope*, no. XXI deals also with "eloquence," a frequent subject in the English papers. The views expressed are in the spirit of *Tatler*, no. 66: "He (Dr Atterbury) never attempts your passions until he has convinced your reason." Less than a month after Addison had begun his famous aesthetic series, Van Effen also writes on the pleasures of the

---

[1] *Tatler*, no. 91, e.g.: "When I first set up I thought it fair enough to let myself know from all parts that my works were wonderfully enquired for, & were become the diversion as well as instruction of all choice spirits in every county *of Great Britain*." There is nothing like a little suggestion!

[2] "Je fais donc du fracas dans le monde," etc., *Misant*. I, no. VI. *Vide* also nos. XII, XIV, etc.

Imagination and the Reason[1], taking, however, a different stand. He treats of wit in *Misantrope*, I, no. XXXI, some eight months after the publication of Addison's views in the *Spectator*.

Van Effen is determined, like Addison, to exalt and vindicate human nature. This attitude is, of course, fundamental to Addison's philosophy and writings, who deprecates the debasing theories of Hobbes and La Rochefoucauld. An essay like no. 108 of the *Tatler*, perhaps Addison's greatest paper, is expressive of his most characteristic convictions. Van Effen is in full agreement. He defends human nature and likewise condemns Rochefoucauld in an excellent paper[2]. Close verbal correspondence need not be sought, because there is sufficient correspondence sometimes of ideas, often of subject and manner. "There is nothing which favours & falls in with this natural greatness & dignity of human nature so much as religion," Addison affirms, and Van Effen gives support with: "Le Christianisme perfectionna l'Humanité." Both are imbued with a wonderful social sense, a humanity and a conviction of social obligation, features which are pleasing characteristics of the eighteenth century. "Nous sommes unis trop étroitement avec nos prochains." "Le grand édifice de la société a besoin pour demeurer ferme de l'estime et de la tendresse mutuelle de ceux qui le composent." But here Van Effen is exhibiting an acquaintance with Shaftesbury rather than with the *Spectator* or *Tatler*, which in their turn had assimilated much of that nobleman's social optimism. When, however, Van Effen writes: "Il y a une harmonie parfaite entre la vertu & le Bonheur général du Genre-humain,...tout ce qui est véritablement utile à la Société humaine est réellement conforme à la vertu," he is paraphrasing from the *Characteristics*. While as firmly antagonistic as Addison to doctrines such as those of Hobbes, he has much to say on the question of *amour propre*. It is in fact the "fondement de la Vertu," a view which the *Spectator* in the person of Henry Grove endorses in no. 588;

---

[1] *Misant.* II, no. XXIX, July 18, 1712.
[2] *Misant.* II, no. XXXII.

this was long after Van Effen's opinion had been expressed, so that the borrowing, if there was any, must have been either by the *Spectator* from Van Effen, or, as is most likely, by both Van Effen and the *Spectator* from Shaftesbury, with whose philosophy both are imbued.

A common subject is that of objectionable types of old men, such as superannuated gallants. Steele had spoken in the *Tatler* of "indecent old age," and frequently a return is made to the subject, as in *Spectator*, nos. 153, 263, 301, 318, etc. Van Effen's paper of September 12, 1712[1], may well have been suggested by Budgell's paper of February 14, 1712[2], on the subject of old rakes who will not resign themselves to the dignity and repose proper to their age. We need not refer to all the points made in regard to this subject by Van Effen and his English predecessors, but two coincidences still remain to be noticed. In *Misantrope*, I, no. IX, for July 13, 1711, Van Effen criticizes opinionated old men who by virtue of their seniority bear down the sound reasonings of younger men, and eight months later in no. 336 of the *Spectator* for March 26, 1712, Steele writes on the same subject. Again, in the *Misantrope* for Monday, September 14, 1711, Van Effen tells the story of the impotent old lover who was put to shame by the pretended compliance of a virtuous young wife, and Steele nearly six months later *tells the same story* in *Spectator*, no. 318, for Wednesday, March 5, 1712. I have not been able to trace a common original and must therefore conclude that Steele had been reading the *Misantrope* before March 1712. It may be noted that no. 336, on the 26th of that month, is also by Steele on a similar subject and particularly on the same aspect of the subject that Van Effen had treated before him. Of course, La Bruyère and others had written on these topics, but the tone and treatment in the *Misantrope* and *Tatler* and *Spectator*, amounting in one case to verbal correspondence, strongly suggest mutual borrowing. Van Effen, with typical eighteenth-century brutality, had the same tendency as Steele to be impatient of senility.

[1] *Misant.* II, no. XXXVII. Cp. also no. XLVII, Nov. 21, 1712.
[2] *Spect.* no. 301.

Another strain of thinking that is fundamental to the *Spectator* and the *Misantrope* alike is the necessity for the harmonising of national culture with the old-established traditions of the country. Sir Roger is the embodiment of this idea, upon which Addison, particularly, was never tired of insisting, as e.g. in no. 103, Thursday (June 28, 1711). Some six weeks later[1] appeared one of Van Effen's most impressive essays on this subject, recommending to his countrymen the good old solid culture of seventeenth-century Holland and deploring the debauched manners imported from France. He frequently returns to this subject later[2].

Misantrope, II. no. III, on Glory and Duelling, recalls the campaign started by Steele against the latter evil in the *Tatler*, and the many papers on the former subject in the *Spectator*[3]. We could thus proceed to enumerate many more subjects that came up for treatment in these two papers and in the *Tatler*. Van Effen has two elaborate essays on modesty, writes on behaviour in church, on common sense, friendship, makes game of the *nouvellistes* like Steele and Addison, and, like Steele, lauds Marlborough and Prince Eugène. He writes also on justice, generosity, happiness, and in *Misantrope*, II, no. XXXIII on the art of doing favours with a good grace, which essay appears to have been developed from *Spectator*, no. 292. In *Spectator*, no. 221, and *Misantrope*, II, no. XXX, Addison and Van Effen repeat the same idea somewhat differently: "a good face is a letter of Recommendation" and "Une Physionomie heureuse est la plus forte de toutes les recommendations." *Misantrope*, II, no. XXXVIII treats of patrons in a vein not unlike that of *Spectator*, no. 214 (or *Tatler*, no. 196). *Misantrope*, II, no. XXX concerns the study of natural bent in training children, and may be compared with *Spectator*, nos. 307, 404, the latter just a month before Van Effen's paper. *Misantrope*, II, no. XXXIV is in the spirit of *Tatler*, no. 242, and *Spectator*, no. 229. Van Effen ventured upon lay sermons, and his

---

[1] *Misant.* I, no. XIII, Aug. 10.   [2] *Ibid.* II, no. XI.
[3] Nos. 99, 219, 224.

dreams and allegorical visions are quite in the style of the *Tatler*. *Tatler*, no. 81 could readily have suggested efforts like *Misantrope*, I, nos. III, V, and II, no. X, the opening of which, as well as that of no. III, is suggestive of *Tatler*, no. 8.

Many of the general features of the *Misantrope* are also in agreement with those of the English papers. Steele's charming gallantry directed the policy of the *Tatler* and the *Spectator* especially to a female audience, and, together with Addison, he may be regarded as a pioneer of the then sadly neglected cause of woman in spite of Mary Astell.

The way in which Van Effen takes the women under his protection as the "moitié du public la plus aimable," warns them, like *Spectator* no. 365, against romances, advises them in love matters, urges a thorough and proper education for them[1], remonstrates with the unfeminine part of the sex for their gracelessness, etc., recalls the whole attitude of the English writers towards the "fair sex," "by the just complaisance & Gallantry of our Nation the most Powerful Part of our People," as Steele said. In fact Van Effen was probably as much in advance of his age in his opinion of women as Steele, but it would be most unlikely if the elder and more mature writers had not influenced the young Misantrope, who likewise writes on sincerity in love and marriage with a view to protecting women[2], and who had the true reformer's perception of the significance to society of the emancipation of women. There is also gentle satire as in *Misantrope*, II, no. XLIX, where the feminine fondness for bravery in dress is remarked on, much in the spirit of *Spectator*, no. 15. Van Effen's chief targets were the *petits-maîtres* upon whom he vented much lively ridicule. He took quite the same stand as Bickerstaff and the *Spectator* against the *beau monde*, the "pretty fellows," the fashionable follies, and the false glitter and insincerity of the libertine's life. The *petit-maître* is perhaps Van Effen's favourite topic in the *Misantrope*[3] as well as later.

The story-telling which is a notable feature of the *Spec-*

---

[1] See, e.g., I, no. IV; II, no. XIV; II, no. IV; II, no. XXXI, etc.
[2] See, e.g., *Misant.* I, II, XX; II, XXXIX.
[3] See, e.g., *Misant.* I, VI and XVII; II, VIII and XLIII, etc.

tator and of which Addison, particularly, was fond[1], figures also in the *Misantrope*. No. VI (I) contains an engaging picture of social manners, which reads like a story. No. XXX on Amsterdam is one of his best. Leyden student-life is also described in narrative manner (no. XXVIII). Nos. XV and XVIII are stories. The former is followed by a disquisition on tale-tellers which seems to have been suggested by La Bruyère rather than the *Spectator*. It may be noted too that the attitude of Van Effen to scientific research is as un-sympathetic as that of the *Tatler*, which cruelly satirizes the Royal Society virtuoso; see, e.g. I, no. II; II, no. XII, in the latter of which Boileau is cited to clinch Van Effen's mean-ing. Van Effen's antipathy to war and its false glories ex-pressed in *Misantrope*, II, no. XXIX, and I, no. XXIV, should be read in close connection with *Tatler*, no. 23, *Spectator*, nos. 180 and 200, and the concluding chapters of *The Chris-tian Hero*. Van Effen's deprecation of the "esprit de Parti" in II, nos. L and XXVIII, recalls Addison's endeavours to assuage this raging beast. Like Steele, Van Effen cannot abstain altogether from politics (II, no. LI). He devotes the paper for July 27, 1711, to the tragedy of Prins Willem Friso just as Steele had bewailed the loss of Prince George of Denmark in *Tatler*, no. 8. In fact there is abundant evidence to show that the *Misantrope* differs as much from the "caractères" as do the *Tatler* and the *Spectator*, which must be held to have suggested the editorial practice and much of the subject matter of the *Misantrope*[2].

[1] See, e.g., *Spect.* no. 123, and Addison's letter to Wortley Montagu on that number: "Being very well pleased with this day's Spectator, I cannot forbear sending you one of them and desiring your opinion of the story in it. When you have a son I shall be glad to be his Leontine...."

[2] The relation of these three papers to this French work, for which in the case of the *Misantrope* see Valkhoff, *De Gids*, Nov. 1717, and Oomkens, *Revue de Hollande*, nos. IV, V, VI, VIII, X, is, of course, less important than their deviation from it in pointing a new way in literature. The *novel* elements of the English papers are the significant thing for literary develop-ment and the *Misantrope* shows all the signs of having appreciated this fact. Valkhoff has done injury to Van Effen by regarding him as a Dutch La Bruyère, whom although he, in common with Steele and Addison, un-doubtedly tried at times to imitate, he nevertheless, in the same degree as the English writers, purposely deviated from. It is easy, therefore, to be unfair to these writers, to compare unfavourably their popular, *enjoué*

Van Effen wrote also on education, a favourite *Spectator* subject, contributing three sensible and original, though Lockeian, papers on that subject. But the great stand of the Misantrope was made against atheism. In no respect does he more resemble his English predecessors than in this. In 1726, Van Effen added, in the manner of La Bruyère, a long section of no less than 139 pages on the "esprits forts" to what he had already said in 1711–12. In effect, this addition did not mean very much. His earlier papers show him to have taken up the pseudo-philosophical, but really popular, attitude of the *Tatler*. He agreed with Steele, who in *Tatler*, no. 3 had expressed himself in no unequivocal terms in decrying a vice "which is almost become popular." "Wretches," "vermin," "vile atheist," "gloomy miscreants," "solemn blockheads," are some of the expressions brutally and indiscriminately slung at the growing section of sincere thinkers. In later essays upon religion it is clear that the position taken is that of Locke, who had reconciled reason with religion for many a puzzled contemporary. This is precisely Van Effen's standpoint, especially in 1726, when he develops it at greater length and with cogent skill. As a contribution to the religious and philosophical speculation of the day, it is by no means negligible. Van Effen seemed for a moment to see, as no reader of Shaftesbury could fail to see, the wedge which the eighteenth century was driving between the concepts Morality and Religion; but the practical significance of this new analysis, which represents perhaps the chief achievement of the eighteenth century in moral philosophy, was lost to him. One cannot be sure whether by 1711 he had thoroughly assimilated Locke or whether the English periodicals had interpreted Locke for him. Although he refers to Locke[1] and the English philosophers in

manner and its necessary comparative superficiality with the incisiveness and serious, searching scrutiny of La Bruyère. The periodicals depended for their very existence as such upon their ability first and foremost to entertain the public, though the writers were careful usually to make the entertainment as clean and instructive as the public taste would stand, and make their audience realize that they would not stoop to carrion or baubles. Cp. Addison (*Spect.* no. 16) and Van Effen's admonition to "Les Amateurs de la bagatelle," *Misant.* II, no. LII.   [1] II, no. XI.

the *Misantrope*[1], we may reasonably suspect that the latter included Messrs Bickerstaff and Spectator and their common philosophy, that of *la raison, le bon-sens* and *le sens-commun*. In this disquisition of 1726 Van Effen is in deadly earnest most of the time and misses both the amusing *outré* raillery of a paper like Budgell's (no. 389) and the lofty disapproval of Addison. The later section, however, was not issued in half-sheets, and does not address itself to a popular audience, so that perhaps we may acquit Van Effen on the score of waxing too argumentative to please a periodical audience, but hardly on that of gravely condemning men like Bayle (whom he otherwise admired[2]) for heinous, irrational error punishable by law, as he had already advocated in 1711 (I, no. VIII).

In 1726 Van Effen also added the readable *Relation d'un voyage de Hollande en Suède Contenue en quelques Lettres de l'Auteur du Misantrope*. He had an interesting and adventurous experience and tells of it in easy, engaging style. But these were additions of the year 1726. The *Misantrope* had run from Monday, May 19, 1711, to Monday, December 26, 1712. On the date of its appearance, no. 69 of the *Spectator* had appeared, and by December 26, 1712, the Spectator already was in the twentieth day of an irrevocable silence, until his mouth was opened on June 18, 1714. We must not be misled by the terms of the Misantrope's leave-taking[3]: "J'ai fait le Misantrope, parce que j'avois la fantaisie de le faire; je ne le fais plus parce que la fantaisie de le faire m'est passée," because he is in a teasing enigmatical mood. For his demise he attributes certain guesses to the public, that are similar to those ascribed by Gay to popular opinion when the *Tatler* was "flung up," viz. the supply of matter was exhausted, officialdom had frowned, etc.

Van Effen refers his readers to the first preface where it was stated that the issue was an experiment to discover the taste of the public for a work of that kind. He now, being fairly satisfied with the result, announced his plan of issuing

---

[1] II, no. XXIII.   [2] *Vide*, e.g., *Bagat.* no. XCVIII.
[3] "Au Lecteur," Part II, *Misant.*

a *Bagatelle* for the reception of which he regarded the *Misantrope* as having cleared the way. He had, indeed, quite auspiciously and successfully inaugurated the literary periodical on the continent. The writer of the *Éloge Historique* tells of its success, and says: "il fut goûté & il s'en est fait depuis une seconde édition[1]." Quérard records in similar strain[2], Verwer testifies to the same, and le Clercq translated most of it and the later French writings into Dutch. The translation[3] included also some pieces from the *Freeholder* and was reviewed with enthusiasm by the *Boekzaal* from 1742 to 1746. Five reviews were devoted to it.

"This work," it says, "shaped on the same last as the Tatler, the Spectator and the Guardian appeared' for the first time like those works in loose sheets, which sold to an incredible number and were read with great enjoyment by everyone who understood French." The bookseller was lucky to get the services of P. le Clercq, the translator of the *Spectator*, and "the good sale of these translations" had justified his choice of translator. The character of the new issue is such as put it above "the great multitude of others which inundate the Republic of Learning." The reviewer, in giving an account of the contents, frequently uses terms such as "the great variety of matter that we here find treated in humorous manner," "gifted writer," considers that the numbers on hereditary succession "cannot fail to please because of the witty turn he has given to them[4]" and recommends the work as "a highly pleasant recreation even for wise and learned people." It has high praise for the *Lettre d'un Homme d'âge* and judges the *Voyage en Suède* "a very neat relation," written in humorous and pleasant style. Thus, finally, the *Misantrope* and van Effen's other French writings entered creditably into their full heritage as Dutch productions.

---

[1] Three editions.

[2] J. M. Quérard, *La France Littéraire* (1827–39): "Le Misantrope est une espèce de feuille périodique à la manière du Spectateur d'Addison qui eut du succès."

[3] *De Misantrope of Gestrenge Zedenmeester Amsteldam*, by Hermanus Uitwerf, 1742, 8°.   [4] *Boekzaal*, May 1746.

There are earlier witnesses too. Van Effen declared himself satisfied in the preface to *Misantrope*, Part II. The *Nouvelles Littéraires* gives the history of the *Misantrope*, and says "le succès qu'il eut a fait naître à deux personnes l'envie de l'imiter[1]." These were the *Censeur* and the *Inquisiteur*.

The review *L'Europe Savante* records the following bit of news from Leyden, March 1718: "Theodore Haak publie ici tous les Lundis une demi-feuille en Hollandois sous le Titre de '*l'Homme démasqué.*' *L'Auteur s'est proposé pour modèles le Spectateur & le Misantrope.*" Van Effen's pioneer work in acclimatizing the new English periodicals had clearly borne fruit.

[1] 1715, p. 21.

CHAPTER IV

THE *BAGATELLE* AND THE *NOUVEAU SPECTATEUR FRANÇAIS*

The projected *Bagatelle* eventually appeared. This is how a merry "correspondent" tells the story of its appearance[1]:

Vous saurez monsieur que ce brillant météore commença de paroître sur notre Horizon le 9 Mai[2] de cette année 1718, & surprit tout le monde. Chacun demanda avec empressement, *qu'est-ce que cela?* Les Bigots en sont effrayés; les Beaux-Esprits n'en font que rire; nos plus savans astronomes observent au travers de leurs Télescopes...; on ne comprend pas la bizarrerie extrême de ce *mouvement*, ni l'origine des *longues Queues.* Les uns disent que c'est un petit soleil enveloppé des nuages, & qui les perce en quelques endroits par la force de ses rayons. D'autres soutiennent que c'est une Planète errante, dont les exhalaisons & les fumées épaisses qui en sortant abandonnent & *réfléchissent une lumière étrangère*[3] & trompant ainsi les yeux sous l'image de Queue brillante. Un petit nombre des plus profonds & des plus experts prétendent que ce Phénomène n'est pas nouveau: ils soupçonnent que c'est le même qu'ils observèrent il y a six ou sept ans, & qui fit du bruit en ce tems là sous le nom de M.[4]...Ils l'ont suivi comme à la piste, & ils en peuvent parler savamment. Il disparut au bout de deux années, & reparoît aujourd'hui sous une forme peu différente, pour continuer toujours le même jeu. Bien plus, ils prédisent hardiment que dans peu (on ne sait pas précisément le mois ni le jour) cet astre sera offusqué par ses fumées épaisses & se dérobera à nos yeux pour se montrer de nouveau plus brillant que jamais dans dix ans d'ici, car selon les observations les plus exactes cette étoile a la double propriété de & fumum ex fulgore, & ex fumo dare lucem[5].

Readers will recognize the motto from Horace[6] which

[1] *Bagat.* no. LXVI, Thursday, Dec. 22, 1718.
[2] The *Bagatelle* actually appeared first on Thursday, May 5, 1718.
[3] My italics.
[4] Probably the *Misantrope*, which ran May 19, 1711–Dec. 26, 1712.
[5] Cp. *Bagat.* no. LXVIII, where Van Effen acknowledges this bit of *jeu d'esprit.*
[6] *Ars Poet.* vers. 143:
"Non fumum ex fulgore, sed ex fumo dare lucem
Cogitat, ut speciosa dehinc miracula promat."

heralded the first *Spectator* on Thursday, March 1, 1711, and realize that a witty turn has been given to it by our correspondent. The new periodical literature had indeed appeared on the literary horizon as a resplendent comet which intermittently irradiated the century. The *Bagatelle* was no unworthy offshoot. The English original, which was now openly and avowedly imitated, had begun to cast a reflection of its halo upon its voluminous offspring. The *Bagatelle* really only sustained the editorial commitments of the *Misantrope*; but it was to be consistently ironic in method and rather merrier and gayer in manner. Van Effen's persuasions had taken a slightly new colour upon the all-important topic of atheism. In a remarkable preface he expresses disapproval of the bigotry and intolerance of the religious, whose orthodoxy is but a cloak for ignorance and intellectual sterility. "Rien n'est donc plus important, que d'examiner de sangfroid si une pareille crainte est bien fondée"; he insists, and urges the necessity for "l'examen" in a "situation calme & tranquille de la Raison" to save us from a "conviction brute & machinale." Van Effen is not far outside the school of Bayle, and is a warm supporter of sentiments such as Addison expressed on enthusiasm in the *Spectator*. So earnest is he that he throws out an open challenge to the world: "je ne refuserai jamais un combat de plume," but this disputatiousness he felt would ruin the pleasantly ironic tone of his *Bagatelle*, so: "je le place dans ma Préface parce que j'en ai trouvé l'exposition un peu trop sérieuse pour entrer dans le Corps de mon Ouvrage." We see then what Van Effen considered was or was not suitable for his work. Like the *Spectator* he is only too conscious of the delicacy of setting up as a moral instructor.

Il n'y a rien qui déplaise plus généralement aux Hommes que *l'Instruction Morale*....Les Sages Amateurs du Genre-Humain ont senti de tout tems cette triste vérité, & ils ont fait tous leurs efforts pour rendre l'Instruction agréable par un déguisement avantageux....Une des ruses dont ils se sont servi, avec le plus de succès, c'est l'allégorie[1].

----

[1] *Bagat.* no. LXXXIII, Feb. 20, 1719.

This is a reference to our Esq., I. Bickerstaff, and his like, whose pleasantries in the giving of advice the *Bagatelle* will strive to emulate. An agreeable allegory in the *Spectator* manner follows. He is sensible that the phlegmatic temperament of his countrymen is fatal to wit[1]. "Nos occupations ordinaires nous jettent dans un sérieux trop épais, pour céder à ce qui est simplement agréable, badin, enjoué." He who would not starve is faced with the necessity "d'avilir son stile jusqu'à" the "burlesque" and the "bouffon." How then would the Bagatellist avoid both heaviness and meanness? He would try to amuse with "une pointe de sel Ironique." He would give "Portraits rians du Vice." The alternative title of the paper ran: "Discours ironiques où l'on prête de sophismes ingénieux au Vice & à l'Extravagance pour en faire mieux sentir le ridicule." But close behind the *littérateur* lurked the reformer. With Addisonian fervour and in Addisonian phrase he insists:

Un livre qui prend le titre de Bagatelle devroit développer la grandeur de la Raison, la beauté de la vertu, & l'extravagance du Vice d'une manière un peu singulière; prendre les Passions de leur côté ridicule, & leur prêter des sophismes. Mon but a été précisément celui-là...j'ai pris exprès le tour ironique pour attaquer le Vice & l'Extravagance de leur côté frivole & puéril.

And how did he succeed in this laudable aim? "La Bagatelle étoit trop sérieuse," "la Bagatelle étoit trop relevée," "la Bagatelle donnoit dans le bas & dans le rampant[2]," the critics said. Another found it "trop métaphysique[3]," and also deserving in some parts the rebuke: "Cessez d'encanailler la Bagatelle." He had to abandon the ironical manner, both because he could not possibly sustain it and because "bien des traits ingénieux furent perdus pour le plus grand nombre des Lecteurs[4]." In a wiser mood Van Effen believed that "l'Ironie n'est point le fait de tout le monde, & qu'en général il y a bien de l'imprudence à un Auteur qui veut être lu généralement, de se servir de ce genre d'écrire[5]."

---

[1] *Bagat.* no. LXXX, Feb. 9, 1719.   [2] Conclusion de la *Bagatelle*.
[3] No. LXVI.   [4] *Éloge Hist.*
[5] *Bagat.* no. LXXXIV.

Je ne dirai rien à cette occasion de mille impertinens raisonnements qu'on a fait dans tout ce Pays sur mes Bagatelles Ironiques.... S'il y a des Lecteurs qui ne savent pas trouver l'Ironie où elle est, il y en a bien tout autant qui possèdent l'art de la fourrer où elle n'est point, & où elle ne sauroit être. C'est l'effet malheureux d'une certaine stupidité subtile, d'une sottise artificielle, plus méprisable que la sottise qui n'est qu'un simple effet de la Nature.... Je pourrois alléguer une foule d'exemples pour confirmer cette vérité[1].

Van Effen was obviously out of humour with his public or with a part of it, and this is a dangerous liberty for an author to take. It is significant that after this only thirteen papers followed before the work was closed. To complete the sense of failure, with incredibly bad taste or, as I am disposed to think, in a mood of pique and irony, he notified readers that a capital "I" would in future announce any ironical number. This letter, "caractère humiliant pour le Public[2]," could not but have helped to alienate the public. He had difficulty over his title[3]. Literal and captious souls would not see the pleasant irony of it and drove him to the defence of it, as in the case of the *Misantrope*. There arose some suspicion that he was serving up second-hand stuff from the English papers[4], although the original imitation of good models was the order of the day and brought credit rather than reproach. Van Effen, of course, soon made it clear that he claimed relationship with the *Spectator*. At first he still had some of the enigmatic air of the *Misantrope* in this respect. In paradoxical strain he sang in the third paper:

> Faisons la nargue aux Spectateurs,
> Aux Misantropes, aux Censeurs,
> Et comme il faut, donnons les étrivières
> Aux fiers Rochefoucaulds, aux sombres La Bruyères,

and at the end of the paper whispered to a correspondent, "je vous dis en confidence, monsieur,...que mon dessein est peut-être,

> Non fumum ex fulgore, sed ex fumo dare lucem,

[1] *Bagat.* no. lxxxv.   [2] *Éloge Hist.*

[3] E.g. Van Effen ironically, no. lxvii: "Mais il y a une contradiction entre le Titre & l'Ouvrage."

[4] *Bagat.* no. lxv.

which is, we remember, the motto of the first number of the *Spectator*. At the end of the sixth paper Van Effen calls for correspondents, saying that the public "ne le trouvent pas bon je m'en écrirai à moi-même, selon usage établi parmi les Spectateurs, les misantropes & auteurs de mon espèce." Van Effen often thus mentioned his own work in the same breath with the English papers. A convenient correspondent says[1]: "Ah! Monsieur, combien seroit-il plus beau de prendre MM. la Bruyère & Addison pour modèles, que d'imiter le badinage même le plus spirituel de Trivelin! Qu'il est glorieux de savoir avec ces messieurs, instruire le cœur en faisant rire l'esprit!" which is a noteworthy tribute to Addison for the year 1713. This remark gives Van Effen the opening to say: "Je vous promets encore, que j'imiterai plutôt Addison que Trivelin[2]." Van Effen was perfectly aware that he was an innovator in his own *milieu* as much as Steele had been in London, and was constantly at pains to defend the new periodical genre. The very first *Bagatelle* opens with:

Depuis trois ou quatre ans, le Public a perdu un certain amusement assez drolle, qu'on lui procuroit toutes les semaines à de certains jours réglés. Le Misantrope a commencé le branle, le Censeur a suivi; & à la fin nous avons eu l'Inquisiteur, Pièce dont, malgré son rare mérite, on oublieroit bientôt son nom, si je n'avois soin d'en conserver ici la mémoire. Le premier ne fut pas goûté d'abord; on ne voulut pas le trouver bon, parce qu'on étoit sûr qu'il ne soutiendroit pas; & il ne se mit en vogue, que parce qu'il fut approuvé par trois ou quatre Beaux-Esprits.... On voyoit ce pauvre homme ne faire pas un pas, sans avoir tâté auparavant si le terrain étoit ferme.

The rest is an appreciation of the *Misantrope* cleverly ironical. Van Effen was in fact slowly opening up the new road that lay before a purblind literary public. Tentative efforts in Dutch and in French followed the *Misantrope*; but more spade work had to be done and the *Bagatelle* did it. The very fact of its appearance was, of course, a new milestone; but it attempted also to clear away im-

---

[1] *Bagat.* no. LXVI.   [2] No. LXVIII.

pedimenta of conservatism. One method was, as we have seen, to appeal to examples and precedents. The extraordinary *mélange* which the papers offered disturbed the contemporary taste, with eighteenth century prejudice against the essay. The *Bagatelle*, says the critic, is "un Cahos indigeste de matières," "vous n'observez pas l'unité[1]," he complains. Van Effen makes a long defence.

Il est vrai que vous cherchez en vain des transitions imperceptibles & délicates, pour passer d'un sujet à l'autre...quand je dis qu'il y a du Plan ou du Système dans mon pauvre Ouvrage je ne parle pas d'un Plan & d'un Système comme il doit y en avoir dans un Traité de Théologie. Non, je ne prens pas ce terme dans un sens si rigoureux.

His general aim is everywhere apparent and "n'est-ce pas-là tout le plan qu'il faut exiger d'un pareil Ouvrage? Y en a-t-il un autre dans La Bruyère, dans La Rochefoucault, dans le Spectateur, & dans le pauvre Misantrope, puisque pauvre Misantrope y a[1]." No. LXXX of the *Bagatelle* is a most interesting one. Van Effen is frankly disappointed that the public has not supported the half-sheet publications and again refers it to English example in a remarkable passage:

Depuis un certain tems les Feuilles volantes sont extrêmement à la mode parmi les auteurs de ce Pays, tant François que Hollandois. Il y a de quoi s'en étonner. Le Public n'y mord guères, & si un pauvre Ecrivain devoit vivre de ce trafic de Bel Esprit, il courroit grand risque de mourir de faim. Ce n'est pas que parmi ces petits Papiers il n'y en ait eu quelques-uns de généralement applaudis de tous ceux qui passoient pour Juges compétens de ces sortes de matières....

And this ill-success is hardly due to the fact that these papers are not in the language of the country, because a "Pièce Hollandoise de la même nature" has had no better success. It is *'t Mensch Ontmaskert*.

Le stile en étoit bon quoiqu'un peu empesé, les matières instructives, & quelquefois assez agréables....Cependant, je ne crois pas que dans toutes nos Provinces il s'en débite quatre cent par semaine.

[1] *Bagat.* no. LXVII.

Le sort du Spectateur a été tout autre en Angleterre. Il paroissoit tous les jours, & chaque fois on en débitoit jusqu'à seize mille. Quand les Dames du premier rang prenoient leur Thé le matin le Spectateur étoit le déjeuner de leur esprit. Les premières Têtes de l'Etat déroboient à leurs occupations importantes le loisir qu'il falloit pour s'amuser à cette utile lecture, & les moindres Bourgeois se cotisoient pour partager ce plaisir avec la Noblesse & avec les Beaux-Esprits.

Where, then, is the rub? As to the authors, he says in the excess of his humility: "J'ose assurer le Public, au nom de tous mes Collègues, les petits Auteurs hebdomaires de ce Pays, que nous n'avons pas un assez sot orgueil, pour croire nos Productions à peu près du même poids que la Pièce Angloise dont je viens de parler." "Pause there, Morocco, and weigh thy value...." Van Effen occasionally shows a curious lack of self-confidence, which can have done his work no good. Still, nous ne nous méprisons pas assez, pour convenir qu'il y ait une juste proportion entre le différent degré de mérite de nos ouvrages & du Spectateur, & entre leurs différens succès. Nous aimons mieux supposer que cette dernière différence, qui est si prodigieuse, procède en partie d'une autre cause, & nous osons bien la trouver dans le caractère de nos Lecteurs.

Then follows an appreciation of the state of English society that is as remarkable as it is flattering to the English and depreciatory (by comparison) of his own people. First of all, the Dutch lack of appreciation of pleasant witticism and refined humour, and secondly, the Dutch parsimony, make the task of the periodical writers hopeless. Van Effen goes out of his way to praise the *Courier Politique & Galant.* Its excellence should have ensured it success, but "le pauvre Ouvrage se trouve arrêté dans sa course, par notre aimable esprit d'épargne. Il est trop cher, tout le monde s'en plaint; c'est un vrai brigandage, de demander jusqu'à un sol pour un quart de Feuille." And yet the *Quintessence,* which "a l'air d'une demi-feuille," can win the field because "elle a plus d'une demi-aune de longueur." The only hope for the *Courier* is to sink to the level of the *Gazette rimée d'Amsterdam* and sell for a farthing. Van Effen is feeling sore over the question, so we must expect a little over-statement. It is worth while to note that the judgment of his public on these early writings was in the main more just than Van Effen's. He was the interested writer, piqued when he cast his thoughts to a neighbouring country where high fame had been won by his prototypes. Yet Van Effen was probably right in so far that if an Addison had appeared in Holland then he would probably have been frozen out too. London society formed the basis of an ideal reading public, large enough to ensure success to him who could command it, and small enough to be retained. Amsterdam was a beehive of industry where the ready public for literary dailies was small. The Hague was too cosmopolitan for any sort of spiritual unity of atmosphere such as made Londoners, in a sense, a happy family in the years when the *Tatler* and the *Spectator* entertained them. Moreover, all the alarming signs of decadence were rising to the surface in Dutch life. Politically their system was hardening into an oligarchy; socially there grew a sharper cleavage between the masses and the cultured class, alienated and distraught by the inundation of French manners and language. There could be neither the national self-confidence nor the necessary balance to produce much in the way of great original literature. And with it all there was the problem of the vulgar new rich, of extravagance and poverty, and of a sharply declining trade. Holland had made its great effort and had, temporarily at least, spent itself, vitiating its national strength in excessive internationalism and Gallicism. England showed exactly the opposite side of the social picture. There was growth in every direction. The wars which had struck a deadly blow at Dutch trade had merely cleared a dangerous competitor out of the way for England. National culture was beginning to assert itself more and more, and the danger of its being submerged had really passed with the Revolution of 1688. Never perhaps has English society attained to the solid balance, the conscious intellectual power and self-confidence which it acquired during the time of Queen Anne. And even in England the *Spectator* would not have been the *Spectator* had it appeared in the time of the Georges and the Jacobite rebellions when national unity was disturbed and self-esteem shaken. Van Effen was unduly pessimistic. His *Hollandsche Spectator* was going to prove it. But in the meantime the early periodicalists were doing uphill work, insisting on their claims to be read, advertising their labours and trying hard to win the public to a relish of the novel literary species. On Thursday, June 23, 1718[1], Van Effen has a clever ironical paper on this kind of writing:

Je ne sai par quel zèle indiscret on travaille continuellement à nous communiquer les réflexions, que certains censeurs bizarres ont faites en d'autres Pays sur les Vices & sur les Sottises des Hommes.

Molière as well as the Misantrope is much in vogue,

qui s'est cassé la tête inutilement à réformer le Genre-humain, selon les fantaisies de sa petite raison. N'en voilà-t-il pas bien assez, pour troubler les honnêtes-gens dans la possession de leurs manières? Y a-t-il de la nécessité à surcharger tout cela de rêveries de certains Anglois, atrabiliaires, & hypocondriaques[2]? Passe encore, si après nous avoir donné du Spectateur par les oreilles[3], on veut bien se séparer de nous quite & bons amis. Mais il est à craindre que tout le reste du Fatras Britannique ne suive, & qu'on ne nous accable encore du Babillard & du Gardien; Rapsodies de la même nature que le Spectateur, & qui viennent à ce qu'on prétend, de la même source. Ce n'est pas proprement que j'aye peur que ces petits Ecrits donnent une âme à ceux qui n'en aient pas[4], & qu'ils causent quelque remue-ménage réel dans nos mœurs. Point du tout, les choses du monde vont toujours leur train, & on seroit bien fou d'aller changer sa conduite pour le beau nez de quelques Ecrivains, dont le but est bien moins de nous corriger, que de nous arracher notre estime & notre argent. Eh bien nous trouvons du génie dans leurs spéculations, & nous payons leurs Livres plus qu'ils ne valent: ne doivent-ils pas être contens comme des Rois?...

C'est pourtant-là le but ridicule de tous ces Faiseurs de Feuilles volantes dont j'ai parlé. Ils veulent rendre les Hommes raisonnables & ils n'ont pas la pénétration assez vive, pour sentir que les rendre *raisonnables* c'est les rendre *malheureux*.

Can we wonder that Van Effen lost patience with a public that was confused by such simple irony? Nos. xxxix and

---

[1] *Bagat.* no. xv.

[2] Another indication that the *Misantrope* was conceived in the spirit of the *Spectator*, etc. Cp. previous chap.

[3] The literal translation of the title *Spectator* did not satisfy French taste. *Vide* introd. to French translation of *Spect.* 1734.   [4] Cp. *Spect.* no. 10.

xl, each a "Lettre à l'Auteur," and the following two numbers in reply, are elaborate attempts of the writer to explain himself and his work to a public which did not seem to know how to take them. These essays have for their text Defoe's " 'Tis a new thing for an author to lay down his thoughts piece-meal." (Cp. also *Spectator*, no. 124.) *Bagatelle*, no. v contains perhaps the most interesting reflections on the new Spectator style. "Lorsqu'on écrit dans ce goût, on ne peut répondre de rien; l'affaire dépend de l'humeur où l'on est, & d'un certain degré de feu qu'on se trouve dans l'imagination...." But these reflections were inspired by the *Spectator*: "Ce que je viens de dire, me rappelle fort à propos dans l'esprit quelques Réflexions du Spectateur Anglois, sur la difficulté de bien composer une Feuille volante." A paraphrase of the opening passage of *Spectator*, no. 124 then follows. But the first part of this *Bagatelle* paper also owes something to *Spectator*, no. 476. Van Effen compares himself with a traveller who "s'amuse dans les campagnes à cueillir tantôt une fleur, tantôt une autre" until night approaches. Addison, when reading rambling authors, fancies himself "in a wood that abounds with a great many noble Objects," and where you may ramble "a whole day together and every moment discover something or other that is new to you." Both authors are discussing their methods of working, and it is in this paper that Van Effen's first borrowing takes place. There is more of it in the sequel. The correspondent of *Bagatelle*, no. lxv openly said: "vos Envieux publient que ce n'est qu'une imitation assez bien tournée d'un Discours du Spectateur sur les Jupes de baleine." The reference is to *Bagatelle*, no. xxii which, out of the many numbers dealing with the petticoat in the *Tatler* and the *Spectator*, may have been most directly suggested by *Spectator*, no. 127. Another correspondent[1] can write:

Voulez-vous bien que je vous dise que je vous crois un peu Plagiaire? Il est fort apparent que c'est le Gardien qui vous a fourni le sujet de votre dernière Bagatelle. Serois-je fort injuste,

---

[1] *Bagat.* no. xciii.

si sur la foi de cette découverte, je vous soupçonnois d'avoir tiré plus d'une fois de pareilles sources, des réflexions que nous avons prises pour être de votre cru, & que nous avons eu la bonté de mettre sur le compte de votre génie? Si vous avouez naturellement la dette, vous êtes à moitié justifié dans mon esprit.

The writer is, of course, Van Effen himself who thus wishes to make an opening for a discussion of the point. The pretended correspondent played the detective. He sent up a translation of Cleora's letter which had appeared on May 18, 1713, in the *Guardian*[1] to prove that its subject had inspired one of Van Effen's papers[2], which he would have esteemed highly had he not discovered that the same idea had been

détaillée fort au long dans un Livre Anglois. C'est le Gardien, ouvrage de la même nature que le Spectateur. Il revient plus d'une fois au même sujet, & entr'autres choses sensées & plaisantes qu'il dit là-dessus il nous donne une Lettre qu'il a apparemment composée lui-même. Elle n'aura pas peut-être la même grâce pour les Lecteurs François, qu'elle a eu pour les Habitans de la Grande-Bretagne....

After this slight apology, not uncommonly made on behalf of English wit at that time, the letter is given, and at the end the contributor says that his aim has been to please the author of the *Bagatelle,* who seems to have a predilection for such foreign *morceaux.* Van Effen replies in such a way as to leave nothing for us to add to the whole question of his borrowings and literary debts:

Vous qui semblez vous plaire à la lecture des Livres Anglois, vous vous souvenez sans doute du Seigneur de Paroisse caractérisé dans le Spectateur. Ce bon homme avoit choisi exprès pour Curé, un Ecclésiastique qui n'étoit pas savant, mais qui avoit une voix claire & forte & une bonne manière de réciter. Il lui faisoit prononcer devant ses Paroissiens tantôt un Sermon de Tillotson, & tantôt un de l'Evêque d'Asaph; & tout le village en étoit aussi édifié, que si ces deux illustres Prélats eussent prêché eux-mêmes.

That Van Effen cites to his purpose from the *Spectator*[3] is an indication how he had familiarized himself with it. Many

---

[1] No. 58.   [2] *Bagat.* no. xcii.   [3] *Spect.* no. 106.

of its ideas had become part of his thought, and many of his own ideas honestly come by found their counterpart in English writings:

Sans vanité, monsieur, l'idée que j'ai tâché de développer dans ma dernière Bagatelle je l'ai eue longtems avant que d'avoir lu l'auteur Anglois dont vous parlez. Il est vrai que le charmant Discours de cet Auteur l'a fort éclaircie dans mon esprit, & que je lui dois en partie ce qu'il peut y avoir de bon dans ma dernière Feuille volante. Je l'ai composée pourtant sans relire le Discours en question, & la forme que j'ai donnée à cette matière est tout-à-fait à moi. Je ne crois pas franchement que cette façon d'agir me doive attirer le titre odieux de Plagiaire. Il me semble que dans un Recueil de petites Dissertations comme les miennes, on peut hardiment mêler les fruits de sa lecture avec ses propres réflexions; & que le Public doit être content, quand on lui donne quelque chose de bon & de nouveau. Que lui importe de quelle source on le tire?...Je confesse, monsieur, qu'il y a dans ma Bagatelle quatre ou cinq morceaux, que j'ai pris tout entiers des Feuilles Volantes Anglaises, mais j'ai toujours averti qu'il n'y avoit de moi que le tour François; le reste de mon petit Ouvrage, quel qu'il soit, m'appartient véritablement; ce sont mes propres petites réflexions, &[1] *quelquefois sans doute ce sont les fruits de ma lecture, si fort brouillés avec mes propres idées, qu'il m'est impossible de les distinguer les uns d'avec les autres....Le seul moyen légitime de s'approprier les idées d'autre, c'est de les digérer par la méditation.* Elles deviennent alors les nôtres, de la même manière que les alimens se changent en parties réelles de notre corps. *Vous savez, monsieur, que le plus grand Génie de l'Univers n'ira jamais loin, s'il ne tire ses pensées que de son propre fond; je suis persuadé que l'Esprit le plus porté à réfléchir & le plus propre à le faire avec succès, quand il seroit soutenu par l'imagination la plus féconde n'acquerra jamais une grande étendue sans la conversation & la lecture.*

These words are most remarkable for the year 1718. They reflect the growing realization of the universality and internationalism of literature and philosophy; but are in expression well in advance of their time and worthy of Saint-Beuve. Van Effen goes on to say that, if every man must discover all his ideas *ab ovo*, little progress can be made. It is better to take a thought already suggested so that "en l'examinant de toutes ses différentes faces, en la combinant avec nos propres

[1] My italics.

idées on l'auroit étendue, embellie, fortifiée.... *Celui qui agit ainsi, lit & médite; mais il ne pille pas, à moins qu'on ne veuille bannir la lecture de la République des Lettres, comme un brigandage.*" No one will be disposed to quarrel with Van Effen over these views, although most people would make the reservation that everything finally depends upon the result. According to this theory art might become hopelessly derivative or might perennially appear with the freshest originality. As an artistic thesis it says little in effect, because it is too wide. Its very truth can be wrested to become untruth. We judge finally by results, but we must know as far as possible what manner of material genius has worked upon to produce those results. To appreciate originality in thought and expression it is necessary to know how much of it is imitation and how much *aus eigener Erfindung,* which knowledge can be obtained only by careful comparative study.

Van Effen's consideration of the point of plagiarism is not unconnected with the frank avowals in the English papers, which, taking advantage of the "late Act of Naturalization," adopted French *pensées* as well as French *réfugiés.* "My precautions," declared Steele in *Guardian,* no. 87, "are made up of all that I can hear & see, translate, borrow, paraphrase or contract from the persons with whom I mingle & converse & the authors whom I read[1]." Such an avowal is very much in the spirit of Van Effen. Nor was Van Effen ignorant of Steele's practice, and the knowledge of it at the same time supplied him with an additional motive and excuse for borrowing.

In *Bagatelle,* no. xxvii Van Effen adopts no. 153 of the *Guardian* (by Addison) and makes the following prefatory remark: "Je ne saurois mieux dépeindre ce qu'il en penseroit, qu'en me servant d'une petite allégorie, que j'ai trouvée dans un auteur anglois. Ce n'est qu'user de représailles; ces messieurs pillent assez les Ecrivains des autres nations, quoiqu'ils ne fassent semblant de rien." It was, we

---

[1] Cp. also *Guardian,* no. 52: "I shall not assume to myself the merit of everything in these papers. Wheresoever in reading or conversation," etc.

see, the morality of plagiarism that worried Van Effen. This explains why he was scrupulously honest in disclaiming what was not his own, within the limits, always, of his theory of what constituted plagiarism and what did not. From Van Effen's answer to the correspondent's accusation already quoted, it is clear that he wished to make no. xcii a sort of test case. The subject is an allegory built up on Berkeley's *Theory of Vision*, and applied in the sense of Addison's exposition in the Pleasures of the Imagination essays in the *Spectator*, of which again Locke was the starting-point. Now Locke and Shaftesbury were probably the first English writers with whom Van Effen was acquainted. The *Spectator* he knew very well and had himself written on the pleasures of the imagination in the *Misantrope* (1711/12) soon after Addison's series had begun to appear. Then the *Guardian* had revived the theme, and Berkeley himself contributed an essay on the subject, showing incidentally that the Addisonian style has a curious trick of appearing in other Queen Anne writers as well. In no. 58 Steele allegorized the subject with his usual rough gaiety. In *Bagatelle*, no. lxiii Van Effen discusses Notions and Images after the manner of Locke. We can therefore well believe Van Effen when he protests: "l'idée que j'ai tâché de développer dans ma dernière Bagatelle je l'ai eue longtems avant, etc." It is in exactly this sense that much but not all of his work from the *Misantrope* to the *Hollandsche Spectator* is derivatively original. Besides the borrowings already noted, a few more direct ones occur that exhaust the "quatre ou cinq morceaux" which Van Effen stated he had utilized from the English papers. No. lxxv is a translation of a *Guardian* number, as Van Effen indicates in no. xc; so for the most part is no. xii a translation of *Guardian*, no. 157. The eighty-third *Bagatelle* is mostly "tirée d'un Auteur étranger," who, one finds, is Addison in *Guardian* no. 152.

There are, however, cases of clear but unacknowledged borrowing on the part of Van Effen, even if it be only for the general idea of an essay. Van Effen's papers on laughers, *Bagatelle*, nos. xliii, xliv, are obviously modelled on papers like *Spectator,* no. 47, *Guardian,* no. 29 and especially *Guardian,* no. 42; nos. xc and lxxv on pastoral poetry are inspired by *Guardian* papers. With *Bagatelle,* no. xlvii we might compare *Tatler,* no. 93 and *Spectator,* no. 364. The opening especially of *Bagatelle,* no. xliii develops the idea of *Guardian,* no. 87. "J'ai remarqué que celles de mes Bagatelles qui répondoient au sens naturel de ce terme, ont toujours été les plus goûtées, quoiqu'assurément ce ne soient pas celles qui m'ayent coûté le plus," etc.[1] *Bagatelle,* no. xliv also shows once more that Van Effen's standpoint was almost identical with Addison's on the subject of reason and the dignity of human nature. To both, reason was an absolute faculty independent of the passions over which it was willing to assume control if we would only exercise it; in such measure as we were reasonable beings we were true men and women. *Cogito, ergo sum. Bagatelle,* no. lxiv on the "Thermomètre de sanctification" must be read in connection with *Tatler,* no. 214 on the "*political* barometer" and no. 220 on the "*ecclesiastical* thermometer[2]." The preacher of *Bagatelle,* no. lxxvi who loves to cite the "original" in his sermons and desists on the advice of a friend, but is entreated by the congregation not to discontinue so scholarly a practice, might claim the preacher of *Spectator,* no. 221 as a kindred spirit. *Bagatelle,* no. xci is distantly reminiscent of parts of *Spectator,* nos. 604, 626 and others, but is developed in an original way. And so there may be found more resemblances which show that the English papers coloured Van Effen's thinking and guided his method.

But the *Bagatelle* by no means reflects English periodical literature only. There is another strain of influence traceable which emanates from no less a writer than Swift. We have said in a former chapter that Van Effen had undertaken to translate *A Tale of a Tub* when he was in

---

[1] "The grave discourses which I sometimes give the town do not win so much attention as lighter matters. For this reason it is that I am obliged to consider vice as it is ridiculous and accompanied with gallantry.... Where I have taken most pains I often find myself least read."

[2] Usually assigned to Addison; but in Holland apparently credited to Swift, e.g. by *Boekzaal,* March 1735—review of le Clercq's translation of the *Tatler.*

London in 1715. The translation appeared three years after the *Bagatelle*, with translations of other famous pieces all amply annotated. Van Effen was in fact working intermittently on Swift while the *Bagatelle* ran. It would then be strange if Swift's wit and energy of invention had left no trace on Van Effen's receptive mind. *Bagatelle*, nos. XXXIV and LIV, on the manufacture of dedications and prefaces, are manifestly inspired by the *Tale*. We are not surprised therefore when the latter paper is wound up with a versified rendering of the story of the "fat unwieldy fellow" in Leicester Fields told in the preface to the *Tale*. It is criticized by a correspondent and defended by Van Effen in no. LXVIII. *Bagatelle*, no. LXXIV, on the project for establishing hereditary succession among the clergy, combines an original idea with the manner of Swift, although Van Effen gives the clergy his blessing in quite Addisonian style at the end. But the very spirit in which the *Bagatelle* was undertaken was the fruit of Van Effen's reading of Swift. We have mentioned that he wished to cast his lucubrations within the mould of irony, and how he found that irony could not be sustained throughout. It was, of course, from the start an incongruous association—the cutting, misanthropic irony of Swift with the amiability of the Spectator and his "tendresse pour le genre-humaine." Irony would do for occasional papers, but would inevitably, if carried too far, freeze out the geniality proper to a Spectator. Van Effen had tried in the *Bagatelle* to combine Swift and Addison, for whom he had an almost equally fervent admiration, and in his own temperament were traces of the characteristic qualities of each. A striking correspondence of Van Effen and Swift in caustic irony is found in *Misantrope*, I, no. XXX, which gives a sombre picture of busy mercantile Amsterdam and depicts the inhabitants as for the most part a species of debased animal. Van Effen never again clouded over his satire so darkly, and gave but a foretaste of that Yahooland with which the English wit was to shock the world later. We have noticed how Van Effen, in the manner of the *Spectator*, was strengthened in the desire to teach, and teach pleasantly, by the frequent expression in those papers of the need to "enliven morality with wit." This was of course a fixed idea of Swift's:

"Having carefully cut up human nature, I have found a very strange, new and important discovery that the public good of mankind is performed by two ways, instruction and diversion"...and "throughout this divine treatise I have skilfully kneaded up both together with a layer of *utile* and a layer of *dulce*[1]." *Omne tulit punctum*.... It might be remembered, too, that the *Tatler* was practically a joint venture by Swift and Steele at first, so that the insistence on the necessity for mixing the *dulce* and the *utile* in that paper and its successors may well owe something to the convictions of Swift upon the point. Nevertheless, without wishing to stress Van Effen's indebtedness to the English writers in respect of this governing policy of his writings, and without pretending to place definitely the source of his indebtedness in this respect, we think it necessary to show that he was familiar with most of Swift's work. Two remarks occur in the *Bagatelle*, somewhat out of place too, as if dragged in, which indicate intimacy with a particular strain of Swift's humour; when Swift exercises "the liberty I have thought fit of praising myself," and "makes his own eulogy," like the proud author who invariably commences: "I speak without vanity[2]." So elsewhere he recurs to the same ironic point of "forcing into the light with much pains and dexterity my own excellences[3]," speaking confidently of the time when "this treatise of mine shall be translated into foreign languages," as indeed it soon was to be.

Van Effen claims ideas as his own in no. xciii, as if he had taken a patent on them; but in no. xv he is bolder:

J'ose prendre cette occasion pour féliciter ce siècle d'avoir produit un homme comme moi, propre à s'opposer vigoureusement aux attentats de la Raison, & à la détruire en la mettant en contradiction avec elle-même. Je m'engage au Public....

---

[1] *A Tale of a Tub*, Section v.
[2] *Ibid*. Preface.   [3] *Ibid*. Section v.

The effrontery of the Bagatellist when he takes leave exceeds even that of the fatuous transcriber of *A Tale of a Tub.*

Ce que je vai vous communiquer à présent consiste en réflexions profondes sur les matières les plus épineuses. J'ai eu besoin de la plus forte méditation pour les creuser; j'y vai répandre des lumières merveilleuses; & soyez persuadés, que personne ne vous a jamais dit ce que vous allez entendre aujourd'hui. Vous êtes surpris de mon stile....S'agit-il d'un savoir immense, d'une érudition illimitée, qui sait mieux que moi en étaler le noble orgueil?

Personne au moins ne me disputera la gloire d'être le premier homme du monde pour l'intelligence des Langues Originales.... Heureux notre siècle, d'avoir produit un Esprit d'ordre du mien, un Esprit propre à dissiper ces nuages ténébreux qui enveloppent la République des Lettres!

Except for some incongruity with the general context, this and what follows is a good imitation of the loud Swiftian style, and is, with the rest of the Van Effen-Swift relations, an interesting incident in the history of eighteenth-century international literary exchange of the second decade.

In addition to the elements from English literature carried over into the *Bagatelle,* there is a fair amount of critical observation and description of English literature and character which rendered the *Bagatelle* a valuable organ for disseminating English culture and spreading its vogue. It was natural that the influence of La Bruyère and other non-English writers should also appear in the *Bagatelle.* Van Effen was too deeply read in French literature not to reproduce, or connect thoughts from it with his own. Bisschop and Valkhoff have indicated some correspondences. But it must not be thought that the *Bagatelle* is negligible as literature because it is useful historically. Apart from avowed translations and some close imitations which hold little interest for readers of Addison and Swift, but were no doubt a pleasing feature to Van Effen's contemporary audience, Van Effen has, with his usual independence of treatment and thought, said many good things well. Bisschop has made quite a fair estimate of the work as a whole, but may have been somewhat more appreciative of the better work in it. There is much good sense, sagacity, observation and description couched in fluid masculine style. No. xciv well illustrates Van Effen's general level.

Le beau tems m'invita, un jour de la semaine passée, à goûter le plaisir de la promenade avec un ami spirituel & éclairé. Il semble que jamais l'esprit n'est si fort porté à la réflexion, que quand les sens, plutôt amusés qu'occupés par la variété d'un grand nombre d'objets rians, communiquent à l'âme une joie douce & paisible, & l'endorment dans une agréable rêverie. Nous nous étions abandonnés pendant plus d'une demi-heure à des distractions satisfaisantes, lorsque par hasard mes yeux tombèrent sur un bon homme assis sur le bord d'un canal, la pipe à la bouche, & une ligne à la main. Il paroissoit être de cette classe de gens qui par le travail le plus rude gagnent précisément ce qui leur faut pour ne pas mourir de faim. Je m'arrêtai assez longtems pour voir la réussite de cette pêche, & je ne vis pas le moindre petit poisson qui daignât seulement donner au pauvre Pêcheur de fausses espérances. Je m'impatientai pour lui, etc....

There is proportion, clarity, and an atmosphere into which the solitary fisherman is admirably made to fit, the picture provided being in deft and sure outline.

No. xcv is an excellent paper on the English. The seventy-ninth paper on scholarship and social life is an admirable one. Nos. xxxii and xxxiii, on the hereditary professorship and kingship, are a worthy contribution of the popular kind to political thought, anticipating revolutionary theorists like Paine, who makes use of the same idea to illustrate the ridiculousness of hereditary succession[1]. The description of the ways of English women in no. xxxix is a good example of Van Effen's lighter, easy, pleasant style. Amongst much else that pleases, there is also some poor, dead stuff, which can easily be found. The paper on the Clapperman of Ternate is the most objectionable one Van Effen ever allowed himself to write, and there is but small excuse for him to say: "cette Pièce m'a été envoyée de Londres, où elle a fait grand bruit; on dit même qu'on l'a traduite en anglois." There is a great deal of poetry which Van Effen has passed off on a

---

[1] T. Paine, *Political Works* (1817).

long-suffering public. It is very much in the manner of
Swift, without the Dean's frequent mordant brilliance of
phrase.

The next venture of this kind was the *Nouveau Spectateur
Français*. The *Letternieuws* from Paris for March 1724 in the
Boekzaal reads: "In addition to *Le Spectateur François* and
Le Spectateur Suisse a third little work of a similar kind has
appeared here which carries the title of *Le Spectateur Inconnu*.
It is said that the work is very well and wittily written.
While such writings seem at present to be very much in the
mode, J. Neaulme, Bookseller at the Hague, began some
weeks since to issue also a *Nouveau Spectateur* or *New French
Spectator*. The sheets that have already appeared are written
with understanding, and people assure us that the author of
le Misantrope and *la Bagatelle*, which some years since were
printed (weekly), is also the writer of this half-sheet."

In 1717 Carlet de Marivaux had taken up something in the
vein of the *Spectator* in several contributions to de la Motte's
Mercure. He did not know English, and therefore must have
made his acquaintance of the new manner through the
French translations of the *Spectator*, which the Dutch press
had speedily put on the market: while at the same time he
was probably familiar with what had been written in French
in similar style, and therefore with the *Misantrope* and later
the *Bagatelle*. Van Effen's general example did not pass unheeded in Paris, which saw its *Spectator* for the first time in
1722. In particular, there is little correspondence, but, if
Marivaux caught the hint from someone else for his clever
skit on the pedant who professes to despise the new literature
of half-sheets, he benefited from the *Bagatelle* (especially
no. xxxix) rather than from no. 124 of the *Spectator*
which is very different. The *Spectateur Français* struggled
on through some two dozen numbers and on the whole
has but little resemblance to the well-sustained and
adroitly managed English paper. Marivaux, moreover, had
neither the requisite equipment nor temperament. He had
no Greek and little Latin and as for modern languages,
Larroumet says: "comment auroit-il songé à étudier

les langues étrangères dont l'utilité ne fut guère reconnue en France qu'un siècle plus tard?" Far from having "examiné à fond les anglois" as Van Effen had, Marivaux knew very little about them, and could import neither classical colour nor English spirit into his lucubrations. Larroumet finds that "Marivaux a pris un titre à Addison mais il ne lui a guère pris que cela." A second La Bruyère was stringing his thoughts on an Addisonian frame. Marivaux was interested rather in being a polished man of the world and cutting a fashionable figure in the *salons*, than in instructing the world how to think, read, speak and behave justly and with taste. In every way Van Effen was the better placed and equipped among continental writers for receiving the mantle of the English *Spectator*. He combined the classical culture of Addison, and the desire for social reform shown by the English writers, with a knowledge of them and their aims that was unusual for the time. If Marivaux has been justly called "un médiateur entre la littérature anglaise et la littérature française[2]," how much more does that distinction belong to Van Effen! In 1724, while at the University of Leyden, Van Effen continued Marivaux's paper under the title "*Le nouveau Spectateur Français, ou Discours dans lesquels on voit un portrait naïf des mœurs de ce siècle.*" He now advertised that he was determined to reproduce the English manner. First of all, plans had been made for the collaboration of a number of wits, no doubt after the English example; but as M. Potin in his letter to the writer of the *Éloge* says, "cet associé lui a manqué dès le commencement." The *Nouveau Spectateur Français* therefore turned out to be as abortive as the *Spectateur Français*, reaching only a few more numbers. It also borrowed largely from the Paris paper, with due acknowledgements, as usual[3]. Van Effen thought highly of

---

[1] *Marivaux, sa Vie et ses Œuvres*, p. 297.

[2] C. Joret, *Herder et la Renaissance Littéraire en Allemagne*, cit. Larroumet.

[3] "Parmi ses Discours j'en trouve d'écrits d'une manière si brillante & si agréable, que je me ferai un plaisir d'en insérer de tems en tems quelques-uns dans mon Ouvrage."

Marivaux's wit, but considered that his attempts in the Spectator style missed the moral tone and reforming qualities which should distinguish the new genre[1]. For the first time Van Effen used the word Spectator in his title but with a degree of humility that was almost timidity.

Je crains bien que le titre que je prens ne rebute les Lecteurs. Il semble annoncer une audace & une vanité inexcusables. Le placer à la tête d'une Feuille volante, c'est promettre en quelque sorte un Ouvrage qui approcha du moins de l'excellence du Spectateur Anglois....J'ai imité la hardiesse de ce Bel-Esprit[2], en me donnant les airs de prendre le titre de Spectateur, c'est une démarche qui mérite d'être justifiée....Je ne prens leur titre, que parce que j'ai résolu d'écrire dans leur goût, & de rendre mon Ouvrage aussi utile aux hommes qu'il me sera possible.

The moral aim was stressed particularly; he would give "Lambeaux de morale," and in everything the English precedent was to be followed. "J'imiterai ici le Spectateur Anglois & le Mentor Moderne en traçant mon propre caractère," he says, and gives a charming account of his father and himself, which must be read to understand Van Effen. Even the Spectator's practice of Latin mottoes was now for the first time followed with an appropriate line from Virgil for the first motto: *Sequitur non passibus aequis.*

"Il paroît en quelque sorte essentiel aux Spectateurs de rêver quelquefois, & il arrive je ne sais comment, qu'en rêvant ils ont plus de raison & de génie, que pendant qu'ils veillent[3]." Van Effen accordingly treats us to a *songe* of his own making. No one, of course, will be deceived. This was no new vein for Van Effen. The Misantrope had already had his dreams in the Spectator manner and had sketched a character of himself to satisfy the curiosity of a Public, which was eager to know if a writer "be a black or a fair man, of a mild or cholerick Disposition, married or a Batchelor with other Particulars of the like nature that conduce very much to the right Understanding of an Author[4]." The Misantrope, too, had given samples of light criticism in Addison's

---

[1] *Vide*, e.g., no. i. [2] Marivaux.
[3] No. xiii. [4] *Spect.* no. i.

manner. The *Nouveau Spectateur Français* gave several papers to the consideration of Voltaire's *Henriade* and La Motte's works, obviously suggested by the famous series on Milton. Van Effen had the good sense to condemn the puerilities of La Motte's fables; but otherwise his laudatory judgments on that author have failed to secure the support of modern opinion. There are papers on the true as well as on the false *philosophe*, who is stupid in so far as his knowledge is allowed to make him less human and sociable. Not only was philosophy to be brought from the clouds, but the philosopher himself was to be dragged from his cell into the light of common day. The *petits-maîtres* and the old men are not forgotten. There are some excellent papers on criticism; coquettes, ministers and fathers have to run the gauntlet; there is a great deal of beausexing—to adapt Swift's impatient expression in regard to the *Spectator*—and subjects such as marriage and love duly and properly come up for discussion. But if one looks for influence from, and for interesting argument upon, English literature, one is met almost everywhere by a preoccupation on the part of the author with French literature. Beyond what we have noticed, interest in English culture and literature is hardly anywhere seen. In no. x "un auteur Anglois" is quoted, and in no. xii, a letter appears which had been translated from the English. Beyond a general correspondence of thought between the English periodicalists and Van Effen, maintained here as elsewhere, it is difficult to point to any expression or hint which Van Effen may be said to have gathered from an English source. So far from writing in the style of the *Spectator*, Van Effen has hardly succeeded in writing the entertaining essay as we know it in the English papers. He is argumentative, expository, and, however popular and concrete he tries to be, seldom amusing. But this does not detract from the real virtue of the *Nouveau Spectateur Français*, which lies in vigorous speculation expressed in clear and lively terms, and the original, open examination of everyday matters, without descent to the commonplace or the vulgar. His remarks in no. iv may, perhaps, be cited as illustrating our point, as well as Van Effen's broad patriotism and humanity. He deprecates the censure passed on entire nations.

"Ces sortes de censures sont odieuses....La vertu est la patrie générale de tous les gens vertueux....Tout l'Univers crève, pour ainsi dire, d'hommes extravagans & vicieux, c'est une vérité aussi triste que palpable...mais si toutes les Nations ont leurs vices distinctifs, toutes les Nations ont aussi de belles qualités qui les caractérisent....Je crois pourtant avoir remarqué que cette corruption est moins générale, & moins excessive qu'on ne la dépeint d'ordinaire. Je ne dirai rien de cette ridicule déclamation qui fait le panégyrique de tous les siècles passés, pour jeter tout le fardeau du crime sur le nôtre....J'avoue qu'une certaine portion d'amour de préférence pour nos compatriotes, est naturelle, légitime, & même d'une grande utilité. Un cœur bien placé & sensible ne sauroit s'en défendre, il ne le doit pas même. Chez tous les Peuples, malgré la variété infinie des caractères particuliers, il règne un caractère général, une certaine conformité de naturel, une familiarité avec les mêmes mœurs, les mêmes coutumes, le même air, la même nourriture, les mêmes sons articulés. L'intérêt de tous les particuliers y découle du même intérêt général & toutes ces causes réunies donnent à chaque individu une espèce de droit de propriété sur toute la Nation....Ce zèle pour nos compatriotes est donc souverainement utile, & digne de plus grands éloges. Cette opinion déplaira sans doute à une classe de philosophes...." But "la Raison ne suffit pas à des hommes placés dans de pareilles circonstances. Il nous faut pour hâter les opérations de notre raison, des instincts, des passions nées avec nous, ou excitées nécessairement par la situation où nous sommes mis par la Providence. Ces instincts, ces passions sont les liaisons de la Société, elles frayent à notre raisonnement la route des devoirs mutuels, qui affermissent la félicité du Genre-humain. Le Sage ne doit point travailler à détruire ces heureux instincts: ils lui sont naturels, il les trouve dans le fond de son être; c'est l'ouvrage du Créateur aussi bien que la Raison."

Nowhere else does Van Effen come nearer to realizing that the eighteenth-century fetish of reason did not compound either the whole duty or the whole nature of man.

In this essay there is a reference to the English character, and the first number contains a panegyric on the *Spectator* which we will not now discuss. But otherwise there is little in the *Nouveau Spectateur Français* to show that Van Effen was interested in and familiar with the English and their literature. Amongst the essays from Marivaux's paper which Van Effen republished in his own, there are some relating the "Histoire d'une Dame Âgée," which probably gave Van Effen the initial hint for his novelette under the heading of *Lettre d'un Homme d'Âge*, which we have discussed above in connection with Van Effen's character. Perhaps we may conclude our consideration of Van Effen's principal French writings with the verdict of Oomkens: "Van Effen est penseur de sa nature[1]"; "Van Effen est un vrai philosophe[2]." "Il est certain que par son esprit éclairé et ses vues larges, il était fort supérieur à la plupart de ses contemporains, qu'il se trouvait à la tête de la civilisation de son époque[3]."

[1] *Rev. Holl.* VIII, p. 855.   [2] *Ibid.*   [3] *Ibid.* X, p. 1059.

CHAPTER V

THE *HOLLANDSCHE SPECTATOR*

I$_T$ would have been passing strange had the Netherlands not made its appearance among the countries which duly produced a *Spectator* and its prolific progeny. For the production of a national *Spectator* Van Effen was by right of precedence and by ability unquestionably the right man. And he did not fail his countrymen. As he had worthily inaugurated the great periodical age on the continent, it was left for him to represent his country worthily in it by his *Hollandsche Spectator*. The first number appeared on August 20, 1731, and the last on April 8, 1735, five months before the author's death. It was, therefore, not only late in the day for Holland, which had absorbed more English literature than any other country, to have its national *Spectator*, but also very late in Van Effen's short career. At the outset[1] he declared: "Of what concerns my person and capabilities I shall not say much. I have travelled much, read much, observed much. I am old enough to be circumspect and thoughtful, young enough to be merry and of good temper." In fact, the period of his maturity was unfortunately rapidly passing now, for digestive trouble had seriously impaired his health before the work had been carried far. It was almost as true of his *Spectator* as of Fielding's *Voyage to Lisbon*, that it was "a work begun in pain and finished almost at the same period with life[2]." He was sinking into

---

[1] No. 10; cp. Addison in *Spect.* no. 10.

[2] In no. 204, Van Effen acknowledges a present of a pot of preserved ginger for his malady, which, he complains in one of his gasping run-on sentences, has "since some time for the greater part deprived me of the desire for writing and the usual pleasure I take in it, without which one produces nothing good, and which has forced me, if I did not wish to discontinue my work when it is still far from completion, to snatch some lucky moments by the hair every day and avail myself of them at intervals, which practice nevertheless never produces such a good result as when one can follow up the linking of one's thoughts in a mood continuously favourable."

a melancholic mood[1] and too many of his lucubrations are "sicklied o'er," which was as much the result of his physical condition as of the contemplative discipline that had now become a habit of his mind. In fact, Van Effen's condition all but spelled—but happily did not always bring—death to the sprightliness and gaiety proper to a true Spectator. His mood on the whole was consonant rather less with the *jeu d'esprit* of the *Tatler* than with the sermonizing of the *Guardian,* a paper which influenced him more than any other English paper because he had translated it. Although the *Hollandsche Spectator* appeared only once and later twice a week, he faltered in its regular output. Verwer indeed says that there were signs that the paper would stop[2], and that, at another time, when the supply of numbers was almost exhausted, the publisher Uytwerf secured his services for Van Effen, who was discomfited at the poor support he was getting from the public[3]. Bisschop has denied Verwer's allegations, but they are borne out by the *Boekzaal*[4], which, in a review of part six of the *Hollandsche Spectator*, says: "We do not doubt that the reader will notice sufficiently well from these samples that in this sixth part the Spectator still maintains himself with fame, in spite of the expectation of many that his fall would occur before the third part had been completed." Van Effen took himself and his task most seriously, too seriously, perhaps, and was worried at the end that he would have to abandon his work without fulfilling the obligations due from him to his many unanswered correspondents and to his countrymen generally. His last Spectatorial words expressed the wish that "some or other younger brother of the Spectator" might take upon himself the commitments of the elder and pay off all debts with interest. There was less of jest than of earnestness when he spoke in no. 34 of "the tender interest that I take in my little work." The spirit was willing enough, but the flesh failed him. It is therefore to be regretted that he had not

---

[1] Cp. *Holl. Spect.* nos. 348, 185, and Verwer & Zuydam.
[2] *Leven,* p. lxxii.   [3] *Ibid.* p. cxvii.
[4] Nov. 1733.

taken up the work sooner. It has been asked, indeed, why he took it up at all. Was it zeal for reform? It is certain that the reformer had as much justification as scope in the Holland of his day. The particular troubles and abuses from which Dutch society suffered had been considerably aggravated since the days of the *Bagatelle*. There was decadence everywhere, of which poverty and extravagance, bankruptcies and false culture were some signs[1]. While at no time were the social evils so grave as those the *Tatler* had to combat; yet French gallantry and English scepticism were now more and more felt as serious dangers which were enervating domestic, moral and religious life. Economically and politically his country was fast approaching the condition described by Chesterfield[2]: "The Republic has now no other title but courtesy to the name of a maritime Power.... Their trade decreases daily and their national debt increases...." He finally commends their police as the only survival of "that prudence, vigilance and good discipline which *formerly*[3] made them esteemed, respected and courted." The Dutch, by a generosity which it would be unkind to call foolish, drained their vital resources, and vitiated their national culture by the exaggerated magnanimity with which they exhausted themselves in order to play a leading part for the freedom of Europe, spiritually and politically. Their history at this period remains a standing warning of the dangers of excessive denationalization and internationalism and of the exaggerated cultivation of foreign cultures. They may indeed be said to have played a noble rôle as *point d'appui* whence international cultural exchanges were effected, but the price which they paid for this distinction was a terrible one. Their country was overrun with foreign elements, especially

---

[1] "'Twere to be wished," remarked le Clerc later *à propos* of Temple's *Observations*, "that what Sir William speaks of its frugality were true. The state of things has been mightily altered within these Thirty or Five and Thirty years & Luxury has introduced itself especially in the Chief Towns to as great an Excess as in other Countries." (Theobald's Version, 1718.)

[2] *Some accounts of the Government of the Republic of the Seven United Provinces*.

[3] My italics.

French, which were not and could not be properly assimilated. Whereas the Dutch had been leaders, they seemed now content to be imitators. In England the French refugees were speedily Anglicized, but in Holland they Gallicized the Dutch and their language, showing indeed an undisguised contempt for the national culture of their generous hosts, as Van Effen tells with indignation[1]. There is something fundamentally lacking in any nation that can allow such an unhealthy state of affairs to continue, however large-minded and rational its people may flatter themselves to be in attempting to be citizens of the world. To regard what is native, and distinctive of themselves, as things to be tolerated only with pardonable indulgence or despised as "canailleuse," as Van Effen says, revealed a lamentable pettiness of spirit, which the inexorable justice of natural law would surely punish. No national life could have maintained its integrity and vitality under the inundation of foreign influences to which Holland had recklessly flung open her floodgates. In adopting the culture of all Europe, the Netherlanders had in the end lost the proper healthy respect for their own. They had made a premature experiment in cosmopolitanism while the rest of the world looked on or wisely followed with less precipitation. England had survived her French period, and was once more attaining greater independence. Anyone who turns from Shaftesbury to the *Spectator* will realize what immense strides had been taken in establishing in its proper esteem the domestic culture of Arbuthnot's *John Bull*. Shaftesbury would have been horrified at Addison's praise of *Chevy Chace* and at the bourgeois tastes of the *Spectator*. As it was characteristic of the *Spectator* to vindicate national domesticity and the fine products of the national spirit and genius, so nothing is more fundamental in Van Effen's *Spectator* than the same zeal for, and determination to restore in general esteem, the home article in every sphere. He, with all his cosmopolitanism, was one of the first to realize that Dutch culture had lost its poise. His very turning from French to his mother tongue for purposes

---

[1] *Holl. Spect.* no. 8.

of literary expression is an indication of his final attitude. Led astray by a desire for glory in the international field of culture and learning, he had used French, because he felt it to be the coming, if not existing, international medium. This was a fixed idea at the time, in which the outrageous French imperialism must have delighted, and which Van Effen retained even to the last. In his final Dutch work he remarked the spread of the French language with satisfaction[1]. "How is it conceivable that although the French language is so common amongst us and with reason becomes more common every day, our folk do not trouble to read, or do not find good to draw their advantage from the fine and well-argued works written in that tongue on the subject of truly wrought wit?" This expression, which occurs in a paper on Gothic taste that would have done the hearts of both Shaftesbury and Addison good and that owes something to them, proves that Van Effen still looked to France as the fountain-head of taste in art, and regarded the prevalence of French as a reasonably good thing. But he could now see the limits better, and would not have advocated what he himself had been guilty of, namely, the cultivation of French as a medium of artistic expression or social intercourse to the neglect of Dutch. That he presented the nation with his excellent periodical must be taken as something in the nature of an *apologia* as well as the belated fulfilment of an obligation.

Van Effen, having first reformed himself, had much to reform among his countrymen in respect of their unnatural defection from the healthy, vigorous simplicity of the life of their forefathers in favour of an extraneous artificiality of manners which sapped their national culture.

Deeply conscious of these facts, he made it his chief endeavour as a Spectator to warn his countrymen of the insidious influences at work amongst them. In company, Verwer says, he spoke "with such ardour of the ancient good faith of the Netherlands that one saw that his heart opened when he touched upon that chord." Van Effen, in fact, added a vigorous nationalism to his internationalism, and his work

[1] *Holl. Spect.* no. 310.

glows with the fervour of a patriot[1]. This is more pronounced in his final periodical, but it was also characteristic of his first. *Misantrope* no. XIII is a remarkable paper which paraphrases most of what he has said in this connection. "Les histoires nous parlent d'une certaine Nation la plus sage & la plus heureuse qu'on ait jamais trouvée dans l'Univers" is the opening sentence of an inspired sketch of the land of his fathers.

Jamais Peuple ne fit de plus grandes actions, & jamais on ne vit plus évidemment que la Liberté est la source de la Valeur. La bonté cordiale, qui paroît si ridicule dans ce siècle, étoit le caractère particulier de ce Peuple chéri du Ciel: tous les malheureux, tous les persécutés venoient de tous les coins de la Terre, chercher dans cette République un asile assuré....Sans finesse d'esprit, ils avoient un Bon sens admirable;

their only gallantry consisted in rendering themselves "aimables aux yeux d'une seule Femme, pour partager avec elle les plaisirs que leur procuroient leur vertu, & les peines inséparables du sort des Hommes." No "luxe odieux" had corrupted their sobriety and "le bonheur de la Patrie étoit le but & la récompense des soins de ces véritables Pères de leur Peuple." But, alas! "cette heureuse, cette sage Nation, n'est plus; la Politesse & les Trésors superflus ont été la Guerre & la Peste qui l'ont efacée de dessus la surface de la Terre," and with startling effect Van Effen points a grave accusation:

"Messieurs les François, reconnoissez-vous, dans le Portrait que je viens de vous tracer, les Ancêtres de ceux qui, gardant encore quelques restes de leur ancienne cordialité, vous ont soulagés dans vos malheurs, & que par reconnoissance vous avez achevé de corrompre." "Il est vrai," he adds with scornful irony, "que par le Bon-air, & par la Politesse, vous avez remplacé les Vertus que vous leur avez fait perdre, & à ce troc ils ont gagné indubitablement. Ah, sans vous ces bonnes gens ne savoient pas seulement ce que c'étoient que les Fourchettes, & ils mangeoient avec leurs doigts, que la Nature rustique leur avoit donnés pour ces sortes d'usages: qui pis est, ils buvoient brutalement tous d'un même verre: quelle grossièreté!... Heureux mille fois, dans leur impolitesse, les Anciens Belges!"

[1] Cp. *Holl. Spect.* no. 10.

The man who wrote thus was clearly not *entêté* with the French and their manners. At the same time his high opinion of French literature (by no means uncritical, however) proves the fair broadmindedness of his outlook.

In the *Bagatelle* it is the same. Van Effen speaks with forcible earnestness of the refugees and their baneful influence[1].

Il en vint surtout grand nombre s'établir dans le petit Pays de Cachemire, où tout le monde, pourvu qu'il se soumit aux Loix de l'État, pouvoit servir Dieu comme il le trouvoit à propos. Parmi ces pauvres Fugitives il s'en trouvoit beaucoup qui joignoient aux manières les plus aimables, une piété sage éclairée: & qui répondoient par toute leur conduite au généreux sacrifice qu'ils avoient fait à Dieu & à leur Conscience, de tout ce qui peut rendre cette vie douce, aisée & agréable.

Il y en avoit une foule d'autres, qui étoient bien éloignés de ce sublime caractère. Quoiqu'ils eussent été reçus des chémiriens de la manière du monde la plus honnête & la plus obligeante, entêtés de la ridicule politesse de leur Patrie, ils morguèrent d'abord du mépris pour les manières d'un Peuple simple.... Heureusement la Médisance, la Calomnie, l'Esprit de basse intrigue vinrent à leur secours; & ils n'employèrent ces nobles talens que pour se déchirer les uns les autres...remuer ciel & terre pour entrer dans les secrets des Familles,...voilà leur amusement, leur occupation, leurs plaisirs les plus vifs....Il y en avoit, surtout parmi ceux-là, qui, fourbes, avares, injustes, sensuels tandis qu'ils avoient vécu dans leur Patrie, continuoient à s'abîmer dans les mêmes vices après leur exil volontaire. D'autres, qui du tems de leur prospérité avoient regardé comme un trait de galanterie, une action de Joli-homme, de débaucher les Femmes de leurs Voisins, & de duper l'innocence de Filles de leurs meilleurs amis, exerçoient encore le même métier détestable dans le lieu de leur réfuge, sans daigner seulement se donner la peine de sauver les apparences.

They seemed to think that by "un seul sacrifice ils avoient racheté tous leurs crimes passés & à venir."

The darkness of this picture seems to have been intensified by the zeal of the reformer in the attempt to rid his people of a fatal prepossession in favour of the manners of the unfortunate strangers who had been unhappily har-

[1] No. LXVIII.

boured in his country. Van Effen saw in this the downfall of his countrymen and left no argument untouched to rouse them to a sense of their danger. The outrageous conduct of the French was exposed, the national self-respect was appealed to and stimulated by panegyrics on the greatness that had been Holland. He turned his back in scorn upon the Anglicized young refugee in England who dared to say that his brethren in the Netherlands would not fuse with the Dutch as those in England were incorporated, because the English were in every way superior. Van Effen shows this to be merely a baseless ungrateful prejudice on the part of those whom they had favoured, saying that if he had a free choice, his reason would induce him to be a Dutchman. His action, he says, is dictated not so much by the desire to muzzle those thoughtless contemners of his nation as "to inspire my fellow-burghers with a rightful self-esteem and thereby spur them on to establish themselves in that degree of worthiness and lustre where they were placed by their matchless forefathers."

These are clearly the tones of the patriotic reformer. But it was not enough to hold up to his contemporaries a picture of the solid worth, simplicity, frugality, sobriety, honesty, industry and valorous achievement of the great men of sixteenth and seventeenth-century Holland. The widespread imitation of the French must stop if cultural and social equipoise and national self-respect are to be maintained or restored.

These themes, commenced in the *Misantrope*, broadened out steadily to become the most conspicuous part of the *Hollandsche Spectator*. There is scarcely any need to quote from the abundance of evidence that Van Effen and his collaborators considered the unnatural Gallicizing of their people as the many-headed beast whom to slay would be the climax of their achievement. Raillery, burlesque, irony and grim seriousness were employed in turn. The Dutch *mamselletjes*, whose Dutch could not be understood by one who did not know French[2], were teased as unmercifully as

---

[1] *Holl. Spect.* no. 8.   [2] No. 13; cp. no. 229.

the *masseurtjes*, who played the *petit-maître*, were gibbeted. Education for any who pretended to *politesse* came to mean the manners and often the morals of the *sallette*. That Van Effen's laudable efforts were not unappreciated and unsupported is shown, e.g., by the remarks of the *Boekzaal* reviewer for September 1733, on a fresh volume of the active *Spectator*.

"We are," the writer agrees, "still so much addicted to the French language and manners at the present time, as to imagine that we exhaust ourselves in drudgery to good purpose if we can but enable our children to acquire these perfections. Therefore we rank above all others those schools which carry the name of French, and resign our daughters to the teaching of a mademoiselle from whom we receive no letter which is not written in the worst crabbed scribble and is in addition so full of misspellings that we are put to great pains to decipher it."

Verwer has recorded the impression Van Effen made by the patriotic paper from which we have quoted above, and by nos. 6 and 13 which are in a similar strain. No. 6, on the open-hearted generosity of the Dutch, established the *Spectator* in the public esteem. In fact these papers were "the foundation of his renown[1]."

The fight against the *petits-maîtres* was perhaps as pronounced in the *Misantrope* as it afterwards was in the *Hollandsche Spectator*. The Frenchified fops that Van Effen had remarked in the Amsterdam coffee-houses, as he tells in *Misantrope*, no. xxx, were of the same tribe as the messieurs of *Hollandsche Spectator*, no. 394, fresh from Paris, with their new suits and strange mannerisms.

The Dutch had deservedly become a laughing-stock on this account. Holberg, with his unrivalled opportunities and powers of observation, has supreme contempt for the Dutch, whom he uses in his autobiography as a foil to the brilliance of the English. He must therefore be read *cum grano salis*:

Imagine an honest Dutchman on returning to his country encumbered with Parisian elegances and refinements. This is a

---

[1] "Grontslag zyner Vermaertheit"—Verwer.

sort of refinement whereat men and brutes may marvel, for it is difficult to refer him to any known class of animal since he has lost his natural character without acquiring that of the foreigner he endeavours to imitate[1].

This was the very type that Van Effen frequently rapped over the knuckles; and once, though he had never been to Paris, he himself came very near being classed with it by the observant Bruys[2].

C'est un homme d'un esprit fin et délié, d'un jugement solide, d'un entretien aimable, d'une conduite sage et réglée....Il est fâcheux qu'il n'ait pas voyagé en France, pour y prendre des manières plus naturelles et plus aisées. Trop d'affectation fait tort à son mérite, aux yeux de ceux qui ne jugent de l'homme que par l'extérieur. Je lui trouve le cœur droit, bon, généreux et compatissant.

Even in this respect we feel the truth of Koopman's conviction that Van Effen has given us an "illustrated self-criticism" in his work.

This is still truer of the moral philosophy expressed in his work, and whatever elements of his thinking may be recognizable as derived from authors with whom we know him to have been familiar, any such borrowing must be regarded as having been sufficiently assimilated to free him from the charge of unoriginal imitation or plagiarism. The much-recommended "self-conversant practice[3]" of Shaftesbury formed in Van Effen too the basis of an unceasing enquiry in all directions.

Again, we might quote from the *Misantrope* in illustration of his attitude.

J'avoue que *l'Esprit d'examen*, cette noble hardiesse qui nous porte à ne puiser nos sentimens que dans nos propres recherches, est une qualité très digne de l'excellence d'une créature raisonnable....Premièrement cette noble hardiesse est plutôt une disposition du cœur, qu'une qualité de l'esprit; elle marque moins une grande étendue de raisonnement, qu'un certain courage, qu'une certaine fermeté[4].

[1] Cp. Sir Wm Temple above, chap. i, p. 38.
[2] Cp. above, chap. ii, p. 57, and Verwer, p. clix.
[3] Cp., e.g., *Advice to an Author* (1710), pt. iii, sect. i.
[4] *Misantrope*, ii, no. xxxiii, ed. 1726.

The deep reflection and meditation urged by the correspondent Philodemus[1] carried the Spectator's approbation.

His introspection also took the form of religious self-examination, as may be seen from the papers on the subject of prayer, e.g. nos. 121, 126. Zuydam, in his study of Van Effen's philosophy, has shown that his standpoint is in the main that of Locke. Revelation and Reason were similarly reconciled. In no. 35[2] this standpoint is clearly expressed. The integrity of the Reason is asserted: "it remains a palpable truth that to affirm the essential and fundamental corruption of the Reason paves the way to a general doubting whence one has no hope of extricating oneself." But Reason and Revelation must be associated:

The Reason that knows not the clear beams of Divine Revelation, or closes the eye of its understanding to the same, is so cramped in respect of the means of elevating itself to the most useful sciences and so scantily provided with the most necessary ideas, that an ordinary Christian is better instructed in the most elevated truths than the Platos and Ciceros who in their groping have discovered a minute portion of the same.

On the other hand

no one will deny but that Reason must pave the way to the embracing of the glorious Revelation as Divine. Reason alone can instruct us that there is a higher Being, whose verity is not subject to the least suspicion, and that the Holy Bible has actually descended to us from that fountain-head of truth....Not a step of progress is made in divine philosophy except by means of reasoning.

Reason is the all-sufficient instrument which God has given man to attain to a sense of His divinity, and Van Effen uses whatever argument he can lay hold of to satisfy his own reason. With the deists, with scientists like Boyle and Newton, with Locke and Addison *extollit deum ex natura*. On the historical proof also he placed much reliance, as e.g. in no. 121 of the *Hollandsche Spectator*.

He accepted, generally, Locke's theory of ideas. It is treated by Van Effen in no. 175 (with quotations from

[1] *Holl. Spect.* no. 269.   [2] *Holl. Spect.*

the *Human Understanding*), and in no. 269 by the good correspondent Philodemus who offers to send the Spectator a copy of Locke. The offer is accepted (rather out of politeness than need, we may be sure) "chiefly to respond to the courtesy of my civil and wise correspondent," writes the Spectator. He had long possessed his Locke, and the clearest exposition of Locke's moral philosophy, as Van Effen was influenced by it, had already been given in the *Lettre sur la manière de Traiter la Controverse* which Zuydam does not appear to have used. It is largely a plea for the necessity of free investigation of all things, especially religion, and proceeds from the starting-point that Faith is an intellectual act, a higher philosophy. In an analysis of the nature of Faith he asserts: "in fact to understand, to realize and to believe are words that have the same meaning." Reason and Faith were identified precisely as Locke had identified them.

Yet Van Effen is more purely rationalistic, as one may expect, than the empirical physician-philosopher Locke, and seems to have admitted the possibility of Shaftesbury's *innate ideas* when it suited his argument. He speaks of "the faculty of Reasoning that solely concerns itself with the speculating of ideas brought forth out of one's own bosom, *or presented by the physical senses*[1]."

Like Locke, Van Effen avoids conflict on knotty points such as predestination, freewill and the Trinity. "Divine predestination is the darkest article of doctrine to be found in natural as well as revealed religion, and has seemed to the acutest spirits to be the most impenetrable."

On education Van Effen and Locke thought very much alike[2]. It had to be practical, giving the child every consideration and scope to develop according to his bent. But Van Effen, we must note, is much more democratic. Children must be taught to ignore class distinctions as far as possible, as these are harmful to the best interests of society. A point on which Van Effen is in the fullest agreement is the sentiment *mens sana in corpore sano est*, which is the

---

[1] *Holl. Spect.* no. 35.   [2] Cp. Zuydam, *op. cit.* p. 157.

central point from which Locke started and to which he returned in his educational theories. Children must not be pampered and must be inured to the most rigorous climatic conditions of their country, the Spectator urges, and recommends to his countrymen "the physical education which is in vogue in a neighbouring kingdom[1]." He gives a striking picture of English robustness, and criticizes fond Dutch mothers for their misapplied care in muffling up their children too heavily.

In politics Van Effen was a confirmed Whig, of course, except that he conceived the state as a strongly theocratic machinery, but without the kingly head that Hobbes invested with divine jurisdiction. For the rest there are, as we have noted before, many traces in Van Effen of the reigning Shaftesburian optimism (in the abstract mostly) with regard to man, God, and the universe, while at the same time a good deal of Van Effen's thinking is both consciously and unconsciously a refutation of Mandeville's pessimism. In no. 36 of the *Hollandsche Spectator*, he openly crosses swords with his Rabelaisian countryman in London, and attempts to controvert the thesis of the *Fable of the Bees* that *Private vices are public virtues*. But Mandeville caught Van Effen, too, in his net of sophistries. The invidious position that small evasions and deceits are morally defensible practices in business is maintained by the Spectator. In no. 47 he returns to the challenge on another point. This time it is Mandeville's *Free Thoughts on Religion*, which maintains that religion is simply a bridle which some astute members of society devise to control the ignorant. This idea became fairly prevalent, and Mandeville appears to have popularized it for eighteenth-century atheism. Van Effen dismisses such an unphilosophical tenet with appropriate scorn, and deals out some hard words upon England and the unbelieving. But Mandeville, who illustrates his economic theories by frequent reference to Holland, touches Van Effen upon one of the most vital points of his social reform. The latter rightly ascribed much of the economic decay in

---

[1] *Holl. Spect.* no. 238.

Holland to the false glamour of that ease and luxury which Mandeville elaborately pretended to see as the basis and stimulus of all prosperity. In this negative way, then, there is some practical philosophy in the *Hollandsche Spectator* which is due to Mandeville. On the whole, Van Effen's philosophy is such as would have been described as new in his day and probably as English. But it is difficult to trace origins amid the hide-and-seek of ideas, common to those who thought at all in the first half of the eighteenth century.

Yet, finally, it must be said that we seldom get far from the *milieu* of thought of the English periodicals when reading Van Effen. I incline to the belief that Van Effen allowed these English papers to interpret for him much of the English philosophy with which he was familiar. In spite of much original working out of argument, of original statement and control of his material and medium of expression, the *Hollandsche Spectator* forces this parallel upon us in many ways and at many points; primarily, of course, it suggests this parallel by its frank imitation of Steele and Addison.

We will allow that it was pressure of ideas, combined with a keen sense of the peculiar abuses of his time, which contributed mainly to induce Van Effen to emulate his English predecessors once more. But such emulation was in itself an inducement that must not be minimized. Van Effen makes it quite clear that the dizziest height of literary fame to which he could aspire was to reproduce in a sufficiently original way the immortal English periodicals. "The English work which I purpose not to translate, but to imitate in my mother tongue"—these are the opening words of the *Hollandsche Spectator*. "Should it be asked me whether I imagine myself able to equal the English Spectator, I should reply with the same frankness that I am not so drunk with conceited presumption as to flatter myself in any degree with that proud hope," he continues[1]. The demand and the opportunity offered fair. "The desire which had long been expressed for such a work in the Netherlands would be

[1] Cp. *Nouv. Spect. Fr.* no. i.

satisfied at last," people said[1], if he would proceed on such lines as the sixth number promised. A genial correspondent writes[2]:

You have undertaken a work which can be nothing but agreeable to the lovers of letters in our fatherland. We have (allow me to address you in the name of many) received the first with great eagerness, and hope to see this weekly feast dished up by you in continuance. Your desire to write appears to us to be the result of a noble zeal which has been kindled by the English and the German writings of this kind. Go on, sir,...[3].

In fact, as in the case of the *Nouveau Spectateur Français*, open avowals of imitation would distinctly favour the work. "In the first paper the reasonings of his project were considered very good. He showed that he did not lack the knowledge of how a *Spectator*, after the model of the English, ought to be written," said Verwer[4]. His correspondents (real or pretended) allowed no departure or omission to escape his notice, they would have the great model followed, and the more strictly the better. There were mottoes, for how could the real thing be written without them? "Is it not somewhat pedantic that the Spectator always places some saying from a foreign language above his papers?" asks our pedant exposed in no. 308:

as pedantic in him as in the English Spectator, who has preceded him in this regard and has so well defended his practice, that also the Dutch Spectator could safely trust himself to that defence, although he, in case anything could rightly be urged against the practice, is much more readily to be excused than his predecessor, because you know how greatly the British Spectator is esteemed here; therefore it was not policy on the part of his imitator to differ from him even in that minute point. It would presently have roused a prejudice against him as if he was an illiterate man, and not to be compared with Addison or Steele in even the thousandth degree.

The fortieth paper opens with the following reminder from a correspondent: "I dare to say that to deserve the title of Spectator you are still lacking in an important gift, to wit,

---

[1] Verwer, *Leven*, p. lxxv.   [2] *Holl. Spect.* no. 21.
[3] *Holl. Spect.* no. 21: "Uw schryflust komt ons voor als d' uitwerking eener edelmoedige jalouzy," etc.   [4] *Leven*, p. lxxii.

the talent of dreaming, in which your British predecessors have so greatly excelled, that one may hold that while asleep they had more intelligence than when awake[1]." An allegory in the Spectator manner duly follows. It reinstals the wise Rhadamanthus of *Guardian*[2] fame upon the judgment-seat to consider the cases of erring defendants. In no. 47 our Spectator declares his hand in the important matters of religion and politics merely by stating: "my intention is to imitate my grand and praiseworthy predecessor, the British Spectator, in this respect."

A correspondent sends an Eastern apologue and trusts that it will be accepted because "the British Spectator has had no scruples about availing himself of these infidel inventions[3]." In this way rich veins were successively opened by the example and prestige of the inimitable "English Socrates" as the original Spectator was christened from the start.

Literary criticism and the appreciation of great works were very proper subjects for a Spectator, and in this respect also: "I shall follow in the tracks of my noble British predecessor who never neglected giving his competitors for the laurel wreath their due[4]." But the Spectator expresses himself even more explicitly[5]. A panegyric on Fénelon's *Telemachus* is introduced:

Some readers will possibly be of opinion that the following panegyric cannot have any proper place in my paper; nevertheless these will be pleased to know that herein I follow in the tracks of my progenitor the British Mentor—never to be sufficiently praised—who in more than ten different places crowns and glorifies the dignified writer of the tragedy entitled Cato with many deserved laurels grown on his own soil as well as on that of others.... Nevertheless I here do not follow the British moralist, merely because he has preceded me, and from a principle of slavish imitation; but because he has taken that course from weighty considerations. It is not enough for a writer in our style to describe vice and imperfection as atrocious or ridiculous, if he does not show also that he takes a noble pleasure in doing justice to true merit in order, as far as possible, to make it prevail and encourage it to happy continuance.

[1] Cp. *Bagat.* no. LXXXIII.   [2] No. 158.
[3] No. 81.   [4] No. 140.   [5] No. 221.

John Philodemus, writing from Amsterdam on February 26, 1733[1], endeavours to get the Spectator to toe the line, and make his attempts at social reform more effective even than those of the "Engelsche Socrates." It is recalled how he fought the vogue of the hooped petticoat, etc., what trouble he took to make the stage more civilized and moral; even he has had little success, so his Dutch follower must be neither careless nor lax, and above all must avoid being flippant. Accordingly, no. 187 opens: "I have in this work already spoken much of the small fruit which, as experience has taught us, the moral lessons of an honest and virtue-loving Spectator can promise." But there is some consolation in his failure, for "what fruitless attempts has my zealous and fine progenitor the British Spectator not made to confine the hooped petticoat within a narrower compass,...!" This paper, it may be noted in passing, is one of Van Effen's best efforts in a lighter vein. In social satire, a correspondent informs him, he must write without pointing a finger at individuals "according to that title of Spectator, as people have learnt to understand it since the appearance of your British progenitor[2]." No. 215 is an extended parallel between the English and the Dutch *Spectators*. Critics should inform themselves of the nature and history of the genre before criticizing, says the correspondent in his letter. Another correspondent writes of a friend who holds that if poetry is to be included it must be introduced strictly in the manner of the English *Spectator*. When the alleged pot-pourri methods of the Dutch paper are defended, the crushing retort is made: "I am not aware that the English or the French who have so praiseworthily succeeded in this kind of writing, have in this way preceded their Dutch imitators."

The *Spectator's* treatment of ministers of religion must also be guided by the attitude of the English papers[3]:

I have remarked, sir, that everywhere in your paper you treat divines (and rightly to be sure) according to their worthiness, and greatly scorn such as abuse their wit by making ministers

---

[1] No. 147.   [2] No. 186.   [3] No. 265.

ridiculous in the eyes of those whom they cannot edify if they be despised; a custom which the English *Guardian* with reason considers to be a proof of a totally corrupt mind when it is practised in regard to reverend ministers. Still they must not be considered as exempt from criticism, for the English Spectator has on occasion rallied them for their ostentation.

Indeed, correspondence itself was invited on strict British precedent. A supporter sends in his effort with the hope that he and others may be allowed to contribute towards maintaining "that praiseworthy institution," the new periodical paper, following thus in the track of the peerless British Spectator[1]." The Gallomaniac of no. 123 writes that he thought that the correspondence of the Spectator was merely an artifice and written by himself "in order to resemble his English, French and German predecessors better." An officious correspondent advises the Spectator not to treat the same subjects frequently, and the reply is: "With your permission I shall in this respect imitate the British Spectator, who, with proper intervals, brings to light everything he finds essential to a subject[2]." This alone might almost serve to correct Dr te Winkel's repeated assertion[3] that Van Effen had learnt the method of "lively intermission" from the French whence he introduced it into his *Spectator*.

After this we must not be surprised that Van Effen finds his too explicit avowals of following strictly in the wake of his hero an embarrassment. In several numbers there are gentle suggestions that even the English papers are capable of improvement; indeed, as a correspondent says, there are papers "that, not only according to my ideas but also to those of many others, sometimes go past the pale of morality, dignity and prudence[4]." When Van Effen, after a comparatively discouraging start, had begun to receive greater support, he took heart sufficiently to say: "The longer I continue the more I have the daring to hope that in time the *Hollandsche Spectator* will hardly be required to give way either to the British writings of the same nature or to

---

[1] No. 111.   [2] No. 34.
[3] *Ontwikkelingsgang de Ned. Let.* (Haarlem, 1908), vol. III, p. 382.
[4] No. 174.

the *Duitsche Patriot*[1]." Finally, the Spectator lost patience somewhat. The occasion was given by the following letter[2] asking for yet more reproduction:

> Mr Spectator,
>   You have to my knowledge not yet spoken of any clubs, although your English model is full of such matters....

In fact, "the majority of correspondents generally begin their letters by expressing their surprise that the material to which they thus direct you has not as yet been treated by you." A sketch of a Société Galante is then offered. The *Spectator* prints it but has something *à propos* to say:

> I own that thus far I have neglected to exhibit to my readers sketches of similar societies. The reason is that I try to make use of my English models with judgment. It is true that most of the British pieces are full of invention and spirit and satirize certain absurdities with the most judicious quaintness. Nevertheless that method of correction is much more applicable to the English than to us.

Also, the English require such correction much more than the Dutch; club-life is the soul of London but not of any Dutch city, and besides, Dutch clubs are very different from the English ones.

Furthermore, I will remark that the greatest crowd of readers have a sickening conception of what constitutes the imitation of striking models. It is as if a *Hollandsche Spectator* cannot be good unless it be shaped upon the same last as the British in everything, whereas it is nevertheless certain that the change of time and place must necessarily be taken into account by a judicious writer, and that his predecessors ought to be imitated only in that which is good and acceptable to the general taste, or in that which can be brought over, without forcing, to the particular taste of every national character, by a change of the sauces. The same foolish opinion also radiates from the practice of certain writers who, exerting fruitless efforts to appropriate the English manner in this type of work, imagine they accomplish wonders, when they fill their paper with *Dreams, Allegories,* and *invented Societies,* and so with rejection of the kernel use the husk only. This sort of writers I class with certain young

---

[1] No. 111.   No. 224.

advocates, who imagine that they are quitting themselves excellently, and are in the right way towards attaining to the eloquence of the most famous pleaders, if they but succeed in adjusting their perukes, taking off their hats, blowing their noses, clearing their throats, and droning out *Noble and puissant Gentlemen* in similar manner. This will give me occasion to indicate the true distinction between original and apish imitation.

This assertion of independence raises the necessary but thorny question of the originality of the *Hollandsche Spectator* as it was executed by Van Effen. We have noted the numerous open professions of imitation scattered through the work, and have considered Van Effen's indebtedness to some English thinkers. The general direction of the paper, its aims and spirit, the kind of subject treated, and the manner of treatment were things for which the *Spectator*, and particularly the *Guardian*, were the models. On all the important topics Van Effen cannot be said to have differed much from Addison and Steele. They were no less stoutly national and anti-French (professedly) than Van Effen himself who considered in fact that the English Spectator carried his antipathy to the French too far[1]. They were hardly less bourgeois, popular and moralistic than he. Their themes were his, while many minor hints were taken from the English papers as well. No. 29 contains a quotation from a *Guardian* paper[2], and is executed *à propos*, in similar vein. As in the Spectator's, there is mystery in his initials[3]. He is not sworn to taciturnity like the British Spectator, his "greatly honoured predecessor[4]"; but has his physiognomy, being "gifted with a solemn, thoughtful" face[5], and he, too, silently overhears political conversation in coffee-houses or visits the Exchange[6]. The Spectator describes a journey by coach to Land's End, so his descendant describes his in a *trek-schuit* on the Dutch canals. But imitation in this case

---

[1] *Vide Holl. Spect.* no. 69. The English Spectator seemed to him to have an anti-French "prejudice sucked in with mother's milk and, whether it be out of complaisance to his readers, which would not be very laudable, he speaks throughout with an unjust disdain of the fine spirits among the French."

[2] *Guardian*, no. 26.   [3] *Holl. Spect.* no. 23.   [4] *Ibid.* no. 88.
[5] *Ibid.* no. 45.   [6] *Ibid.* no. 9.

does not prevent the Dutch paper from making excellent reading, and being very differently turned. In no. 83 the *Guardian* is cited, and the whole paper keeps close to *Guardian* sentiment. He touches on the masquerade[1] with a reference to the English Spectator, who pitted his strength against its great vogue in London; but in spite of promises of further examination of this *divertissement*, he allows the subject to drop. No. 182 is inspired by *Tatler*, no. 86, and similar papers on ceremony and precedence; but, though the phraseology is reminiscent, the execution is divertingly original. The topic of congregations and Latin appears in different forms in *Spectator*, no. 222 and *Hollandsche Spectator*, no. 203. Both *Spectators*[2] happen to tell the story of Molière submitting plays to his house-keeper's approval, and Van Effen, by the context, appears to have taken his cue from Addison in praising the naïve judiciousness of uninstructed taste. In no. 268 Van Effen imitates the *Hamburger Patriot* by opening a competition amongst his readers for the best allegory. The practice is derived from the *Spectator*, of course, but we may note in passing that this German paper seems to have served also to remind Van Effen at the beginning that a Dutch *Spectator* still remained to be written[3]. The campaign against the *harddravery* was probably inspired by papers like *Guardian*, no. 6 and others on cruelty to animals, especially as Verwer says that nobody was aware that such an abuse existed in Holland. Van Effen has two numbers on false wit[4]. He writes on dancing[5] and vindicates a proper use of it; like his predecessor, he recommends physical exercise to his readers, his exercise consisting chiefly of dancing privately, while the Spectator swings dumb-bells and Mr Bickerstaff had been constrained to take up fencing.

There are several papers on superstition, a subject which was suggested to him by the English *Spectator*, for in no. 333 Van Effen writes that he might have told of a divine and his

---

[1] *Holl. Spect.* no. 125.
[2] *Ibid.* no. 258, and *Spect.* no. 70.
[3] Cp. *Holl. Spect.* no. 21.
[4] *Holl. Spect.* nos. 310, 312.
[5] *Ibid.* no. 321, etc.

fear of sitting down with an unlucky number of diners, had not his "English predecessor abundantly and very wittily already exposed these[1] and other fantasies as to the last degree foolish and ridiculous." As Verwer has told, Van Effen's assurances on this topic at one time did much to allay public feeling when it had been superstitiously excited. *Guardian*, no. 20 is quoted and recommended to readers, indicating whence Van Effen had taken the idea for his papers on revenge. No. 279, on pets, is better done than anything in the English papers on the same subject. Other minor correspondences will not escape a careful reader, but we have given most of them. The whole list of deliberate imitations here compiled looks formidable enough. It is, in fact, misleading to one who has not read the whole of the *Hollandsche Spectator*. But it is a very striking feature of this periodical as a whole that it contains surprisingly little that may be closely paralleled in detail and in length with the matter of the English papers. Van Effen had spoken out at last in no. 224 from which we have quoted above. We must allow him to speak again. His subject[2] is plagiarism or "letter-thieving."

The case of the *letter-thieves* is like that of some other pirates who can so change and rough-hew what they steal, that it can scarcely be recognized any more and can sometimes be passed on to the owner himself without danger. As these are capable of metamorphosing a mantle into a dress, a piece of cloth into a camisole..., so the other kind often exercise the art of stripping a serious sentence of its outer garments and covering it again with a jack-pudding suit; of trimming with the finery of fustian an elevated thought couched in simple expressions, as a scintillating jewel is enclosed in a little rim of humble silver, and finally— a device which is employed with the best results—of changing verse into prose and prose into verse. But I may possibly encounter the objection: you, who here have so much to say about that sort of knavery daily committed by your fellows, are you yourself not somewhat addicted to that practice? and is it not to be readily believed that, should research be applied to the fountain-heads whence what you have thus far written has flowed, it would be found that in respect of the best that you have com-

---

[1] *Spect*. no. 7, etc.   [2] *Holl. Spect*. no. 69.

municated to us, you have not come by it very honestly? To put my reader in a position to pass a fair judgment himself in regard to this question, I will here make it my business to examine carefully into the true nature of letter-thieving, of which few people form a just opinion.

To begin with, it is certain that no one can ever be accused with the slightest semblance of justice of that sort of theft, when he generously acknowledges that what he is serving up for us is not the fruit of his own wit. This is not stealing, but borrowing in honest wise, and by the naming of the true owner, borrowings are restored again to his possession. Should such quotations, even though they be fairly numerous, add strength, light and ornament to the original ideas of a writer, then we owe him no less obligation than if everything had flowed forth from his own mind and imaginative faculty. Why, we even owe him no less esteem, since by the acquaintance which he shows with the excellence of what is quoted he gives us evidence of his judgment, and convinces us, by the witty variegation of the borrowed blooms, which beautifully show up his whole work by their charming variety, of the neatness of his understanding and the sprightliness of his imagination.

It is also very unreasonable, though not at all unusual, to suspect a writer of plagiarism as soon as the same thoughts and ideas are found in his writings as have been noticed in his predecessors'. This can often happen, although the author in question has never even heard the works mentioned which he is accused of stealing from. Indeed, there is nothing more natural than that sensible folk, reasoning on the same grounds and without bias, should in respect of certain subjects discover the same truths and bring to light the same ideas. Still I must admit that such correspondence must be fairly suspicious if it should extend to the arrangement and expression, which, though by no means impossible, is not at all likely. But does one not at least perpetrate plagiarism as often as one passes off as original that which has been drawn from the writings of others? Not in the least; there is a certain manner of making profit out of what is read, which gives us an absolute right of proprietorship over such profit. Consider for example that a sensible and attentive reader finds somewhere a piece of reasoning which supplies him with new concepts, or limns and illuminates concepts which he already has; he views the argument from all sides, he analyses it, he observes and investigates all the parts of which it is constituted, and, after having grasped it in its fullest relations, he strips it of all material expression, and makes it altogether spiritual. As such it is transplanted into his mind, and there in all its purity, planted as if anew, shoots deep roots, enriches itself with new strength and brings forth fruit which, coming from the new soil, absorbs a new national flavour and which, like the tree that bears it, belongs in indisputable ownership to the new master.

Van Effen continues in the same strain as in *Bagatelle*, no. xcii[1], and altogether he has faithfully expressed the truth about his own work. As literary artists and as thinkers it is equally unreasonable to dismiss either Addison or Van Effen as mere imitators. Van Effen was imbued with the idea that his paper had to draw its nourishment not from England, but from the home soil. He had made it clear that he intended to adapt English invention in his own way to his own and his country's uses. This thought recurs constantly. In fact, it was the chief point made in the first number. An objector is made to say: "Why then have you undertaken this work? The excellent work of which we dare not expect any satisfactory imitation from your abilities, we already possess in our mother tongue. To what purpose would an inferior one of the same kind be of service to us?" "Such reasoning would not be valid," returns Van Effen. "Every nation has its special customs, morals, codes, manner of behaviour, virtues and vices. Many teachings and admonitions strike the British and have no bearing on us. It is with this, as with the translations of foreign comedies, which we put on our Dutch stage...," etc. He realized fully that it was the distinctively national, the particular and personal, and not the ubiquitous generalization which achieved artistic universality. Sir Roger pleases all the world because he is so thoroughly English. Van Effen has given no characterization as good or as full as that of Sir Roger, but he has given social sketches superior to anything in the *Spectator*. We obtain flitting but perfectly satisfying glimpses into Dutch interiors, there are clever and amusing pictures of tea-parties, and other social gatherings, lifelike revelations of Dutch household economy. In the first volume, nos. 14, 15, 17, 18, etc., give a good sample of the excellent portraiture that

---

[1] Cp. above, chap. iv, p. 131.

any nation would rightly class amongst its good and superior work. ·No. 42 is not excelled, even by Sam Trusty's visit to Mrs Feeble's[1]. No. 68 gives an excellent domestic picture of birthday festivities in a solid and respectable burgher's home. Nos. 154 and 157 again depict the manners of the time and are of excellent literary and artistic quality. Another good example of his wonderful domestic sketches is no. 174.

No. 294 is a good paper. It gives an illuminating glimpse into simple city life with mellow thought thereon. Then there are the excellent papers on the *Burgervryage*[2] (bourgeois love-making), and the *Kobus* and *Agnietje* papers which created a very great sensation amongst Van Effen's public. These depict, with unerring psychology and in firm outline, the course of an artless love affair, from its beginnings to the happy consummation, between Agnietje, the young daughter of a widowed sempstress, and Kobus, a carpenter's apprentice. Agnietje is pacing up and down the *stoep* waiting for her mother, and the youth, for all his boldness, is suddenly stricken with an unknown fear, but tremulously requests the favour of being allowed to light his pipe at the chafing-pan she is carrying under her apron. Thus the ice is broken. Developments follow; Agnietje, not wanting in the instinctive sagacity of her sex, is mistress of the situation (for a time), but yields before our patience is exhausted and soon the two lovers are fast bound in formal betrothal. The humour is exquisite, the style clear, firm and more than adequate, the description characteristically Dutch in its realistic sufficiency, the conversation lively and excellently controlled, the narrative well managed and ended by the happiest little climax. The final number is perhaps the best. The scene round the dinner table where the company of eight had gathered to arrange and celebrate a happy union combines the art of a Dickens with a classic simplicity of which the early eighteenth century seemed to have learned the secret. The attorney, an old friend of the family and the

---

[1] *Tatler*, no. 266.
[2] *Holl. Spect.* nos. 209, 264.

observer, is the guest. Kobus, the lover, is on his best behaviour, and uses his fork.

Father looked attentively upon this civility in his son, and said:
"Well, my lad, now where would you have learnt to eat with
a fork? and you seem to be getting away with it too! Well, then,
you stick to your courtly fashion; I might perhaps have joined
you; but am too old to change habits; I have not been educated
up to such magnificence...."

This and the rest of his remarks, with the conversation that
follows, could not be improved upon. Then there are toasts,
later a roundel "of olden times" that contained "something
about kissing," and soon, after our friend the attorney had
assured the maidens that it was "the fashion among the
most honest daughters," kisses came as "thick as hail." Then
comes a charming episode much in the manner of Goldsmith
mellowed by the sweet sentimentality of 1730 still unmarred
by the sickliness of later sentimentalism. When the fun
had continued for some time, "father rapped on the table
with his knife, and requested the company to keep quiet a
bit as he had something to say.... 'Hark 'ee, friends,' spoke the
good man, "a truce to all jest " says Klaasbuur and..." Here
mother broke in: 'Come, husband, rather let me say it'"—
and the subject of the match is put to the attorney. He,
with general approval, waives all necessity for a marriage
contract "especially as Agnietje's mother can contribute
little or nothing to her daughter's portion." "How now—
'little or nothing,' ejaculated Kobus's old aunt Motje, 'no,
no, that will not do, that I entirely fail to understand, and
I will not allow it either, even if it were so, no, not at all.'"

Here was a pass. But startled faces began to clear as
the good woman offered to give as a marriage portion to
her future niece the savings she would not be able to spend.

"Well, how now, what do you folks stand staring at me like that
for, you aren't thinking, I hope, that Motje is in such a generous
mood because she has had a glass too much. What I have said,
I mean, come...."

Scarcely had she said this when Kobus, beside himself at such
an unforeseen occurrence, flew to Motje in tears and hugged her.
I signed to Agnietje to do likewise and she, though deeply moved,

acquitted herself of that duty with unaffected and tender gratitude, in which she was followed by all of us. Tears escaped my
eyes in spite of myself, and so too with the rest. Motje wept with
us for joy. . . .

A notary was fetched, everything arranged, Agnietje, faint
with joy, was in her lover's arms, and that night redoubled
merriment resounded in a happy home.

Such is the nature of Van Effen's immortal story of how
Kobus courted Agnietje. It is an admirable effort in a new
kind. In it the domestic novel stands on tiptoe on the
threshold. Add to it the colour, the compression and swift
flexibility of style which translation has dissipated and then
a just estimate of Van Effen's best can be made. No wonder
that his friend was so powerfully affected[1]:

One of my dearest friends who possesses glowing imaginative
power, though directed by an excellent judgment and who has
resigned the honour of having an immovable disposition to the
illacrimabilem Plutona and his like, has confessed to me that the
unexpected magnanimity of the good drudge Motje has so
powerfully worked upon his mind that his heart impels him to
embrace the fine old woman, and that he cannot restrain himself
from shedding tears of joy with the weeping company.

We detect here and elsewhere in Van Effen a wholesome,
legitimate sentimentality of which Prinsen[2] regards him as
one of the chief founders before it had become a sickly,
European fashion. In this respect again Van Effen holds
a significant place in the growth of modern Dutch literature, and has handed on the torch to the novelists Wolff
and Deken. How much his artistic temperament had been
affected by his association with the early English sentimentality of Steele, e.g., cannot be gauged, but must not
be ignored. Van Effen, here too, is somewhat of a mediator
between the literature of Holland and that of England.

In the above story there naturally are imperfections.
The hero is unheroic, the story is sketchy, and contains an
element which has become almost offensive to modern taste.
In spite of the tender humanity which lights up the words,

[1] No. 209.
[2] *Gesch. der Ned. Let.* chap. "De Nieuwe Renaissance in Nederland.'

there is also a feeling that the author was condescending to his subject. We must remember that *everyday* low or simple life had still to fight its way into polite literature against refined artistic prejudice, and Van Effen's attitude is tinged with the cautious conciliatoriness of Addison recommending the *Babes in the Wood* to polite readers as good literature. Assertion goes boldly before, but apology shuffles behind, and appears easily in the form of condescension. Van Effen's attitude was somewhat complex. The lower middle classes interested him intensely. "He showed himself not averse from associating with the commoner, especially when he was writing the *Spectator*. What respect he entertained for him, he had already avowed in an early paper. Thus, he also had the means of collecting a variety of characters and rendering his writings pleasant to all classes, *but it never caused him to fall into meanness*[1]," and this remark suggests a doubt characteristic of an age when the domestic novel was tentatively evolving. The passage referred to by Verwer occurs in the third paper:

Recently I have, by chance, had the pleasure of making the acquaintance of a respectable citizen, who, although his manner of living is quite near to earth, possesses a good deal of money gained by his application and good economy. Methinks that among all nations the middle sort of people are the best, and this I well think to have experienced especially in our national character. I will gladly avow that I much prefer to associate with such people. My new friend is not openhearted, frank, honest; he is honesty and openheartedness itself.

A eulogistic *character* of our honest burgher follows, which reminds us somewhat of the sketch Van Effen gave of his father in the *Nouveau Spectateur Français*. There is little doubt, however, that we have here another equivalent of the solidly national element in the English *Spectator*. We have indicated that this aspect of the English papers was appreciated and imitated by Van Effen from the time of the *Misantrope*. In fact this pronouncedly patriotic strain became the distinguishing feature of most of the Spectator

[1] Verwer, p. clviii.

literature on the continent, from the *Misantrope* and the *Hamburger Patriot*, to the *Borger* of Elizabeth Wolff, Van Effen's illustrious follower at the end of the century.

Van Effen's "burgerman" was a somewhat more bourgeois Sir Roger. But we may refer this aspect of Van Effen's depicting of lower middle-class types to our remarks above on his national aims, and consider here the literary aspects.

That which perhaps qualifies me better than many others for the exercise of my function of Spectator, is my fixed habit of enquiring with the greatest attention into the nature of everyone I meet without distinction of rank, in order to increase and illuminate my knowledge of the human heart by the variety of my observations. When in that frame of mind I take almost the same pleasure in speaking to a farmer, to a nobleman, to a child and to a philosopher. No wonder then that I have formed a familiar acquaintance with Casper the shop-clerk of my apothecary....

This is the opening of paper no. 280.

Van Effen was an observer of things and men. He is in his element on the canal-barge where he finds congregated "a promiscuous mingling of the most various classes that constitute human society." And we must not regard him as merely hunting for copy among the simple folk. He clearly had a real love for them. It is, of course, the great achievement of the eighteenth century that it made possible the sympathetic literary treatment of bourgeois domesticity; but, as usual, Art like a Colossus seemed to stand with one leg firmly planted in the Past and the other in the Future. Van Effen was, with Steele and Addison and Defoe, and even Richardson and Fielding, much in advance of his time. Listen to a "correspondent[1]": "The characters, if they do not go outside the nation and do not appear foreign to the Dutch sense, all have their use, when considered observantly, to edify and amuse. I have on occasion heard it remarked: 'How can a man of so much circumspection, understanding and judgment occupy himself with such mean subjects, derived from the humblest folk?'" But, "even if some or other wiseacre says: 'that is too *canailjeus*,' such papers

[1] No. 160.

sell the best." There were critics who had to be considered[1], and a careless public that wished only to be amused and did not fully grasp the writer's intention; so, in a free talk[2] with his readers, Van Effen informs them of the purpose of his papers on the courtship of the "handsome" Kobus and the "sweet" Agnietje.

The great mass of readers have clung to the outer portrait work, without penetrating to the true significance, although it was covered with but a thin crust. What has pleased them in those little pieces is merely the living fidelity of the painting, which has been able to make a low subject novel and pleasing even to those who are accustomed to associate familiarly with it.

Other superficial judges "imagine that there is nothing simpler, and that they could without trouble imitate me in something of the same kind. Nor do I in the least doubt but that soon enough some specimens will be placed in my hands." But more discerning critics "find a certain flexibility of wit in the art of representing the small without meanness as well as the great without inflation." But few have surmised that his real aim was

to place before our eyes, with the greatest force, the just and essential worth of men in its proper nature, divested of all the trimming that is lent by birth, wealth and greatness of condition, and, protecting it from an extravagant contempt, to enable it to obtain all the reverence it deserves.... Who would not notice, however slightly he may examine this subject, that true desert, that everything worthy of respect and love, is bound to no rank but cleaves to the human being only, and that, although appearing in different forms, it possesses the same essential nature in all degrees of life and ought to draw to it the same inclination and respect? Who, *by me brought into the way of being observant*[3], will not clearly see in the scene which I have depicted,...that humble manners can be accompanied with a tender and disinterested love, with decency and generosity, nobility, thankfulness, modesty and unfeigned friendship, nay, and what is more, with good judgment?

[1] Cp. nos. 204, 205, where Van Effen defends himself against a polite critic who exclaims: "Now is that a writer to mention to people who understand la politesse!"

[2] No. 165.   [3] The italics are mine.

This and what follows reveals a full consciousness, remarkable for the year 1733, of artistic aim in the direction of simple realism beautified. It shows again our writer's convictions on the subject of bourgeois life, and indicates the real nature of Van Effen's contribution to, and through him of English influence upon, the development of Dutch literature. Yet Van Effen was not free from the attitude of his time, and seemed to wish to propitiate it by giving an impression of amused indulgence. When lower domestic life is portrayed, Van Effen creates a humorous atmosphere by a profuse use of diminutives. In the first-rate attempts at vernacular writing in character, the letters from the cobbler, the "weevertje" (little weaver), from Geertje Levens[1], and in the *Kobus* and *Agnietje* papers and others, the excessive use of diminutives has the note of condescension on the one hand and of amusing pettiness in the characters displayed on the other—a fact which seems to have roused the wrath of Prinsen[2]. On the whole, however, there is not the slightest doubt of Van Effen's honest appreciation of simple life as worthy of respect in life and in literature.

That Van Effen and the *Hollandsche Spectator* command excellent humour will have been suspected from what we have already said. For a purely diverting social sketch we may quote no. 178, on over-fond mothers. No. 252 will always raise a hearty laugh. No. 3 is a great and amusing paper. It is true, on the other hand, that Van Effen's humour is not the *Spectator's*, nor does it flow as freely or as frequently. It generally has a more intellectual quality, and drollery is seldom made to jostle with serious reflection, as in the English papers; these latter indeed were criticized in Holland on that account.

One feels, however, that Van Effen has not retained the true balance of humour and seriousness and that he allows the preacher and thinker to obtrude too much on the artist. But we have the compensation that whatever Van Effen

---

[1] These two are, however, not by Van Effen.
[2] *Handboek der Ned. Let.* in voce Van Effen.

has given us of his meditation is generally well worth the tasting. His allegories have been laughed at; and although his efforts in an unfamiliar style are indeed very tentative, a paper like no. 192 is certainly a well-executed piece of imaginative construction. Of his less philosophic but serious papers, no. 319, on war, might have been written in 1924. The points are well maintained, the transitions well managed, the style is simple, disengaged but not discursive, the manner earnest but not oppressively so. There is no fulmination; only sober disapproval expressed with good sense and taste on the whole. Van Effen misses the "divine effulgence" of Addison, but we find in his sober work more substance and ripeness. No. 328, on national prejudices, shows no decline in this power or in that of expression. Referring only to the great variety and control of subject and the adroit management of the paper as a whole, and the happy alternation of mood, we may sum up with Verwer:

On these lines Mr Van Effen wrote his *Spectator* with much praise, and regard for him grew more and more as time went on. His lively and most familiar papers, as has been said, were the most enjoyable to the greatest part of the readers, as commonly happens to this sort of writing, but the learned, serious, and devout essays pleased others no less[1].

The hoax over the *Bato*, one of the best of literary jokes, should also be recalled. Van Effen had long tried to educate his public in the matter of true literary appreciation, especially in prose fiction, and resolved to test them. A pretended project was formed of publishing a romance entitled *Bato*, and some foretaste of it was given in no. 255. There was general consternation and surprise. Some readers considered it a mark of their taste to abjure both the *Spectator* and the projected *Bato*. But the great majority thought differently and besieged the publisher's office. "Even folk of advanced years, who did not wish to be known as people who concerned themselves with the reading of romances, came in the dusk of the evening, and betimes of a morning, to subscribe secretly, with a request that their names be not divulged," tells Verwer[2]. The whole object, he continues,

---

[1] *Leven*, p. cxvi.   [2] *Vide Leven*, pp. cxxxi–cxxxiv.

was but to make ridiculous the "Romanziekte[1]" which then seemed to be raging still. Van Effen had exposed it even in the *Misantrope*, where he condemned romances for their lack of verisimilitude, immorality and bombast, and deplored their vogue as an infallible sign of the decay of taste[2]. Perhaps the eagerness of the public may be excused. They were merely expecting something from the writer of the Kobus and Agnietje story, which was to come later from other pens, and which unfortunately, so far as Van Effen is concerned, remains only one of the attractive might-have-beens of literature.

For the literary instruction and reform attempted in his work Van Effen had, of course, the best *Spectator* precedence, but critics agree that he cannot be said to have made the great use of it that his English predecessors did; in particular they cannot forgive him his attempt to exalt the domestic poet Cats at the expense of the divine Vondel. But there is little doubt that Van Effen had great respect for Vondel, although his own taste in poetry was too intellectual and unmusical to allow him to appreciate the great master properly. Van Effen correctly pointed out some of his weaknesses, such as an insufficient knowledge or consideration of what was fitting to the stage; but the motive that prompted Van Effen to take up the attitude he did was to knock down a false idol which dilettantes had erected under the name of Vondel. Dutch poetry just then was suffering from a spell of heroic afflatus, proper control of which none of their daring spirits may be said to have commanded[3].

"Instead of softly flowing on with Catullus we fly up in the air with Pindarus, with no small danger...of hurtling down with Icarus," says Van Effen in no. 37. On the other hand, the sober, domestic Cats was being outrageously treated as mean and trivial, and Van Effen's defence of Cats strikes one as sane and calculated to influence Dutch

---

[1] Sickly craze for romances.
[2] Cp., e.g., *Holl. Spect.* nos. 14, 116, 215, 274, 255.
[3] *Holl. Spect.* nos. 217, 24, 118, etc.

literature in the right direction of domestic portraiture which was being taken elsewhere in literature, especially in England. Verwer, who is himself but half converted, remarks that many felt that Van Effen was making a useless attempt against the current, but the *Boekzaal* reviewer for October 1733 was pleased that Van Effen "had restored this entertaining and instructive poet to his deserved honour[1]."

In at least two other respects, Van Effen had a salutary influence on his age similar to that of his predecessors. He may, in the first place, be said to have done almost as much towards extending the reading circles in his country as did Addison in England. Nothing pleased him more about the *Spectator* and the English character than that the reading of that paper was so general. It spread from the "Dames du premier rang" and "Les premières Têtes de l'Etat" to the meanest *batelier*. "Il se trouve peut-être à Londres plusieurs milliers d'Artisans, capables de goûter du moins en partie le Spectateur & l'on peut juger de-là à quel point il doit être à la portée des Honnêtes-gens & des Gens de qualité, dont la plupart ont fort bien étudié dans leur jeunesse[2]."

He deplored time and again the small encouragement given in Holland to fine writing of a nature that depended on wide public support. In his last work he decided to write for a public socially wider and more numerous if more restricted geographically, and from all sides we have testimony of the growing circulation of his Dutch paper, although he always expressed himself in modest terms and the actual sale is nowhere given. But this would have been but small indication at a time when dozens of readers could be reckoned to every copy sold. The *Hollandsche Spectator*, in its attractive homeliness, its sociability, its democratic,

---

[1] Cp. Southey's poetic lines on Cats: where

"father Cats
The Household Poet teacheth in his songs
The love of all things lowly, all things pure,
Best poet who delights the happy mind
Of Childhood, stores with moral strength the heart
Of youth, with wisdom maketh middle life rich
And fills with quiet tears the eyes of age."

[2] *Bagat.* no. LXXX.

patriotic atmosphere, was indeed a powerful educative force in spreading reading over class-barriers and among the busy mercantile classes in cities such as Amsterdam where, as Holberg says in his autobiography, "trade occupies every man's thoughts" so that "it is impossible for a man with literary talents to get on in Amsterdam." But Van Effen did get on there, and he greatly helped to lay the foundation for conditions described by a descendant in the *Spectator* line—the *Denker*[1] for September 28, 1772.

"For some years the desire for writing has greatly increased in proportion to the growth of the desire for reading which is certainly more general than it was 20 or 30 years ago." As Professor N. G. van Kampen[2] has said: "Van Effen's *Spectator* was read by rich and poor, young and old, upper as well as lower classes and his writings have had an incalculable influence on the culture of the nation."

But the element which perhaps contributed most towards popularizing both the *Spectator* and reading in general, and which is at the same time of great value for Dutch literature, was Van Effen's style. He deliberately addressed himself from the outset towards re-shaping Dutch prose. The Dutch had long been noted as linguistic purists. Holberg, for example, speaks of this trait. He praises the copiousness and assimilative power of English and with inevitable comparison contrasts the poverty of Dutch which was being daily denuded by excessive purism. Van Effen casts a glance[3] at the English practices of *laissez faire* and word-appropriation and strenuously resists the purists, while at the same time advocating rigorous selection of proper existing Dutch words, and avoidance of Gallicisms. He was naturally taking a middle course, vindicating the stately Dutch language against slanders, such as Holberg repeats, of its poverty, unsuitability "to serious and tragic composition," and fitness only for low comedy. A discouraging friend[4], on the other hand,

[1] No. 509.
[2] Lecture before the English Literary Society at Amsterdam, Feb. 1832, on: "The Influence of English Literature upon Dutch Literature."
[3] *Holl. Spect.* no. 202.　　　　　[4] *Holl. Spect.* no. 10.

expressed the opinion that Van Effen's undertaking would not succeed in the Dutch language, which was "as well adapted as any other to the treatment of earnest, grand and elevated subjects," but lacked "a certain lightness and ease." Van Effen, in words remarkably reminiscent of Huygens's famous retort to Charles II, replied:

"All languages when properly understood possess all the necessary colours to depict the low as well as the grand, the pleasant and the serious, jest and earnestness. It is not the nature of a language that makes a style forced and stiff, it is the inflexibility of the writer's wit and imagination. It is true that if I should use the manner of writing most in vogue amongst us to-day, I should have much trouble to produce such drollery, as would be fit to amuse great minds. But that (style) I intend to avoid as far as is compatible with the nature of our language."

"Since my aim is to bring entertainment and profit to all my fellow citizens, I will apply myself specially to considerations of intelligibility and perspicuity," and "although I shall endeavour to flex my expressions according to the matter, I will throughout strive to avail myself of the familiar style such as has been established by usage among people of birth and education." Accordingly, "I will watch for long extended periods, in which it is the custom, after the Latin, to bring up the verb, upon which the whole sentence depends, at the end.... Also I will, for the sake of clarity, carefully eschew those long parentheses... which in some of our writers, enclose and again enclose within themselves other parentheses like nest-boxes[1], and necessarily produce confusion in the mind of the reader."

It is to Van Effen that Dutch literature looks for the first successful and sustained use of what in English is vaguely called "modern prose." It was upon the classic creators of this English prose that the mind of Van Effen dwelt; it was they whom he admired, translated and imitated. The thrustful energy of Swift's conciseness, the refined, simple, but rather loose urbanity of the *Spectator's* style in which the seventeenth-century Latinized ideals of prose style were effectively and least obtrusively made "to inhabit among men," the man-to-man colloquialism of *Robinson Crusoe* rising up, as it were, from below, to take its place in literature and make

---

[1] An idea probably from Swift, *Tale of a Tub*.

the new style, all these qualities did not escape the translator[1]. Well did Van Kampen say[2]: "he presented us with a treasure of the highest value in the *Hollandsche Spectator*, a work written in imitation of the English *Spectator* and which contributed in a very high degree to the improvement of our style in prose." It is "the first classic composition in the familiar Dutch prose style." In his selection from Van Effen, Van Kampen again treated this point. He agrees with Ypey[3], the linguistic historian, that Dutch prose was in an exceedingly bad way at the opening of the eighteenth century. Describing the modern style, he says: "thirty years after the beginning of the eighteenth century a certain man for the first time created such a style for the Netherlands. It was Justus van Effen." And truly in no direction was the influence from England more salutary, necessary and formative than that of having induced through the clever mediation of Van Effen not only a reform of style, but also an introduction of new elements of style which were sorely needed, but so little employed in Holland that Van Effen remained a lonely pioneer until his great successors Wolff and Deken appeared half a century later. Before that time there were of course others who wrote good prose of the new kind, but for artistic purposes most of it is negligible. Indeed, Van Effen had assistants whose prose is good for the time, but rarely, if ever, better than Van Effen's average, so that we can pardon an enthusiastic correspondent who says:

The free, easy and flowing style which seems to be peculiar to you only, enables me at once to recognize your productions amongst those of others, in however lively a manner they may be executed. It is possible that I deceive myself but methinks that the difference in style and language nowhere appears so clearly as in your fourth part where I guarantee to point out with the finger which papers have proceeded from your pen and which have been contributed. The latter, nevertheless, also deserve praise...."

[1] Cp. below, chap. vi, the critical estimate of the style of the English *Spectator* in the *Journ. Lit.*
[2] *Op. cit.*
[3] *Geschiedenis der Nederl. Taal*, e.g. pp. 502–504.

The writer continues by remarking how contributors consider and depend upon the Spectator's judgment.

One of Van Effen's staunch supporters was the poet and theologian Th. van Snakenburg[1], who, if we are to believe a writer to the *Nederlandsche Spectator*[2], assisted his principal in the technicalities of Dutch language and style, in which the latter was unversed. But, if this be true, the divine's influence seems to have been in the wrong direction, and the critic becomes suspect when he speaks of the frequent offence caused to choice readers "by a careless word or a detestable error" in Van Effen's style. It is true, of course, that Van Effen might have sifted out his Gallicisms better, and that he could be drawn into heavy trailing sentences; but there is greater probability, judging by results, that he showed the way to his coadjutors rather than they to him, and that our critic is merely a purist of the old school. On the question of the Spectator's assistants there is little to say. The first indication of assistance (except for a previous letter) begins with no. 56[3]. Out of a total of 360 papers, Zuydam, after a careful examination of the evidence, at best uncertain, has attributed a proportion of about four-fifths to Van Effen[4]. Snakenburg contributed most of the poetry; W. Suderman (minister), P. Verwer, Jan van Ryssen, the poet Lucas Pater, Gerhard Schroeder (Doctor of Laws), and Pieter Merkman contributed several good things. These were men of note, and altogether they formed a group which materially assisted in shaping public opinion and taste in the new directions to which Van Effen was pointing. Verwer is best remembered by his excellent memoir of Van Effen, but he carried on the tradition of his principal and became a Spectatorial writer of some note and a busy translator of English books. Van Ryssen was born and bred in England, so that it is not strange that he should have joined the pioneer band of the *Hollandsche Spectator*. Suder-

[1] This is probably the "certain profound intellect" without whom Van Effen, according to the same periodical (vol. I, p. 6), would not have been able to accomplish what he did; a claim which has puzzled Bisschop (p. 265).
[2] *Ned. Sp.* vol. III, 1751.   [3] Verwer, p. xciii.
[4] *Ibid.* "Aanhangsel."

man likewise received his education in England and both he and Van Ryssen had as Verwer says "from their youth occupied themselves much with the writings of the English." Suderman especially was responsible for several good translations from English literature. But perhaps the most notable member was Pieter Merkman, the son of a literature-and music-loving textile manufacturer, and a figure of some importance for our subject. He had long been an admirer of English thought and letters and of Van Effen. Of this the *Mengelstoffen*, issued in six parts by him and a friend Govert van Mater from 1724, gives ample evidence. The work is one of those parasitical papers which were becoming common. It fed mainly on the products of Van Effen, Steele, Addison and La Bruyère. It translated and re-hashed many a paper, anecdote or thought from the *Tatler*, the *Guardian*, the *Misantrope*, the *Bagatelle*, etc., and altogether the work breathes the newer literary interests. The opening tribute to the English periodicals is characteristic. "No one in any way conversant with books is ignorant of the fame which those eminent English wits, writers of the *Tatler*, the *Spectator* and the *Guardian* have won for themselves, and truly..."; then follows a panegyric in which terms such as "famed minds," "illustrious men" occur. "The excellent wits of other nationalities not only in France, but also in our *Nederland*" have followed their example; "who, instructed in the French language, does not know the *Misantrope*, the *Bagatelle* and the *New French Spectator*? not to mention now the *Mensch Ontmaskerd* and the innumerable other Dutch writings that have followed the same trail, although with unequal steps and unequal result." In the preface for 1728 Van Merken would have it known, for he was an odd, proud little man, that he used no Dutch version of the *Spectator* but the original English itself! And indeed Van Merken had gone to the fountain-head—to London—whence after "a lengthy stay[1]" he returned to Holland to preside over a talented coterie of fine spirits at Haarlem, who met to enjoy

---

[1] *Onze Eeuw*, Nov. 1910. Dr A. H. Garrer, *Een medewerker van Justus Van Effen*.

music and literature, often of their own making, as was the custom.

In that circle the *Spectator* of Van Effen, which appeared in 1731, was received with pleasure, and this was natural. Had not Merkman and Alberti some years since in the *Mengelstoffen* taken up Van Effen's French essays from the *Misantrope* and the *Bagatelle*, were they not adherents and admirers of the English philosophical currents that also found expression in the English *Spectator*, would they not, as sincere Dutchmen, be attracted by the sound Dutch prose which the choice stylist soon gave them twice a week to enjoy[1]?

Consequently Merkman is one of the first to send an excellent attempt (no. 58) and later he contributed some clever things with which, as Verwer says, the Spectator was highly pleased. Some of the racy colloquial pieces are from his pen as, e.g., in nos. 188 and 273. Comparing the style in the sketches from lower bourgeois life given by Merkman and by Van Effen, Garrer says that "one feels that Van Effen puts his heart into his sketches and loves his characters," while "Merkman never forgets that he is superior in culture to his subjects"; but, at the same time, "he may be named as one of his best collaborators in his love for pure, pithy Dutch and in his truly national taste for the depicting of bourgeois life."

It is clear that Van Effen was helping to direct literature and impressing others with a sense of new aims, new methods and new values.

The encouraging lines sent to the *Hollandsche Spectator* by a correspondent[2] are a fitting conclusion to this chapter:

> Proceed with equal steps and zeal untired;
> Though *Netherland* could once not have aspired
> To claim a writer she but now has won
> Who treads the manly steps of Steele and Addison,
> Of whom Great Britain justly boasts the fame,
> We you may ne'ertheless their equal name.

---

[1] Garrer, *op. cit.*   [2] *Holl. Spect.* no. 215.

CHAPTER VI

THE REVIEWS AND THE FURTHER SPREAD OF ENGLISH LITERATURE

DISSEMINATION of the knowledge of English literature in Holland proceeded apace in the years that lay between the English and the Dutch *Spectators*. It was an important and interesting process, which opened up new vistas for European progress, even though the new ideas did not always take root and spring up so lustily as in Van Effen's papers. In such activity the refugee and Dutch reviewers took the chief part. J. Texte[1] has given an excellent general account of their work, but the voluminous results of their tremendous industry deserve the close attention of students of this period. The beginnings of the new journalism have been discussed in the first chapter, and the discussion must now be continued. During this time there were at least a dozen important reviews labouring ostensibly to promote the spread of learning and letters, but serving actually to satisfy and stimulate at the same time the public appetite for English works. The pioneer *Nouvelles de la République des Lettres* ran on into the year 1718, when its chief editor Jacques Bernard[2] died. "Il avait aussi profité en quelque manière des lumières de Philosophes anglois; & il abandonnoit le Cartésianisme." He was a great friend of le Clerc's.

In 1713 the *Bibliothèque Choisie* came to an end, and the excellent le Clerc was soon prevailed on to commence an important new review, the *Bibliothèque Ancienne et Moderne*, 1714–27. Friends assured him that they could not do without his paper, especially on account of his habitual practice "de lire les nouveautez," and these *nouveautez* we

---

[1] *Jean-Jacques Rousseau* (Paris, 1895), chap. i.
[2] "Pasteur & Professeur en Philosophie & aux mathématiques dans l'Église & l'Université de Leiden."

are given to infer are such as come from over the channel. Then Philippe Masson, "ministre de l'église réformée à Dort," conducted his *Histoire Critique de la République des Lettres* from 1712 to 1718 at Utrecht and Amsterdam.

In 1713 appeared at the Hague the celebrated *Journal Littéraire*, "le mieux écrit... et l'un des meilleurs qui existent," as Hattin[1] says. It was begun, he adds, speaking in paraphrase of Marchand, a collaborator who left a full account of this journal in his *Dictionnaire*, "par une société de jeunes gens tous distingués par leur génie et leur savoir, et étroitement unis par les liens de l'estime et de l'amitié." Marchand has told us how this anglophile—for they were that—society met on Friday nights[2] to distribute its labours and consider the articles or reviews contributed by each member, when they carried out their determination to be impartial and unafraid of censure, even in the case of original works of the members themselves.

This journal speedily came into the limelight and into the forefront of papers of its kind. "Ce livre s'acquit en peu de tems beaucoup de réputation," said *L'Europe Savante*[3] in 1718. Their Whiggish Republicanism and their outspokenness, for, as they assured a Paris correspondent, they were "une société composée de gens qui se disent fort naïvement leurs véritez," soon made the *Journal Littéraire* a suspect paper in France. From the club was issued the *Chef-d'œuvre d'un Inconnu* with Van Effen's *Parallèle* appended, a work which in its droll burlesque of pedantic commentators well expressed the spirit and merry common-sense of the club. It achieved a great European reputation. Communication was speedily established with a large number of centres. Among the correspondents were Keill, Professor of Astronomy at Oxford, de Crousaz of Lausanne and J. G. Eccard, Historiographer Royal in England. It made enemies, too, in addition to the Paris authorities, and when Van Effen's article on Dutch poetry appeared, matters grew lively. He had said some ill-judged things about Vondel,

---

[1] *Les Gazettes de Hollande.*   [2] *Vide* Bisschop, *op. cit.*
[3] Preface.

which brought the Dutch critics about his ears[1]. He was, as Zuydam too had urged, one of the chief contributors and a leader[2] of the circle with 's Gravesande, who also had some publications to his credit. The latter was chiefly responsible for the leading scientific articles in the paper and in later controversies gave the journal a wide reputation[3]. Van Effen's forte, we have every reason to believe with Bisschop, was literature, and it is to him that several important articles may safely be ascribed. That some importance was attached to the reviews is also illustrated by Ditton's protest against a review of his work on the Resurrection. In the first volume it was announced that this book and Clarke's *Sur la Trinité*, "deux livres Anglois fort estimez," would be considered in the next issue, so a review (vol. I, pp. 391–485) by 's Gravesande duly appeared. Ditton wrote to Johnson the publisher (who had also published the *Misantrope*) complaining of "misrepresentation," "disingenuity," etc., upon which he received a reply which closes as follows[4]: "As for them, they will always observe such rules as they think a due regard for truth and for good manner [*sic*] requires of them; and not think themselves obliged to answer the clamours of every writer that does not find himself praised so much as he thinks he deserves." The estimation in which the journal was held is shown by Verwer who, writing several decades later, says, "The writers gained great praise by their labour, and their work is still read with pleasure at the present time." Among the Wetstein papers preserved in the British Museum, is a letter of the middle of the century in which this famous Amsterdam bookseller offers Lord Dysart in England a complete set of the *Journal Littéraire*[5].

But what makes the *Journal Littéraire* particularly important for our purposes is that, as its name indicated,

---

[1] *Vide*, e.g., Te Winkel, *Ontwikkelingsgang*.

[2] As to Van Effen's share in the work, compare Bisschop, who, however, wrongly contradicts Verwer who makes a statement which is based on the following one by *L'Europe Savante* in 1718: from Jan. 1716 "M. v. Effen se chargea de la continuation de ce Journal."

[3] *Vide* Marchand, *Dict.*   [4] Bisschop, chap. VI.   [5] Add. MSS. 32414, vol. I.

it was more of a real literary journal than any other of the time. It contains a number of valuable reviews of English literature of a nature not to be found in the other journals. Indeed, it may be emphasized here that on the whole these journals were still devoted to English science and philosophy, for which there appeared to be an almost unlimited demand. In the preface to his *Bibliothèque Ancienne et Moderne* le Clerc, speaking of scientific works that contain "beaucoup de Véritez qui sont par elles-mêmes, très-belles, très-sublimes & très-utiles," giving new light to scholars, adds, "J'en prens à témoins ceux qui ont lu dans la *Bibliothèque Choisie* les Extraits de divers Livres Anglois...."

The following *avertissement* by Masson in his *Histoire Critique de la République des Lettres* prepares one for solid fare:

On se propose entr'autres, de parler ici de ces excellens Ouvrages de *Littérature* & de *Critique* qui ont paru depuis qu'on a vu renaître les Belles Lettres; surtout de ceux qui sont & les moins communs & les plus solides en même temps. On aura aussi soin de rendre compte au Public de plusieurs Livres Anglois *qui ne sont guère connus au-deçà de la mer* & qui sont pourtant très dignes de l'attention de tous ceux qui cherchent un solide sçavoir. La Grande Bretagne a été trop fertile en grands Hommes, pour ne lui pas rendre toute la justice qui lui est duë. Cette sçavante Nation nous a fait part d'un trop grand nombre de beaux Ouvrages, pour souffrir qu'ils demeurent à jamais inconnus au reste de l'Europe.

After this highly interesting and fairly promising prelude what do we find? Explanations of passages in Pliny and Clement Alexandrin's *Remarques sur Eupolême*; an essay on the life of David with comments on the Psalms, and reviews on *Les Epîtres d'Ovide traduites en Vers François* by C. G. Bachet, and Cudworth's *Discourse* on the Lord's Supper. This is the only English work treated. It is followed by a *Dissertation Critique sur le prix que l'on donnoit autrefois aux Vainqueurs dans les Jeux Phythiques*; a commentary of seventy pages on three passages in the New Testament, and a *Dissertation Historique & Critique sur une Médaille de*

Drusus. At the end, Livres Nouveaux are announced. They are mostly commentaries on either the Bible or the classics, or theological works in Latin such as those of Limborch. A work by J. Perizoni on the *Origines Babylonicae,* etc., is strongly recommended to all who have a taste for "la belle Littérature" and "pour la bonne Critique." Madame Dacier's translation of the *Iliad* is also noticed. Such, then, is a sample of the fare these *recueils littéraires* mostly provided. No wonder that Masson's had but a struggling existence, as *L'Europe Savante* tells us[1], and no wonder that an objector appears who complains[2]: "il y avoit trop d'Érudition dans votre 1ère Volume." But our reviewer snaps his fingers at these people. "Il y a une infinité d'autres Livres composez à cet usage auxquels ils peuvent avoir recours. Pour nous, nous ne nous sommes engagez qu'à rechercher & à publier ce qu'il y a de plus solide & de moins commun dans les Lettres & dans les matières sçavantes." Here indeed the aim of most of these papers is justly stated; but there was no "infinité d'autres Livres" where readers could become *au fait* with fine literature, and the work that satisfied most of this need was unquestionably the *Journal Littéraire.* Then there was the *Nouvelles Littéraires,* an international literary newspaper which battened largely on the current journals and often contained interesting news from London. It appeared at the Hague from 1715 to 1720, and at the same time there also appeared the *Mémoires de Littérature* of Sallengre[3], a member of the *Journal Littéraire* club: but this contains little of interest for us. Then comes a paper which openly avows its aim to be that of popularizing English literature on the continent. It is the *Bibliothèque Angloise* of Michel de la Roche who had already figured prominently in refugee literary activity. Writing from London, he makes some very interesting remarks in the *avertissement,* vol. I:

On peut dire en général que les Livres Anglois ne sont guère connus hors de cette Isle, & ceux qu'on traduit de tems en tems

[1] Preface.   [2] Vol. II, Avertissement.
[3] Member of the Royal Society, visited England in 1719, was intimate with Lord Whitworth, and a nephew of the Dutch poet Rotgans.

en François ou dont les Journalistes parlent, ne sufisent pas pour donner une juste idée de l'état où les Sciences s'y trouvent aujourd'hui ni pour satisfaire la curiosité du Public. De sorte que le dessein, où je suis de rendre compte, non seulement des Livres nouveaux à mesure qu'ils paroissent, mais aussi de quelques-uns de vieille date & fort curieux, dont les Journalistes n'ont rien dit jusques-ici, ne sera pas désagréable, si je ne me trompe, aux Personnes qui aiment les belles Lettres.

"I shall endeavour to make my foreign readers as sensible of the merit of our English authors as I am," he declared in English[1], speaking of "my French Journal at Amsterdam." But de la Roche also disappoints. The first book which he reviews is a *History of the Jews*, by the Dean of Norwich, after which he considers a volume of Blackmore's essays; and then follow considerations of Bentley's *Horace*, and of historical, biographical, political and antiquarian works. Indeed, in the whole of the *Bibliothèque Angloise* there is, except for a short defence of Addison's *Cato*, a review of the notorious *Fable of the Bees* and a few desultory references to Pope, Locke and a few others, very little that has anything to do with the artistic side of English writings. Science, religion and philosophy were its matter and its chief interest. As Armand de la Chapelle had taken over the management of this review at Amsterdam, de la Roche started another—*Mémoires Littéraires de la Grande Bretagne*, which appeared at the Hague, from 1720 to 1724, filling sixteen volumes. But previous to this Van Effen had again entered the journalistic field with *L'Europe Savante* (1718–20) from which we have quoted above. With him was associated Themiseul de Saint-Hyacinthe, the principal author of the *Chef-d'œuvre d'un Inconnu* projected by the *Journal Littéraire* club. The review runs into nine volumes, and although it contains several articles of great interest, it was largely preoccupied with science and philosophy, as the title indicates.

In 1726 Van Effen again conducted a review entitled *Histoire Littéraire de l'Europe* "contenant l'extrait des

[1] *Mémoires Littéraires*, etc. Feb. 1717, Art. v, review on R. Blackmore's essays.

meilleurs livres, un catalogue choisi des ouvrages nouveaux, les nouvelles les plus intéressantes de la république des lettres, et les pièces fugitives les plus curieuses." It fills six octavo volumes. Strict impartiality was to be observed. "Il faut que l'auteur écrive comme s'il n'avait ni religion ni patrie; *c'est de la science seule qu'il s'agit dans un journal*," and the last remark is again fairly well descriptive of the atmosphere of these journals. Van Effen, therefore, as we have seen, took a very considerable part in the journalism of the day, and where *belles lettres* are concerned, his share for this period is exceptionally large and important.

Perhaps the most influential journal published in Holland at this time was Sewell's Dutch *Boekzaal* which was still flourishing. It compares favourably with the best reviews in French and was really even more literary than the *Journal Littéraire* itself. Treating all the usual material, it allowed very little of any importance in English fine literature to escape its notice, so that it was one of the premier journals for acquainting the Dutch public with English literature, and forms to-day a mine of information for the literary investigator. As it was one of the first of the eighteenth-century reviews, so it lasted to the end, running into more than 200 octavo volumes of over 700 pages each. For our purposes it is almost invaluable and will often be quoted, for in it are notices of most of the historic eighteenth-century works, especially of English books. Although the bulk of the reviews deal chiefly with matters outside pure literature, they form nevertheless a highly significant chapter in the growing cosmopolitanism of European literature and particularly in the eastward movement of English literary influences, for which indeed they were in some part responsible. The several volumes may frequently disappoint those who would seek evidence of the interest taken in English works, but there is no doubt that in the aggregate they are usefully informative. These journals together continued to provide an excellent and wonderfully well-informed course of instruction in English history, thought and manners—

a necessary preliminary to the more intimate study of English poetry and *belles lettres*. This literary spade-work was not only necessary but was also acceptable to the public, who, in spite of the somewhat conflicting statements made, were strenuously applying themselves to the study of things English. In English history and domestic politics, for example, interest was still very keen, and the excellent popular works of Rapin and Leti excited the greatest possible enthusiasm at any rate among the journalists. In February 1718, *L'Europe Savante*, reviewing Rapin's *Dissertation sur les Whigs & les Torys*, says:

Avant la Paix d'Utrecht la plupart des Etrangers regardoient ces Différens entre les Whigs & les Torys comme une matière simplement curieuse. Mais cette Paix a désillé les yeux à une infinité de Gens parce-qu'on a vû clairement qu'elle étoit une suite de la Révolution arrivée à la Cour d'Angleterre par le changement des ministres Whigs en ministres Torys. Depuis ce tems-là on a commencé à disputer sur cette matière. *Les Etrangers même ont pris Partie.*

Rapin was everywhere received as an authority, and his works were constantly recommended. The *Journal Littéraire*[1], in a review, gives a masterly exposition of party government in England with a full explanation of the names Tory and Whig, and the rise of these parties. Anticipating Montesquieu, it declares that the government of England is "un composé salutaire de tous les autres Gouvernemens connus dans le monde." The *Actes Publics d'Angleterre* were most copiously treated, especially by le Clerc in his *Bibliothèque Choisie* and the *Bibliothèque Ancienne et Moderne*. In the latter (1717) he reveals that the reviewer was the famous Rapin himself and

il n'y a personne qui puisse faire aussi bien ces Extraits que lui qui non seulement a extrêmement étudié l'Histoire d'Angleterre mais qui l'a même écrite.... Il y a eu plusieurs Anglois qui m'ont témoigné qu'ils avoient lû avec beaucoup de plaisir les Extraits que j'en ai déjà publiez, & qui ont manqué même de l'impatience

---

[1] 1717, vol. IX.

d'en voir la suite. D'autres personnes de différentes Nations, qui sont dans le même goût, m'ont aussi demandé plusieurs fois, si l'on ne continueroit pas ces Extraits jusqu'à la fin.

English theology continued to be widely read. "Whoever has any knowledge of theological writings knows how Mr Tillotson has made himself illustrious therein," says the *Boekzaal* in 1726, commenting on a Life of Tillotson with commentary by le Clerc. The latter had always been an admirer. In discussing Dutch and French translations of Tillotson's sermons in 1713[1], le Clerc had said of him and Burnet: "Ces deux Prélats ont tant rendu de services non seulement à leur Patrie, mais encore à tous les Protestans, par leurs ouvrages, qui ne périront jamais, que tout ce qui les regarde s'attirera toujours." The *Boekzaal*[2], commenting on a Dutch translation, spoke of "the noble work of the renowned Mr Sherlock." Lufneu, Van Effen's friend, translated "the renowned work of the famous Dr Derham," as Verwer[3] says. So Clarke, Ditton, Toland, Collins, Blackmore, and others, were at least as well known in Holland as in England.

English ecclesiastical history was no less eagerly read, and Burnet was still a favourite.

M. l'Evêque de Salisbury est si universellement connu par le rang considérable qu'il occupe depuis long-tems aussi-bien dans la République des Lettres que dans l'Etat Ecclésiastique & Civil que son nom seul suffit pour exciter la curiosité des lecteurs. On sait assez que son Histoire de la Réformation de l'Eglise d'Angleterre est une des plus considérables productions de sa plume & en même temps une des Histoires les plus estimées tant à cause de l'habileté & de candeur de l'Historien qu'à cause de l'importance du sujet qu'il a traité. Les différentes éditions qu'on en a faites tant en Latin, en François & en Hollandois, qu' en Anglois en sont de bonnes preuves[4].

In 1715 T. Johnson published a great edition at the Hague by subscription. In 1723 the *History of my own Times* was "read with eagerness by everyone[5]." In English science, of

---

[1] *Biblioth. Ch.* vol. xxvi.
[2] July 1726.
[3] *Leven.*
[4] *Journ. Lit.* 1714.
[5] *Boekzaal.*

course, great interest was being maintained; the Clarke-Leibnitz controversy filled these journals; in 1721 appeared 's Gravesande's work on the elements of the Newtonian philosophy, which was very well received by the reviews.

In May 1723 the *Boekzaal* reviewed a translation of Clarke's *Enquiry*... by J. Suderman (probably a relative of William Suderman, the Anglophile who was later to assist Van Effen with the *Hollandsche Spectator*) and some verses on Newton are appended, beginning:

> O England's everlasting honour,
> Illustrious Newton, chosen
> To pierce the Wisdom of the Highest....

The reputation of Locke was still growing, if that were possible. His treatise on education was reviewed in the *Boekzaal* for Feb.–March 1722 in the following terms:

As this work has been printed and reprinted in various countries in the original language, as well as in French, one should conclude from this that it must have some merit, even if one were uninstructed as to the marvellous judgment and understanding of the writer. That great man has made himself immortal by his *Essay on the Human Understanding*, wherein amongst other things he has untied the Gordian knot of innate ideas, having demonstrated the impossibility thereof with such clearness and strength that, according to the saying of one of the finest intellects [Barbeyrac, professor at Groningen] of our time, no one can believe in their existence any more, unless he perversely would close his eyes to the clearest possible light.

No one is better equipped for a work of this nature than Mr Locke...and it will be seen that his views are in correspondence with Reason in so much as they are opposed to the wrong prepossessions in vogue.

The tendency to extravagant eulogy in these reviews is symptomatic of later ecstasy, and already this period was feverishly exploiting English ideas. Even the notorious get-rich-quick John Law must needs be allowed to teach the Dutch how to run lotteries *à l'Anglaise*, for, says the *Boekzaal*[1], lotteries "were still unknown in Holland." In short, there was no department, including that of the best

[1] Aug. 1722.

current fine literature, in which the public in Holland did not manifest the keenest interest and could not but have had adequate information. The existence of such a swarm of newspapers, *petits-journaux* and reviews is perhaps the best index. We may contrast the situation of England in this respect. The London correspondent to the *Journal Littéraire* for November to December 1714 announced that de la Roche had discontinued his *Memoirs of Literature* which, though dealing mostly with foreign literature, contained also "plusieurs bons articles touchant les Livres Anglois & les Affaires de Littérature de ce Païs." The reason for its discontinuance is:

qu'il n'en trouvoit pas assez de débit, *quoique ce fût le seul Journal Littéraire que nous eussions en ce Païs*, où il ne vient même que fort peu de Journaux étrangers. Cela fait voir que le nombre des Savans curieux n'y est pas fort grand à présent. La Raison en est que l'Esprit de Parti & d'animosité a tellement saisi presque tout le monde ici, qu'il semble qu'on a négligé tout autre soin.... !

In 1722 there was some slight improvement. Observe how Armand de la Chapelle[1] greets the arrival of the *Bibliotheca Literaria* ("...printed for...Th. Woodward at the Half-moon against St Dunstan's Church in Fleet street 1722"): "On doit apprendre avec plaisir dans les Païs étrangers qu'il s'établit, dans la Grande Bretagne, un nouveau *Journal Littéraire*. Bien des gens étoient surpris de ce que cette sorte d'Ouvrages, qui a si bien réussi parmi les autres Peuples, n'avoit presque pû se maintenir chez une nation si libre, si savante & si curieuse [*sic*]." And one reason for this "mauvais succès" was "que les Anglois ont, en général, pour les Etrangers, un mépris naturel qui s'étend jusque dans la République des Lettres." How very different was the atmosphere in Holland at that time! On the value of the innumerable translations which rendered almost every contemporary book or pamphlet accessible to the learned and general public, we need scarcely insist. What was perhaps overlooked by the translator, was generally given to

---

[1] *Bibliotheque Angloise* (Amsterdam 1717), vol. x, p. 502.

the public by the journalists in copious extracts. The following may be taken as an interesting example of how the interest was spreading. *"Verdediging der Poezy uyt het Engelsch van den Ridder Philip Sidnei vertaalt door J. de Haes."*

"Mr de Haes," says the reviewer[1] of this translation of Sidney's *Defence*, "est un de ces exemples bien rares: c'est l'exemple d'un marchand, qu'un Négoce & des biens assez considérables n'empêchent pas de s'appliquer avec ardeur aux Belles Lettres; & qui par conséquent devroit servoir de modèle à tous ceux de sa profession qui peuvent l'imiter[1]."

It was of course an age of translations as much as the twentieth century. In Holland, the Eldorado of the bookseller, translators were no less active than in England. The London correspondent of the *Journal Littéraire*, May–June 1714, wrote:

Il n'y a guère des Livres estimez en aucune autre Langue dont on n'ait fait des Traductions Angloises, & on continue d'en faire encore tous les jours. Nous avons à présent une nouvelle Traduction de Caractères de Théophraste, qui est fort estimée. Elle est de M. Budgell, homme d'esprit qui a fourni plusieurs bons morceaux de Spectator.

Then a new edition of Grotius in English is announced from the Oxford press.

Of the many books descriptive of England, that of Muralt published at this time (1725) is the best; it created some sensation[2], and was well known. It was, however, not up to date, having been written some thirty years before. The *Bibliothèque Angloise* (vol. XIII, 1725) holds a discussion on English humour and appeals to Muralt on the point, but disapproves of his stricture that it is "une certaine fécondité d'Imagination qui d'ordinaire tend à renverser les idées des choses, tournant la vertu en ridicule & rendant le Vice agréable." "C'est définir la signification du mot par l'abus qu'on fait de la chose," objects the reviewer. But the misanthropic Muralt may be pardoned. He had to judge of

---

[1] *L'Histoire Critique & l. Rep. des Let.* vol. III, 1715.
[2] *Vide* Texte, chap. II, pp. 36–44 and references.

English humour as he saw it on the stage mostly during the time of King William.

But what was the actual state of knowledge of English? It was at best uncertain and is difficult to estimate; yet since the period we have reviewed in chapter I above there was great improvement. We have quoted from Masson's and de la Roche's convictions as to the greatness of, and the need for popularizing, English writings. The latter had also said in the *Bibliothèque Angloise*: "L'Angleterre est un Païs, où les Sciences & les arts fleurissent autant qu'en aucun Lieu du Monde; elles y sont cultivées dans le sein de la Liberté." This statement was endorsed by Van Effen's journal *L'Europe Savante*, which adds: "Il est important pour les Gens de Lettres d'avoir quelqu'un qui soit capable de les informer de ce qui s'y passe[1]." The sixth article for February 1718 is a review of de la Roche's *Bibliothèque* in which his opinion: "personne de ceux qui aiment les Sciences ne doit négliger la langue Angloise," as well as that about English books being scarcely known outside England is expressed. The reviewer comments:

Le public doit donc recevoir avec beaucoup de Reconnaissance un journal qui rend un compte fidèle & exact de tous les excellens Ouvrages, qui s'impriment en Angleterre; *quoique la Langue Anglois soit maintenant plus étudiée des Etrangers, qu'elle ne l'a jamais été*[2], il y a cependant un grand nombre de Savans qui l'ignorent, et ceux qui la savent ne sont pas toujours instruits des bon Livres que les Anglois publient.

Over against this must be put a statement made by the *Journal Littéraire* four years[3] earlier that: "Il y a un bon nombre de habiles gens qui savent l'Anglois & le François," who can therefore themselves be judges of the merits of translations.

Le Clerc often refers to "ceux qui entendent l'Anglois." Henry Scheurleer[4] assures us that knowledge of English language and manners is looked upon "as an additional Ornament...especially considering to what height all true

[1] Vol. I. [2] My italics. [3] Jan.–Feb. 1714, p. 211.
[4] Dedication to Addison's *Travels*, published at the Hague.

and polite Learning has arrived in that Nation." In 1718, again, a correspondent, who is particularly impatient to see a promised extract from an English work on the liberty of man, adds: "Il seroit à souhaiter que cet Ouvrage fût traduit dans une Langue plus universellement connue que l'Angloise." And again the London correspondent of the *Journal Littéraire* (1715) says significantly: "C'est un malheur pour les beaux Esprits de ce païs que leur Langue soit en quelque sorte restreinte dans les mêmes bornes que leurs isles; c'est en même temps un bonheur pour les auteurs François qui peut-être cela seul restent en possession de surpasser les autres peuples en matière de bel Esprit."

In 1718 le Clerc[1] asked:

Combien peu de Gens y a-t-il deçà la mer qui sachent l'Anglois? Cependant il y a une infinité de bons Livres dans cette Langue, qu'on n'a point traduits, & qui ne le seront apparemment jamais; dont il est néanmoins très-avantageux au Public d'avoir au moins quelque connoissance....On voit ici des Livres qui sont rares deçà la mer, & qui n'y seront jamais communs, comme quantité d'ouvrages Anglois.

As to the knowledge of English literature outside works like the *Spectator* or Locke, discussed frequently in these journals, it is safer not to be too sanguine. In 1716 the reviewer of Pope's Homer in the *Journal Littéraire* finds it necessary to put in an explanatory footnote that Milton and Shakespeare were "deux Poëtes Anglois dont l'un a excellé dans l'Epique & l'autre dans le Dramatique." In December 1715 the *Boekzaal* announced that an edition of *Spencer* [*sic*] had appeared in London "who was an old English poet and an example of the art of unrhymed poetry" [*sic*]. Indeed, some four years previously le Clerc confessed: "The English poets indeed are not so well known to us because few men on this side of the sea understand English well enough to read those poets[2]." But le Clerc's eagerness on behalf of English writings may have made him unduly pessimistic. Shortly before this[3] he had also said somewhat ambiguously:

---

[1] Avertissement, *Biblioth. Univ.* vol. XXVI.
[2] *Biblioth. Ch.* vol. XXI, review of Shaftesbury's *Advice to an Author*.
[3] *Biblioth. Ch.* vol. XIX, review of Shaftesbury's *Letter conc. Enthusiasm*.

"The ear is not the same in all languages, and what appears strange to the French or Dutch, who do not understand the English Language nor are accustomed to English books, would not seem so in the original, which is very well writ."

As *L'Europe Savante* states, the parts which relate to English poetry as well as those whose relish requires a knowledge of English life were omitted from the first translations of the *Spectator*. This seems to imply that people were ignorant of or indifferent to English poetry and domestic ways. The *Nouvelles de la République des Lettres* (1718), in reviewing the third volume of the *Spectator* which had just appeared in French, observes: "On en a retranché plusieurs dans cette Traduction, parce qu'ils n'auroient eu aucun agrément en François & divers autres qui contiennent une Critique fine et judicieuse du célèbre Poëme de *Milton*, intitulé *le Paradis perdu*; parce-qu'il n'y a pas d'apparence, qu'il soit jamais traduit en François."

Le Clerc remarked[1]: "On ne pourroit néanmoins pas traduire en François les Poësies Angloises, qui se trouvent en divers endroits tirées de Poëtes qui avoient déjà paru & quelquefois avec de petites remarques comme sur le *Paradis Perdu* de Milton ou qui n'avoient jamais été imprimées." There is, however, no need to insist on the point that the *Spectator* must, nevertheless, have played a very important part in making foreigners acquainted with English literature and manners. "L'ouvrage est plein d'allusions à leur manière de vivre & à une infinité de choses qui leur sont singulières," said le Clerc[2], and did not Voltaire say that "Mr Addison, the best critick as well as the best writer of his age, pointed out the hidden beauties of the *Paradise Lost* and settled for ever its reputation[3]"? Yet again, when we think of Steele's fine literary criticism, especially on Shakespeare, in the *Tatler*, it is rather disheartening to find the *Boekzaal* for October 1724 making the following remark in reviewing the *Tatler*: "The writer of this work frequently speaks of theatre-pieces which were played from time to

[1] *Biblioth Anc. et Mod.* vol. i, 1714.　　　　[2] *Ibid.*
[3] Preface, *On the Civil Wars of France.*

time at London when these leaves were issued. We will not hold up our readers, who would be bored, with what he says of these things." Yet T. Johnson evidently considered that there was a public interest in these things when he advertised in 1720[1]: "Toutes les meilleures pièces des bons Poëtes Anglois & les meilleures pièces du Théâtre Anglois, le tout à meilleur marché, & mieux imprimé qu'en Angleterre."

[1] *Journ. Lit.*

CHAPTER VII

VAN EFFEN AND ENGLISH LITERATURE IN HOLLAND

It is evident from the foregoing that, in spite of some advance, much still remained for Van Effen and his *confrères* to do. Though by his periodicals he may be said to have made his most striking comment on English literature and culture, he also expressed himself, as we have partly seen, in more explicit terms. As critic and reviewer he is prominent in the history of the reputation and influence which many English books and writers, especially Addison, gained on the continent.

We have remarked the growth of this writer's fame up to the time of the *Misantrope*, which was in itself, and contained, as we have seen, a striking tribute to the English genius. His fame was to become the meteoric blaze allegorized by the *Bagatelle* correspondent[1]. With the name of Addison, that of Steele was closely associated; therefore we shall treat the foreign reputation of these two wits together.

There had been a curious lull in the interest taken in Addison, while Steele, it seems, was still unknown. Le Clerc's *Bibliothèque Choisie*, which ran to 1713, is silent as to the *Tatler* and the *Spectator*; Masson, whose *Histoire Critique* began in 1714, likewise ignored them. The first intimation comes from Addison himself: "As I have of late found my name in foreign gazettes upon less Occasions, I question not but in their next Articles from *Great Britain* they will inform the world that *the* Spectator's *mouth is to be opened on the twenty-fifth of* March *next*[2]." The gazetteers do not appear to have taken the hint and, except for the *Misantrope*, we have to wait until 1714 before notices begin to appear. The *Journal Littéraire* for May–June of this year

---

[1] Cp. above, chap. IV, p. 120.
[2] *Spect.* no. 550, Dec. 1, 1712.

has: "M. Steel qui s'étoit acquis une très-grande réputation par le Tatler & par le Spectator où il avait grande part, a depuis écrit un autre ouvrage apellé le *Guardian* ou *Tuteur*, qui n'a pas été si estimé & en suite *l'Anglois* qui l'a été encore moins." Then follows a long account of Steele's political activities and literary projects such as a history of the last war. *This, for the first time, made the continental public acquainted with Steele and his career.*

But in this number occurs also the first foreign review of the *Spectator*. It bears all the signs of being from Van Effen's pen. There is much praise, but the reviewer is not blind to faults. He hints at the *surchargé* nature of some papers and administers to Steele a deserved reproof for his impolite reference to Dutch beauties in *Spectator*, no. 82: "Ne peut-on pas dire qu'il y a dans cette belle rèmarque bien de la présomption & une affectation de mépriser les autres nations, ce qui est fort du génie des Anglois? Il y a dans ces Provinces tout un Païs où les simples Païsannes pourroient faire parole à toutes les Dames Angloises sur la finesse de la taille." "Le Génie du Spectateur brille surtout dans l'allégorie," a perfectly true remark which occurs in a review of the second volume of the *Spectator* two years later in the following form. The "Vision of Myrza" "peut aller de pair avec tout ce que les auteurs de tous les âges ont écrit de meilleur dans ce genre."

But other reviews were soon on the trail. On the front page of the first volume of the *Bibliothèque Ancienne et Moderne* one reads among the "Livres nouvellement imprimez": "Le Spectateur ou le Socrate moderne où l'on voit un Portrait naïf des Mœurs de ce siècle par monsr. Richard Steele, 12, 1714." This announcement was immediately followed by *La Crise ou Discours*, "par M. Richard Steele" and also *L'Esprit de Whigs*, etc. In the second volume for this year le Clerc distinguishes himself by giving the best review of the *Spectator* I have read in any of these journals. It fills no less than 67 pages! "C'est ici un Ouvrage qui a paru par demi-feuilles & qu'on a vendu à Londres comme la Gazette" he explains.

Comme il n'y a point de ville que l'on sache, où il s'imprime tant de feuilles volantes qu'à Londres, ceux qui ont travaillé à ces pièces détachées ont profité de cet usage pour instruire tantôt en badinant & tantôt d'une manière sérieuse une infinité de gens à qui les livres font peur, & qui lisoient avec plaisir ces demie-feuilles en buvant du Thé ou du Café. Comme il est extrêmement bien écrit en Anglois, qu'il est plein d'esprit & de bonnes matières, non seulement il s'en vendoit une très grande quantité en demifeuilles mais....

Only one person is named, he continues: "C'est Mr Steele," while under the letters *C.L.I.O.* "on trouvera beaucoup de fines recherches de morale & de leçons très-utiles pour la vie."

But le Clerc's French taste is sometimes offended. "La Langue Angloise d'ailleurs a des libertez & même quand il s'agit de choses sérieuses qu'il est très-difficile d'en représenter l'énergie en une autre Langue." And here he expresses a fixed idea of the time. It was considered a feat of scholarship to translate many of these English books. Speaking of the translator's difficulties, le Clerc had said in 1713[1]: "Ceux qui connoissent le génie de la Langue Angloise, & la liberté extraordinaire que se donnent les auteurs Anglois à se servir de nouvelles expressions & de figures hardies & mêmes violentes en conviendront facilement[2]." But, to return to the *Spectator*, le Clerc finds that it contains also

une infinité de choses générales qui sont également bonnes, pour toutes les nations & qu'on peut lire en François avec plaisir & en profiter ailleurs aussi bien qu'en Angleterre. Ceux qui ne savent pas l'Anglois pourroient s'en convaincre en lisant ce qui en a été traduit.

Il seroit à souhaiter que chaque Nation eût quelqu'un qui lui fît sentir de même le ridicule de ses défauts d'une manière enjouée & qui formât ses mœurs & son goût sans l'offenser & sans prendre le ton de maître.

Le Clerc now further enhances the interest of his excellent analysis by exploring the whole of the *Spectator* of which

[1] *Biblioth. Ch.*, Avertissement.
[2] Cp. le Clerc's review of Chamberlaine's articles on: "Le Génie & la Force de la Langue Angloise." *Biblioth. Ch.* vol. xvii, 1709.

only one volume was known to his public. "Comme on ne traduira apparemment de longtems les derniers Volumes je mettrai ici quelques articles tirez du V, VI & VII où je prendrai toute la liberté nécessaire pour les faire goûter en François...." Nos. 381, 387 are given and discussed with excerpts from other papers. Le Clerc saw what is perhaps the most significant historical feature of the *Spectator*.

Je voudrois pouvoir mettre ici les onze Discours sur les plaisirs de l'Imagination, où l'Auteur a traité d'une manière très-fine & très-ingénieuse un sujet, que personne n'avoit, que je sache, examiné avant lui, au moins de cette manière & dans cette vue. Mais il faudroit les traduire tous entiers ou à peu près comme j'ai fait les précédens, & c'est ce qui ne se peut pas faire dans un Ouvrage de l'étendue de celui-ci. Je envoye les Lecteurs qui entendent l'Anglois à l'original, qu'ils liront avec un extrême plaisir. Si celui qui a commencé à traduire le *Spectateur* continue, ceux qui n'entendent que le François pourront aussi en être régalez.

Le Clerc always did love to dangle the delectable morsels of English genius before his readers.

"Il y a dans cet ouvrage quelques songes ingénieux," he says, giving a taste of no. 483. There are also "beaucoup de plaisanteries qui font voir la sottise de l'Homme à divers égards; que l'on fera bien de lire dans l'Original dans lequel elles ont meilleure grâce." He gives most of nos. 410, 507, 512 and concludes: "Je n'irai pas plus loin dans cet extrait. J'ajouterai seulement que le grand succès seul que cet Ouvrage a eu en Angleterre peut faire comprendre qu'il est très digne d'être placé dans les Bibliothèques de ceux qui entendent l'Anglois. Mr Steele a encore fait d'autres ouvrages de cette espèce; mais comme je ne les ai pas vus, je n'en parlerai pas." The *Journal Littéraire*[1] followed this up with a eulogistic appreciation of Addison.

M. Addison ne triomphe pas moins dans ce genre d'écrire, que M. Newton sur les mathématiques & sur la Physique. Le nom du premier pourtant n'a pas fait autant de bruit qu'il méritoit parmi les estrangers, & sa modestie en est en partie la

---

[1] *Nouvelles Lit. de Londres*, 1715.

cause. Ce qu'on trouve de plus excellent dans le Tatler & dans le Spectateur est dû à son Génie; & c'est à lui que nous sommes redevables de la belle Tragédie intitulée *Caton*. Des personnes d'une capacité distinguée, qui entendent notre Langue, quoique accoutumés à n'admirer que les Tragiques François, conviennent que tout au moins cette pièce va de pair avec ce que Corneille & Racine ont fait de meilleur dans ce genre. M. Armand du Bordieu avoit, à ce qu'on dit, entrepris de traduire cet ouvrage en vers François; mais on n'en parle plus, & il y a de l'apparence que la difficulté de l'entreprise l'en aura rebuté. Quelque bonne que soit cette pièce de Théâtre, il y a à douter si c'est ce que M. Addison a fait de meilleur, son Esprit ne brille pas moins dans le genre Héroïque que dans le Tragique; témoin son Poëme appellé *The Campaign*, dans lequel il décrit la Campagne de Hoghstet d'une manière digne du mérite des Héros qui y ont commandé nos armées & de la gloire que les Alliez y ont acquise. Parmi un grand nombre de pièces fort estimées qu'il avoit faites auparavant, il y en a une qui est d'une beauté & d'une richesse admirable, c'est une Epitre à mylord Hallifax, le Maecenas d'Angleterre, dans laquelle M. Addison étale toutes les beautez & tous les charmes de l'Italie d'une manière incomparable. Rosemonde, Opéra de sa façon, a eu aussi un bon nombre d'admirateurs. Les Poètes Anglois ne s'attireront plus de Réputation par ces sortes de Poëmes; les droits des Oreilles ont prévalu ici sur les droits de l'Esprit. Les Opéras sont tous en Italien, langage fort peu entendu ici & les gens de bon sens qui les entendent, les trouvent impertinents au suprême degré.

For a time the public were content, it seems, with the first volume of the *Spectator* and such accounts. This volume was reprinted and in 1716 a second appeared, which was enthusiastically reviewed. Le Clerc said[1]: "c'est très-bien débité," meaning the first volume, and gave further extracts from vol. II, but he complains characteristically that "la Langue Angloise est si abondante en termes & si hardie, qu'il est fort difficile qu'on l'égale en François & les Versions ne paroissent jamais si vives que les Originaux." The *Journal Littéraire*[2] is impressed by the great success of the first volume of this "ouvrage incomparable," but "tous les Tomes de cet excellent ouvrage" have an equal merit, and the translator is to be congratulated as all who know both

Biblioth. Anc. et Mod. 1716.　　　[2] Vol. VIII, 1716.

languages will admit, only more notes should have been added "afin de mettre au fait les Lecteurs qui ignorent les manières Angloises." Then follow many extracts, the reviewer being delighted with Sir Roger and other *caractères*. His raptures on the "Vision of Myrza" have been quoted. In the following year, vol. III duly appeared and the reviewers did not miss it. The *Spectator*, said le Clerc[1], "est si connu à présent deçà la mer & les deux volumes qui ont déjà paru s'y soient si bien vendus, qu'il n'est plus besoin de le faire connoître ou de le recommande à ceux qui ne l'ont pas encore lu." The translation has nothing "qui choquât trop les manières de la Langue Françoise." As usual, he finds that "l'Angloise est si hardie & si énergique, comparée à la nôtre; qu'il est très difficile de rendre partout beauté pour beauté. On est obligé d'y laisser bien des traits qui se ressentent encore du terroir," and he adds a very interesting remark as to the local colour of English books: "on doit aussi voir avec plaisir dans leurs Livres l'air de leur païs." *L'Europe Savante*[2] said: "Il n'y a personne qui ne sache à quel point cet ouvrage a réussi." The translation of the first two volumes "a été si bien reçue que l'Edition qu'on en a faite en Hollande a été suivie d'une autre en France, ce qui n'arrive que très rarement," and the third volume is just as good as the earlier ones. "Il semble," they said, "qu'il y a chez eux beaucoup plus de Caractères originaux qu'ailleurs," again a significant remark expressing what soon became one of the most popular pet ideas ever entertained of the English by admiring continental peoples. Holberg[3] summed it up thus: England is "one of the most singular countries in the world...which scorns all mediocrity." But in the *Bagatelle*[4] Van Effen has well expressed what afterwards became the conventional view:

Si les Dames Allemandes sont pour la plupart des copies, le caractère des Angloises au contraire est tout-à-fait original: elles ont leur tour d'esprit—à part, des modes, des airs, & des manières qui leur sont particulières & propres.

[1] Vol. VIII, 1717.　　　[2] Nov. 1718.
[3] *Autobiography*.　　　[4] No. 87.

Tous ceux qui ont examiné à fond les Anglois conviendront avec moi qu'ils constituent le Peuple le plus sage & le plus fou de l'univers. On découvre dans leur Pays, jusques chez les marins & les plus vils artisans, de la pénétration du raisonnement, & de l'esprit; mais en même tems une bizarrerie excessive qui vient de l'amour outre qu'ils ont pour la Liberté. Tout ce qui gêne, tout ce qui contraint, leur est insupportable. Il n'y a point de gens au monde qui soient moins imitateurs; chacun se livre à son humeur particulière, sans se mettre en peine des autres. De-là vient que quoique tous les Anglois se sentent du caractère général de la Nation, ce caractère est varié de cent mille façons & qu'il n'y a point de Peuple où se trouve tant d'Originaux différens. Le fond du caractère Anglois est toujours un assemblage monstrueux de beaucoup de bons-sens & d'une bizarrerie incompréhensible, qu'un Etranger prendroit souvent pour un *Fanatisme réel*.

Had not the *Spectator* said that they were a "nation of Humourists"? And the *Spectator* exercised great influence in spreading such and other ideas.

By this time Steele and Addison were enjoying the greatest publicity in Holland. Steele aroused some interest in his favour as a politician, the *Crisis* being speedily translated into Dutch, from which it was turned into German. The *Nouvelles Littéraires* (1715), writing on Bentley's article against the freethinkers, has: "Le la Bruière Anglois je veux dire M. R. Steele me fourniroit des traits excellens pour tracer le Portrait des personnes dont il est ici question." The *Tatler* (nos. 3, 12 and 85) is then cited in support.

In that age of solid reading and attention to the education of women, the *Ladies' Library* excited a tremendous interest, most journals devoting reviews to it[1]. The *Journal Littéraire* for 1717 speaks of *le fameux Chevalier Steele* in a very favourable review of the French translation of this work. The *Boekzaal* for the same year says in its review: "That renowned gentleman Mr Steele, an ardent supporter of the present Government in Great Britain, is named as the editor of this work. His name will not cause it to decline in our estimation...."

As for Addison, his personality and political preferment

[1] Cp. *Nouv. de la Rép. des Let.* Sept.–Oct. 1716.

were exciting the liveliest attention, in addition to his fame as a writer. Le Clerc, in 1717[1], wrote as follows:

Le traducteur qui n'avoit point nommé l'auteur des meilleurs Discours, qui soient dans ces Volumes & à la fin desquels on voit les Lettres du nom d'une des muses, je veux dire de *C.L.I.O.*, n'a pas fait difficulté de le nommer dans sa Préface. Comme toute l'Angleterre le savoit déjà & que cela étoit passé il y avoit longtems en Hollande, il n'étoit guère possible de le cacher. Outre cela ces Discours seront autant d'honneur à l'Illustre Mr Addison présentement Secrétaire d'Etat à Londres, hors de la Grande Bretagne qu'ils lui en ont fait dans cette île. Il y a des lieux où l'on s'imagine que l'étude des Belles-Lettres est obstacle à la Prudence & que les Gens Savans sont aussi peu propres à servir l'Etat; que ceux qui n'ont point d'étude, à enseigner les Sciences, qu'ils ne savent pas. On croit que la portion de Bonssens qu'on a reçue de la Nature, cultivée par quelque Expérience sans aucun savoir, est suffisante pour remplir dignement & avec succès les plus grands Emplois...mais je suis persuadé qu'un homme qui a joint à l'Etude de Belles Lettres le soin de cultiver son Jugement par la connoissance des choses & non des mots seul & qui a aussi fréquenté le Monde peut mieux servir l'Etat, qu'un homme, qui ne sait rien....Cette petite digression n'est que pour applaudir au choix de sa majesté Britannique Le Roi George dans la personne de Mr Addison pour Secrétaire d'Etat.

The *Nouvelles de la République des Lettres*[2], reviewing vol. III of the *Spectator*, has:

Ce troisième volume du Spectateur contient soixante & dix Discours qui plairont sans doute à tous ceux qui ont goûté les précédens & par conséquent, à un très grand nombre de personnes.....
Le traducteur (qui a été long-tems en Angleterre)[3] nous aprend que c'est l'Illustre Mr Addison qui s'est élevé par son mérite jusques à l'importante charge de Secrétaire d'Etat, qui est l'Auteur...

of the numbers marked *C.L.I.O.* Four years[4] previously the London news in the *Journal Littéraire* announced: "C'est assez la mode chez nous depuis quelque tems d'employer des Poëtes & des beaux Esprits dans des Postes publics," and

---

[1] *Biblioth. Anc. et Mod.* vol. VIII.   [2] Jan.–Feb. 1718.
[3] Le Clerc, *Biblioth. Anc. et Mod.* vol. VIII, 1717.
[4] May–June, 1714.

the names of Prior, Rowe, Philips, Fenton, Harrison and Addison are instanced. In fact nothing among all the praiseworthy English practices impressed minds on the continent more deeply than the support and honour accorded to scholars and literary men; and it cannot be denied that in this respect that age came up to the best traditions of what was implied in the proudly-claimed title of "Augustan." The outstanding examples were Addison and Newton, the latter, as Holberg and Voltaire tell in admiration, being laid to rest with the state of a king. "The Arts and Sciences must not be patronless," Shaftesbury had said with decision[1]. But the magnificent support of the general reading public supplied whatever deficiencies there may have been in state and private patronage and similarly impressed foreigners. The *Spectator* again was an outstanding example, and also Pope's Homer. The *Journal Littéraire*'s[2] London correspondent, announcing this translation, says: "Sur un Catalogue publié le 1 mai, on voit déjà des souscriptions pour plus de 2000 Guinées. Vous voyez que la réputation d'homme d'esprit et de bon auteur est bonne à quelque chose en Angleterre." The review, in 1716, of this translation opens with an account of the imposing list of subscribers and the large amount of money concerned in the enterprise which, *mirabile dictu*, is going to benefit the author. The reviewer, who is probably Van Effen, exclaims in wonder and admiration: "un tel encouragement est assez rare dans tous les endroits où l'on estime les Belles Lettres & l'on peut douter auquel il fait le plus d'honneur, ou à Mr Pope, ou à la Nation Angloise." These were some of the things which captured the imagination of foreigners and stimulated their curiosity very strongly. Addison's *Travels* was re-edited and published at the Hague *chez* Henry Scheurleer, who says in the dedication:

If I mistake not this was the first Piece which the ingenious Mr Addison published and whereby He deservedly purchased the Character of a Polite and Learned Gentleman. He has since made publick several other things, some of which have been translated into French, that have gained him the reputation of an extraordinary genius with all persons of Taste and good Sense on this side of the Water....

[1] *Advice to an Author.*   [2] May–June, 1714.

In every department of literature, including that of scholarly guide books for the "Grand tour," Addison, it seems, was considered pre-eminent.

But perhaps the summit of Addison's continental fame was achieved with his *Cato*. It had indeed been translated into French before the *Spectator* and was creating no little controversy. In 1713 T. Johnson had published it *in English* at the Hague. It became the one play to which Anglophiles pinned their faith in the ability of Englishmen to write a proper play, and was made a sort of test case in the lively dispute for literary pre-eminence between England and France—a dispute which had now taken the place of the battle between the Ancients and Moderns. In 1714[1] the *Histoire Critique de la République des Lettres* takes up the cudgels for Addison and states the case clearly:

M. Armand du Bordieu travaille à une traduction Françoise en vers de Caton, Tragédie Angloise de M. Adison. Vous aurez apparemment vû sa traduction en prose, qu'on attribue à Mr Boyer. Je ne sais si l'une ou l'autre de ces Versions sera suffisante pour convaincre M. Dacier que les Anglois sont capables de faire de bonnes Tragédies. Vous savez sans doute le jugement que le Grammairien François a porté de toute la Nation Angloise dans la Préface de la nouvelle Edition des Œuvres de Horace. Il ne se contente pas de condamner tout ce que les Anglois ont fait jusqu'à présent dans ce genre de Poësie. Devenu Critique inspiré, il prophétise que l'on ne doit attendre de l'Angleterre ni grandes préceptes ni grands exemples pour la Tragédie, dont elle est en possession de violer les Loix des plus fondamentales. Mais, de peur qu'on ne le mette au nombre de ces Enthousiastes dont le cerveau n'étoit pas toujours bien réglé, il nous donne deux raisons dont il appuye cet Oracle si mortifiant pour toute la Nation; soit, dit-il, que la coutume ait prévalu, ou que le Poëte Anglois ait naturellement l'esprit trop tragique pour s'assujettir à la sage régularité des Grecs & des Romains: nam spirans tragicum, nimis infeliciter audet.

.Je ne vous enverrai pas présentement une longue réponse à ce jugement injurieux. J'espère que M. Adison en nous donnant Scipion, autre Tragédie qu'il prépare pour le Public, châtiera ce hardi Censeur comme il le mérite. En attendant notez que la première de ses raisons ne vaut rien, pour juger de l'avenir.

---

[1] Vol. v, p. 381.

Custom may change in England, as in other countries where Tragedy has been improperly cultivated, and as for the second reason, "on espère que Mr Dacier & ses compatriotes reconnoissent présentement que toute la Nation Angloise ne pousse pas toujours le tragique aussi loin qu'il pourroit aller & que la pitié & l'humeur pacifique s'emparent quelquefois de leurs esprits." Ever since Bernard (in the *Nouvelles de la République des Lettres*), J. F. Cramer, and others had defended Germanic culture against the slanders of father Bouhours, the journalists of Holland had taken it upon themselves to rebuke Gallic presumption. The matter was soon carried further. The news from Paris in the *Journal Littéraire*, 1715 (p. 204), runs:

Nous avons une autre Pièce de Théâtre qui est assez estimée; c'est Caton d'Utique, Tragédie par M. Deschamps (on trouvera bientôt cette Pièce chez T. Johnson avec un parallèle de la Pièce Angloise de M. Addison avec celle-ci & un examen de toutes les deux). Nous préférons cette Pièce de beaucoup à celle que M. Addison, Poëte Anglois, a faite depuis peu sur le même sujet. M. l'Abbé Abeille a aussi pris le même sujet pour une Tragédie qu'on dit être fort belle; mais il ne la veut pas donner au Public. Nous croyons généralement qu'il n'y a aucune Nation qui puisse comparer son Théâtre & ses Pièces Dramatiques avec les nôtres. Les Anglois se croyent généralement autant au-dessus de nous à cet égard, que nous nous croyons au-dessus d'eux & des autres nations. Il y a sans doute de la prévention de part & d'autre; mais, il y a aussi des Régles dont on pourroit aisément convenir & par lesquelles on pourroit décider cette question. On nous a donné ici depuis peu la Traduction d'un Livre Anglois, écrit sur ce sujet, il y a 20 ans, par un Théologien nommé Collier, qui est fort peu favorable aux Poëtes de la Nation....Mais on dit que les Poëtes Anglois ne reconnoissent pas pour Juge compétent ce Théologien outré, qui s'est fait une affaire de ramasser toutes les ordures de leur Théâtre dans le dessein de le décrier.

From the Hague the literary news[1] is: "Il a aussi imprimé Caton d'Utique par M. Deschamps...," at the end of which is "un excellent parallèle entre le Caton Anglois de M. Addison & celui-ci, où l'on fait voir par un bel examen des deux pièces selon les règles du Poëme Dramatique

---

[1] *Jour. Lit.* 1715, p. 510.

combien cette Tragédie de M. Deschamps est préférable à celle de M. Addison."

In August of the same year the *Boekzaal* has a similar announcement of the parallel between Deschamps's play and *Cato* "made in English by Mr Addison and translated into French and Dutch. In this comparison, which is written with much judgment and a great knowledge of the art of the theatre, it is demonstrated that the French *Cato* of Mr Deschamps is to be ranked far above that of Mr Addison." No further comment is made.

The nature of this *parallèle* between the two *Catos* may be understood from the following:

If he [Dacier] had examined into the English genius he would be convinced that it is very tragical and that there is perhaps no Nation more capable to bring the terrible pieces of the Greeks on the stage. Moreover the English tongue hath a Force, a Copiousness, a Freedom agreeable to the Stage. I must own that the English restrain a little their fiery Imagination by Rules, that they don't allow [*sic*] themselves any warm metaphors, that they fall in certain low actions which the Greek poets have enough avoided; that they ruin themselves by Romantick Ideas. If they come to correct these faults (and they will) the English stage will equal the French. It hath not yet equalled it, allow me to say it: allow me also to prove it by a Parallel of Mr Addison's *Cato* with Mr Des Champs'[1].

Then follows a lengthy comparison not to the advantage of the English work. Sewell, who had already published *Observations upon "Cato,"* returned to the attack in 1716. But the chief contribution to this quarrel was made by Van Effen[2] in the *Journal Littéraire* in 1717. His "Dis-

---

[1] Anon. English Translation, London, 1716.

[2] This important dissertation is ascribed to the refugee journalist de la Roche by Mr C. Haines in his essay on *Shakespeare in France* (London, 1925). M. de la Roche is not known to have had any connection with the *Journ. Lit.* and Van Effen, one of its leading editors, was well informed and well equipped for writing an article of this kind. The first piece of literary correspondence of any length to the *Journ. Lit.* from London coincides with Van Effen's visit there, and from the close correspondence of many remarks as well as of style we may conclude that the new London correspondent is also the writer of the dissertation. Again, on considerations of style and opinion, as in Van Effen's known work, we agree with Bisschop that the dissertation may safely be ascribed to him. In the *Hollandsche Spectator*, too, some views of the writer of the dissertation reappear. Furthermore, the

sertation sur la Poësie Angloise" is "of paramount importance for the spread of English literature" upon which it remained "virtually the only source of detailed information[1]" until Voltaire's *Lettres*. It approaches its subject from the point of view of the fast developing *querelle*. "Les deux nations qui peuvent avec le plus de droit s'arroger le premier rang dans les Sciences & dans les Belles Lettres sont sans doute l'Angloise & la Françoise, et il se rencontre que les mêmes peuples sont justement ceux qui ont le plus profond mépris pour tous les étrangers." But these two nations themselves are in violent rivalry in every department and it is necessary that one should be neither French nor English to be able to judge "sainement de cette dispute." Speaking generally, the writer should say that the English are superior "sur ce qu'il y a dans les Sciences de plus grave & de plus utile," and the French in the things "agréable" and "brillant."

These two peoples profess a sovereign contempt for each other, and it must be said at once that the French have done "le plus grand tort du monde de mépriser les productions du génie Anglois, qui a brillé dans tous les genres d'écrire tant en prose qu'en vers." "Le feu de l'imagination brille autant chez eux que chez le Peuple du Monde qui se distingue le plus à cet égard," and if "c'est dommage que ce feu ne respecte pas toujours les règles que le bon sens lui prescrit," "l'Esprit des Anglois est apparement aussi ennemi de l'Esclavage que leur cœur & ils attachent une idée odieuse à tout ce qui ressemble à la Contrainte." Then there is the *Spectator* "où les plus beaux esprits d'Angleterre ont employé toutes les forces de leurs réflexions avec toute la déli-

writer expressly states that he is a disinterested party, neither a Frenchman nor an Englishman, being free from the suspicion of partiality. The sidelong glances at Dutch literature betray a Dutchman rather than a French refugee in England, and the parallel drawn between Shakespeare and Vondel is in perfect keeping with Van Effen's views on Vondel as an untutored romantic genius. To Van Effen is due the pleasant distinction of having effected, as Professor Robertson says of this dissertation, "the first real introduction of the English poet (Shakespeare) to the continent."

[1] Prof. J. G. Robertson, *Mod. Lang. Rev.* vol. I; e.g. the translator of *Spectator*, vol. III into French referred his readers to this "très judicieuse" article for fuller information hoping that the able writer would continue his account.

catesse du stile & tout le feu de l'imagination. Le *Tatler* ou *Babillard* vient de la même source, & il n'est inférieur en rien à cet Ouvrage admirable, qui a gardé une grande partie de ses grâces & de sa beauté dans la traduction Françoise." Then Van Effen gives an account of English style which is of great interest in the mouth of the reformer of Dutch prose, chief founder of the modern style in Holland.

Les meilleurs Ecrivains Anglois, qui ont écrit dans les autres âges, uniquement occupez des choses, ne se mettoient guère en peine de polir le stile. Par là ils tomboient dans des périodes d'une longueur fatigante, évitées avec tant de soin par ceux qui écrivent bien en France; les auteurs modernes dont je viens de parler, ou guidez par le goût des François ou plutôt par la Raison même, se sont gardez de donner dans un pareil défait & leurs Ouvrages sont si beaux & si achevez de toutes les manières, ils sont si variez du côté du stile & du côté du sujet qu'on peut avancer que les François n'ont rien à opposer à cette production qui puisse la valoir en tout. On peut croire que la Poësie Angloise aura bientôt le même sort que la Prose, & que la correction y sera jointe à la force de l'expression & au feu des pensées.

As to their language,

jamais Langue ne fut moins scrupuleuse à adopter des expressions étrangères; elle s'approprie non seulement des mots, mais des tours de phrases, tout ce qui est expressif & propre à abréger le discours obtient d'abord droit de bourgeoisie chez elle. Cette grande richesse ne contente pas encore l'amour des Anglois pour l'énergie, & pour la laconicité; ils sont aussi hardis dans leurs écrits que dans leurs combats.

Van Effen then deals separately with poetry, satirical and epic, comedy and tragedy. The English profess to despise the French, and not entirely without reason, for slavishness to rules; and, though they themselves take unwarranted liberties with rhymes, their blank verse is worthy of imitation by the French. On the other hand, English poetry has developed under the guidance of French, but the English either vehemently deny their debts or disguise their borrowings. They are "trop orgueilleux pour s'avoüer imitateurs des François," but nevertheless "ne laisseront point de les imiter dans ce qu'ils seront forcé à reconnoître bon &

raisonnable"; while "la langue Françoise commence à être de plus en plus en vogue dans ces Royaumes."

With their extreme and blind prejudice against the French "ils ont encore trop d'orgueil pour reconnoître leur larcin" from French drama.

Jamais ces pièces ne sont traduites; elles sont toujours faites par tel ou tel. Il est bien vrai qu'on insinue quelquefois dans la Préface que le sujet vient de France, mais on ne daigne pas seulement nommer l'Auteur à qui on en est redevable. Ils voudroient faire croire qu'ils en agissent à peu près avec ces petits Poëtes François, comme un maître qui s'exerce sur un sujet qu'un écolier a traité, & qui n'a d'autre dessein que de lui faire voir comment il falloit s'y prendre pour réussir. Quelques-uns de ces messieurs se contentent de piller l'intrigue d'un Ouvrage François, & d'y en ajouter une seconde de leur propre invention pour paroître du moins fécond à multiplier les sujets de leurs pièces. C'est comme en agit M. Dryden, dans sa Comédie apellé *Le Chevalier Gâte-tout* ou *La Fausse Innocence*; ce sont deux Comédies en une dont la moitié est à fort peu de chose près l'Etourdi de Molière....Rarement se contentent-ils de faire valoir par leur génie un sujet simple & unique, ils semblent plutôt vouloir soutenir leur génie par la variété d'actions & de pensées qu'un double ou un triple sujet peut fournir. On diroit que cette pauvreté véritable leur paroisse une richesse d'imagination; c'est ce qu'ils font voir dans les Pièces qu'ils copient, ou du moins qu'ils imitent des François....Un bon nombre d'autres pièces qui sont des inventions des Anglois sont encore pleines de morceaux empruntez des François; & ce qu'il y a de plus merveilleux dans cette affaire, c'est que souvent ces Plagiaires ne s'occupent dans leurs prologues qu'à déchirer ceux qu'ils ont pillés, & à les traiter d'Arlequins ou de Scaramouches; comme si ceux-ci ne fussent que des bouffons, & les Anglois des comiques très sérieux & très morales. Ils considèrent ces vols à peu près comme s'ils étoient faits dans le Païs-ennemi; mais il faut avouer que les Poëtes sont moins humains en Angleterre que les Brigands qui y volent sur les routes & qui se contentent de détrousser les passans sans les maltraiter.

In tragedy, Dryden and the rest of them are equally "grands plagiaires," and altogether this outrageous English conduct disgusted and amazed Van Effen, who returns to the point in his other writings. We have seen how he has treated the subject of plagiarism and imitation especially in the *Baga-*

telle and in the *Hollandsche Spectator*. In no. 69 of the latter, his predecessor, the Spectator, is again accused on this score. "If he should be forced to make them[1] restitution of everything he has taken from them, one may be assured that it would make a considerable gap in his work. It must nevertheless be said to his honour that these thefts are disguised with more adroitness than those of most of his countrymen[2]." The French themselves are great pillagers of the Italians, largely because Italian is scarcely known in France and the risk of discovery is small.

The piracy of the English writers upon the French will probably have a similar origin. For it is known that the language of the latter is not at all common among the former, and that, through a prejudice springing from inborn hatred and contempt, French writings are condemned without examination by the general body of the Great Britannic nation and rejected as being more flowers than fruits and as containing more wind than weight. To remove such plagiarism from the danger of the suspicion of the multitude, these writers not infrequently employ one of the most malicious subterfuges that can be imagined. In the preface of a play, which they sometimes piece together from two or three French ones, they do not stop at showing the utmost contempt not only for French poets, but what is more, for those whom they are actually robbing.

A paraphrase of some comments in the *Journal Littéraire* then follows and Van Effen resumes:

I must nevertheless admit that all the plagiarists among that sensible nation are not equally wanton. Some of them take pleasure in palpably imitating a French piece from beginning to end and adapting the whole matter of it to their national customs, without doing the original writer the honour of even naming him. I even know an almost literal translation in English[3] of one of the most excellent plays of Racine which the translator, without mentioning anything of this so famous man, coolly claims as his own work and as such puts it into the hands of his countrymen. Such ill-treatment could make one think that English authors regard their hated neighbours as born enemies, and without de-

---

[1] The French.

[2] Cp. *Bagat.* no. xxvii, where he excuses his borrowing with: "Ce n'est qu'user de représailles...." *Vide* chap. iv.

[3] *The Distressed Mother* (Ambrose Philips). Steele, in the preface, speaks of it as an ideal compound of French correctness and English fire.

claring war, claim to themselves a natural right to practise piracy on them.

And nowhere was this pilfering more rife than in the Drama, in which Van Effen, judging "sans passion & par connoissance de cause," considers: "il faut avouer que les François l'emportent sur les Anglois à plusieurs égards." "Ce n'est pas faire une injustice aux Anglois que de soutenir qu'ils ignorent absolument l'art dont nous venons de donner une idée abrégée. L'intrigue fait chez eux toute l'essence de la Comédie & le caractère y est pour la plupart absolument négligé." This remark touches a general weakness of English art for story-telling. Their comic dramatists from Beaumont and Fletcher and Ben Jonson to Congreve, while not inferior to most of the French, are none of them equal to Molière. And since Charles II the English stage has been ruined by incredibly low taste and obscenity as well as shameless plagiarism. A vivid sketch then follows:

Au lieu de la fine plaisanterie & de la force comique, il ne règne dans la plupart des pièces Angloises qu'une licence débordée; les paroles les plus obscènes & les actions les plus infâmes s'offrent sur le Théâtre Anglois à tout moment aux yeux & aux oreilles; de sorte qu'il paroît plutôt qu'on veuille reveiller le goût brutal des Laquais & des Femmes masquées que satisfaire à la délicatesse & aux bon-sens des honnêtes gens de l'un & de l'autre sexe. Non seulement les acteurs prononcent les discours les moins modestes mais les actrices, même lorsqu'elles joüent le rôle d'une honnête Femme, sont forcées à dire des équivoques si grossières qu'à peine un débauché les pardonneroit à une Femme, à qui il pardonne de renoncer essentiellement à la pudeur. A peine ces belles expressions sont elles lâchées, qu'on en reconnoît le prix par des applaudissemens & des cris qui font trembler toute la maison; les Laquais, qui sont en Angleterre la plus vive image de l'insolence donnent le signal; quelquefois leurs maîtres les suivent & ne se font pas une honte d'augmenter le bruit affreux que ces Canailles ont commencé si mal à propos. On peut s'imaginer dans quelle situation peuvent être alors les Femmes sages....

Some incidents from various plays are then cited. Happily there were signs of improvement:

Le Spectateur qui a travaillé avec autant de génie & de succès à réformer le ridicule de ses concitoyens n'a pas manqué de dépendre avec leurs propres couleurs, des infamies si publiques & si pernicieuses, mais il n'a pas réüssi à faire revenir les Auteurs d'un égarement si scandaleux[1]: ils craignent apparemment de diminuer le nombre des spectateurs en donner plus de mérite aux spectacles; mais ils devroient bannir cette crainte mercenaire & servile....

Van Effen finds that the comedies ignore poetic justice which, in respect of tragedy at least, he properly understood to mean "les malheurs qui suivent la Vertu même, si elle ne précautionne pas contre certaines foiblesses." When he examines *Sir Fopling Flutter* in the first class, we will not stop to follow his inevitable analysis: but it is somewhat strange that he should have been blind to Shakespeare's fine use of poetic justice in *Hamlet* and *Othello*, which are examined at length. Nevertheless, the discussion of over ten pages devoted to Shakespeare is highly interesting for this time—1717, sixteen years before Voltaire's. By way of introduction, there is a good restatement of the principles of dramatic construction which are well known in England, says the writer, for "les Savans de la Grande Bretagne estiment infiniment plus les Anciens que ne font les François" and "la Poëtique d'Aristote est fort respectée chez eux aussi bien que les Euripides & les Sophocles." Nevertheless, English dramatists have contrived to flout all classical precedent.

Sur ce pied-là ce ne sont point des Tragédies que les pièces de Théâtre faites par *Shakespear* que la plupart des Anglois regardent encore comme le plus admirable écrivain dans ce genre-là, & à qui dans tous les prologues de ceux qui l'ont suivi, on dresse des autels comme à un Dieu du Théâtre: on convient bien qu'il n'a pas observé les règles, mais on le lui pardonne, comme à un génie au-dessus des règles, & qui n'en avoit que faire pour frapper & pour enlever le Spectateur. Ils ont tort & ils ne croyent pas eux-mêmes ce qu'ils disent. Cet Auteur avoit à coup sûr du génie infiniment, comme il écrivoit pour ainsi dire à tout hazard; il attrapoit de tems en tems des traits inimitables, mais souvent— ils sont accompagnés de choses si peu nobles, qu'on peut douter si dans ses écrits la bassesse relève le sublime, ou si c'est le sublime qui fait sentir plus fortement la bassesse.

---

[1] Cp. *Holl. Spect.* no. 147: "What pains has the English Socrates not taken to make play-acting more civilized and cultured...."

And in this remark we are very near the truth. But Van Effen's French classical taste had received too severe a shock not to have reacted and retaliated in sharp criticism. Of the presumptuous freedoms Shakespeare allowed himself, none was more objectionable to Van Effen than the mixture of pathos and pleasantry. The grave-diggers' scene, particularly, was offensive in this way. The diggers with their "combat de quolibets" "chantant une chanson des plus bouffonnés & même des plus libertines," the feigned madness of Hamlet and other things, "remplissent cet Ouvrage de tant de sottises nécessaires au projet, que les larmes sont plus rare parmi les Spectateurs que les éclats de rire." "Ce qui plaît le plus au parterre, c'est l'ombre du vieux Hamlet," and many of his pieces are filled with "pareilles puérilitez" to please the "peuple de son tems apparement de ces sottes fantaisies[1]." At the same time he admits that "le discours qu'on entend faire ici à l'ombre de Hamlet est extrêmement fort énergique aussi bien que les réponses de son Fils."

He sums up by saying "ce qu'il y a de bon, & même d'excellent, dans cet Ouvrage est noyé dans un nombre infini de fadaises & le tout paroît plutôt la production d'un cerveau déréglé que d'un génie du premier ordre." But *Hamlet* is "plus supportable" than *Richard III*. From this play he proceeds to "un de ses plus fameux Ouvrages intitulé Othello," of which the story is told to illustrate Shakespeare's horrible practice of making people's blood run cold. He fails to understand, too, how the heroine is allowed to make such a long speech on her deathbed. It is noticeable that Voltaire[2] likewise mentions this point as an incongruity, as he also complains of the grave-diggers' singing "vaude-

---

[1] Van Effen was equally unsympathetic to this sort of thing in Art as in Life. In no. xci of the *Bagatelle*, he is proud of the high level of intelligence of his countrymen, saying: "Heureusement notre Patrie est le Pays de l'Univers où toutes les opinions superstitieuses sont le moins de ravage.... On n'y voit, ni Spectres, ni apparitions, ni Enchantements, parce que personne n'y ajoute foi: on n'y brûle jamais de Sorciers parce que les Petites maisons y sont destinées à ceux qui ont perdu la raison." Holland fortunately had its compensations for this sober rationalism, e.g., by being rid of the demon of witch-burning long before this devilish practice was discontinued in England or Germany.   [2] *Lettres sur les Anglois.*

ville," while *Hamlet* and *Othello* are the very pieces selected by him for closer analysis. Shakespeare is the Vondel of the English, both "modèles de toutes les espèces de beautez & de défauts: La plupart des Anglois pourtant sont résolus de ne rien rabattre de l'estime exorbitante qu'ils ont conçuë pour leur Héros, & de lui savoir gré de ses défauts, au lieu de se contenter de les pardonner à la grossièreté de son âge & à son manque de savoir." Van Effen, it is clear, writes as an eye-witness, and seems to have been very much interested in the English theatrical practice and drama. In two good papers[1] of the *Hollandsche Spectator* he gives his countrymen some wholesome advice on these matters and wishes them to learn some things from the English.

To what is it due that at Paris and in London so many new pieces of various kinds appear, which attract inhabitants as well as foreigners to the theatre in veritable floods? The chief reason for this is that several consecutive shows are given for the benefit of the writers, whereby it not infrequently happens that such a new play, if it should find favour with the public, is worth five or six thousand guilders to the author[2]. Would it be impossible to introduce the same practice among us? And may it not well be expected to have a similar result? In my opinion, at least, no fitter measure could be devised to excite and encourage poetic spirits. There honour and profit lend each other a hand to spur on the poetic temper in the most efficacious manner....

In England actors were held in much higher esteem than in Holland, and Van Effen puts in a good word for Dutch actors, asking people of social standing to take more notice of them.

But to give the theatre its most efficacious support, there is still another measure which I know was formerly put into operation in London. To the English Spectator, Mr Steele, a considerable annual salary was given to take upon himself the management of the Theatre Royal under his absolute authority. To his judgment compositions were submitted before they were played, in order that he might change whatever they might contain that was dangerous to morals. It was that wise writer himself who

---

[1] Nos. 27, 28.
[2] Perhaps as many pounds sterling, at present-day values.

allotted the parts according to the nature and talent of every player, to whom he gave lessons and instructions to which they adapted themselves, thereby enabling their natural ability to shine out with increased brilliance. The same expedient could be introduced here with a great deal of good effect and in case such a task were offered to one of my best friends(?) upon reasonable conditions, I have no doubt that he would accept it, and I am assured that he would employ such wise and infallible measures that within six years our theatre would not be inferior to any in Europe....

Furthermore, with his usual insight he advocated a national domestic drama.

Addressing himself to the actors, he says, "In foreign countries I have found the most famous actors to be people of schooled minds, of whom many were able to compose a pleasant and regularly constructed theatrical piece themselves."

In *Hollandsche Spectator*, no. 174 a correspondent recommends that playwrights add prologues and epilogues to their pieces "in imitation of many English plays," so that any false impressions may be duly corrected. The subject he is discussing happens to be that of theatrical suicide, and more particularly *à propos* of Addison's *Cato*. Van Effen replies, saying that he agrees with his correspondent in regarding such a display of suicide as objectionable unless the writer can, by some master-stroke, devise means "whereby the emotions may be armed against so destructive an impression." And this, we may be sure, Van Effen believed Addison to have accomplished. In him, our critic believed ("that excellent tragedy entitled Cato" we read in *Hollandsche Spectator*[1]), lay the promise of a great future for the English stage. Him he did not hesitate "de mettre en parallèle avec tout ce que cet âge a produit de plus excellent, tant pour les vers que pour la prose," as we read in the *Journal Littéraire*. And Van Effen's view became the conventional one. Well on in the century it was still considered that, as Moreau de Brasey expressed it, Addison "dans son

---

[1] No. 140.

admirable Cato" had perfected what "un certain Shakespeare" had begun. Van Effen continues:

A l'égard de M. Addison, les Etrangers peuvent juger de son génie par les volumes qu'on a déjà publiés en François du Spectateur; mais nous ne sçaurions lui refuser les plus grands Éloges, quand il n'auroit fait de sa vie, que son *Caton*. Nous ne savons pas comment dans un de nos Journaux on a glissé parmi les Nouvelles Littéraires de la Haye des louanges excessives pour le Caton François & très injurieuses à la pièce de M. Addison. Nous sommes si éloignés de les approuver que nous croyons que le parallèle que les François ont fait de ces deux Ouvrages, égale tous les mépris injustes que les Anglois de tous les âges ont fait éclater contre les François. Ce n'est pas une exagération; il ne se peut rien de plus outrageant que de mettre au-dessus d'un Ouvrage des plus parfaits que la Nation Angloise ait produit, une pièce qui ne peut pas seulement aller de pair avec le plus foible Ouvrage de Pradon.

Cela s'apelle aller plus loin que M. Dacier, qui par une présomption digne de lui a décidé, qu'il ne falloit attendre rien de bon des Anglois dans le Genre dramatique. On verroit bientôt le contraire si dans ce tems si fécond en beaux Esprits Anglois, un Protecteur des muses vouloit établir une Académie, telle qu'on voit en France, arbitre du langage, & juge des pièces d'Esprit.

Strong language this, it may be said, but Van Effen could always command it whenever his hero, Addison, came up for discussion.

Addison was equally an ornament to English verse. The account of English poetry concludes:

J'aurois tort d'oublier ici un Poëme de M. *Addison* qu'il a intitulé *the Campaign*. Ce n'est pas proprement un Poëme Épique dans les formes mais c'est un Ouvrage incomparable, en vers héroïques par lequel l'auteur célèbre avec toute la magnificence possible l'heureuse campagne de Hogstet, & les grandes actions du Héros Anglois, qui mit par là le fondement à cette haute réputation qu'il a acquise dans toute l'Europe. On peut dire qu'il ne manque rien dans cette pièce, & que M. *Addison* soutenu par la beauté de sujet, y est autant au-dessus de M. Addison, qu'il est supérieur dans toutes ses autres pièces, à la plupart des autres Poëtes de quelque nation qu'ils puissent être. Je ne crois pas donner à cet auteur un éloge outré, en lui osant promettre que si les belles Lettres ne tombent pas entièrement dans le mépris en Angleterre, cet Ouvrage sera un monument plus illustre & plus durable de la gloire de mylord *Marlbourg* que le Palais de Blenheim, que le Parlement lui a fait bâtir, pour transmettre à la postérité les faits Héroïques de ce Héros, & la reconnoissance de sa Nation.

Wherever Addison and his work are mentioned, Van Effen prostrates himself. Addison was the one literary personality who completely inspired reverence. Did Van Effen not say: "Nature is not liberal of Addisons[1]"? Indeed, the world had not to wait for Macaulay to make an ardent admiration for Addison the occasion for reducing Steele to a mere foil. Van Effen had fully done this. Taking Steele's words with cruel literalness, the *Journal Littéraire*, as we have seen, ascribed all the best things in the *Tatler* and in the *Spectator* to Addison. In 1717 the same journal writes in a review of the *Ladies' Library*: "Tout le monde sait qu'il a composé plusieurs pièces de Théâtre dans lesquelles il a plus consulté le goût du parterre Anglois que les Règles de sagesse & de la modestie." Steele had indeed carried his humility too far in his "confessions." We have seen how, in the review of the first volume of the *Spectator*, Steele was reproved in the *Journal Littéraire* for his remark about Dutch women, and we may be sure that Van Effen would not have relished his other contemptuous references to the Dutch. The few occasional criticisms of the *Spectator* for plagiarism and flippancy are probably meant for Steele who, of course, was the Spectator, being the sole and responsible editor. We are now fully prepared for the following account with which Van Effen opens his *Hollandsche Spectator* on August 20, 1731:

The English work which I have determined not to translate but to imitate in my mother tongue owes its first origins to a noble friendship. Mr Steele found himself by his own loose conduct as well as through the extravagance of a careless housewife in a very great embarrassment, from which he could not possibly be rescued by any small assistance. The renowned Mr Addison, his bosom friend, furnished with as many virtues as gifts of mind, was too tenderhearted and accommodating to allow the man to pine away and perish in the unhappy situation into which he had

[1] *Holl. Spect.* no. 1.

precipitated himself partly through his own weakness. Love for the unfortunate one sharpened his wits and caused him to devise a measure which would provide his friend with sufficient and regular support. What did he contrive? He roused some other fine wits, inspired them with the sympathy he felt for the clever Steele, persuaded them to the determination of supporting him actively, not by means of the purse, the which according to the common fate of the learned would have been of but little avail, but by the fine products of their minds. To carry this into execution these gentlemen daily gathered together with the object of their sympathy. Each brought with him some fruits of his genius, some entertaining, and others serious, yet all of them adapted to the taste of their fellow-citizens. They were divided into several letters as if written from different quarters and Coffee-houses in London, and so published under the title of the *Tatler*. That work immediately created an incredible sensation and brought Mr Steele, to whom alone the honour and benefit of the same were left, as much profit as fame.

After some time the same society then proceeded to produce the *Spectator*. We do not know whence Van Effen derived his information, but he appears to have made the *Spectator* Club into another *Journal Littéraire* Club, where Steele was but "gentleman-usher" in reality.

Another exceedingly interesting feature of the *Dissertation* is the discussion of Milton. A full eight-page summary of *Paradise Lost* is given. Milton is considered supreme among the moderns with his "chef-d'œuvre des Anglois en matière d'Epopée." As for the French, they "entendent mieux les règles de l'Epopée qu'ils savent les mettre en pratique & qu'ils critiquent très-bien les Anciens, mais qu'ils ne les égalent pas." *Paradise Lost* is altogether an extraordinary poem in which the poet astonishes one by the "manière heureuse dont il a exécuté un dessein si téméraire & si inconcevable." The English make a great fuss of it and "l'on doit convenir qu'à prendre ce Poëme en général, il mérite l'estime & l'admiration dont il a été toujours honoré."

When we are told that the poem contains "un grand nombre d'heureuses imitations d'Homère & de Virgile," we suspect that the critic has been reading Addison. It is too much to expect, of course, that Van Effen should have been entirely converted. He, not unreasonably, finds Milton *trop Théologien*, suspects his orthodoxy, and considers him "trop amateur du merveilleux & trop Poëte dans les combats entre les bons & les mauvais Anges"; while he agrees with Addison in finding that "le merveilleux qu'on en peut tirer ne sauvoit que orner un Poëme par des discours ouides de sens, & qui n'excitent pas la moindre notion dans l'Esprit." We feel, however, that the critic is thinking of Milton when in his criticism of the English language he continues:

point de bornes pour la hardiesse de leurs métaphores, sans que par là ils s'attirent la moindre critique, pourvu que la grandeur du sens réponde à la magnificence des paroles & qu'on ne s'élève pas sur des riens. On ne sait pas trop bien de quelle manière accorder ce goût de la Nation avec son admiration constante pour les Anciens, & sur tout pour Homère où les Métaphores sont aussi rares que les comparaisons y sont fréquentes....La diction de la Poësie doit surprendre l'imagination, toucher & remplir le cœur & l'esprit, par conséquent elle ne sauroit être trop hardie, pourvu qu'elle ne s'écarte point de la clarté & du bon sens....

Indeed, "point de belle Poësie sans la hardiesse," from lack of which the French suffer. With this we should compare *Bagatelle*, no. LI, where Van Effen expresses Addisonian, unconventional views on poetry. "Nous sommes trop ennemis du naturel. Nous...voulons à l'esprit de l'homme & non pas à son imagination. Nous...formons ce qu'on appelle des pensées, c'est-à-dire de petites idées métaphysiques & sententieuses."

To the *Faerie Queene* a paragraph is devoted. It is a torso of a projected epic, which those who understand the "vieux langage" of the poem say is equal to that which "tous les Auteurs ont fait de plus digne d'Admiration," and this remark gives an interesting sidelight on English opinion at a time when Spenser appears to have been neglected.

In burlesque the English are perhaps superior to the French, Samuel Butler surpassing Scarron, but "dans les pièces galantes," the English "ressemblent assez aux Hollandois" in being nowhere. This is not due to lack of wit, of which the English have probably more than any other nation in Europe, but merely lack of natural gallantry, "soit par raison, soit par une rudesse naturelle." The latter appeared to Van Effen to be a prominent constituent of the English character. With regard to women, the Englishman had so little gallantry that "les sentiments qu'il a pour une Maîtresse sont de la même nature que ceux qu'il a pour le vin[1]." Burnet is quoted on the point that the English character is not "susceptible du badinage poli & naturel." Coarseness became brutality. When the English divert themselves, "il semble qu'elles changent entièrement de naturel; le bruit, le tumulte, & des espèces de transports succèdent à leur sérieux & à leur sagesse ordinaire."

In the *Bagatelle*[2], Van Effen speaks out. Mentioning the Roman gladiatorial combats with abhorrence, he continues to say:

mais ce qui approche le plus des Gladiateurs Romains, & que j'ai vu une fois en ma vie avec étonnement & avec horreur, c'est ce qui se passe dans la capitale d'un Royaume voisin de notre Patrie. On y voit au milieu d'un Amphithéâtre, où vous avez placé pour trente sols un échaffaut sur lequel paroissent d'abord plusieurs jeunes gens de dix-huit à vingt ans, qui nuds jusqu'à la ceinture, se battent à coups de poings, mais avec tant de férocité qu'ils ne cessent d'attaquer & de se défendre, que quand ils restaient sur le carreau faute d'haleine. Ces Athlètes font place à plusieurs couples de Champions, qui s'assomment à coups de barre, & qui divertissent le Peuple merveilleusement, en se cassant la tête les uns aux autres.

Après ce cruel prélude, paroissent les véritables Héros de la Pièce, tout prêts à vendre leur sang aux Spectateurs. Ce sont deux espèces de maîtres d'armes, qui se sont défiés dans les formes. Ils se mettent en chemise d'un air flegmatique, & après s'être donné la main en signe d'amitié, ils tirent le sabre, & mettent en usage toute leur adresse & toute leur force, pour se taillader de la manière la plus cruelle pendant plus d'une grosse heure. Une tête fendue remplit toute l'assemblée d'allégresse; l'or & l'argent se répandent de tous côtés sur celui qui vient de faire un si beau coup; les plus grands Seigneurs du Royaume l'honorent par des présens & par des acclamations; & ils confondent leur murmure avec les plaintes de la Populace, quand la Scène n'est pas assez ensanglantée. On peut juger à quel point ce jeu barbare doit

---

[1] *Misant.* no. LXXXVI, 2nd ed.   [2] No. XCV.

paroître innocent à ce Peuple, par le formulaire du Cartel que ces Gladiateurs répandent dans le Public pour l'instruire du Combat futur. En voici à peu près le contenu si je m'en souviens bien[1].

From this interesting first-hand account it is clear that Van Effen had done other things besides going to plays and attending the Royal Society meetings when in London in 1715! Curiosity had drawn him to the bear-garden.

Je sais qu'on prétend excuser cette barbarie, en soutenant qu'elle excite le Peuple à la bravoure & à l'intrépidité. Mais j'ai toujours remarqué que plus on est brave, plus on souffre à voir combattre les autres, parce qu'on peut être engagé par son courage dans le même danger. Au contraire, un Poltron s'en fait un divertissement, il en sent plus le plaisir d'être lui-même en sûreté & la lâcheté se rassure par le péril où il voit les autres.

In the *Hollandsche Spectator*, too, he deprecates the brutality of English sport. "And so we see a custom still in vogue in a neighbouring Kingdom where prizefighters and sometimes women also, hew one another to pieces with the naked sword for but small money, and are greeted with applause as brave and steadfast creatures not only by the common people, but also by the greatest of the land, to such an extent that the more blood there be shed, the more entertaining the scene is considered to be." Van Effen now suggests the kind excuse that delight in such things flows from mere vacancy rather than innate savagery of mind! So elsewhere he notices English roughness and horseplay as leading to brutality. In Letter XI of the *Voyage en Suède*, he describes their entertainment aboard the English man-of-war:

Revenant dans la chambre de poupe, j'y vis régner une joye bruyante & tumultueuse; la plupart des convives sans distinction de rang dansoient pêle-mêle, chantoient, s'embrassoient, se baisoient, crioient, sautoient, tout comme s'il n'y avoit plus eu de Russiens au monde....Les Anglois ont le vin folâtre...; ces Messieurs, après avoir bien badiné avec les Suédois, commencent à jetter dans la mer les chapeaux & les perruques des derniers. Voilà bientôt les perruques & les chapeaux des Anglois qui vont

---

[1] Cp. *Spect.* no. 436.

le même chemin. Ensuite on se mit à s'arracher les uns aux autres les manchettes & les cravates.

Van Effen was plainly amused at this fun, but took care not to join in it. The conduct of some English officers in the opera-house at the Hague[1] went further:

Un Censeur rigide iroit déclamer ici contre le rôle tragi-comique que ces jeunes gens ont joué en plein Théâtre; & il ne manqueroit pas de traiter leur conduite d'insolente & de honteuse au suprême degré! Mais pour moi, qui me fais un plaisir de rendre justice au mérite, j'avoue que je trouve du merveilleux dans cette action, & que j'en tire d'heureux augures pour la conduite future de ces jeunes Gentilshommes. Comment Messieurs, prendre des loges d'assaut! escalader un Théâtre....

And so he continues in ironic raillery. They had clearly gone too far in their English boisterousness.

In English courage there is "plus de férocité & plus d'intrépidité naturelle" than in French valour[2], and even English pride is "insolent & l'insolence est un mélange de sottise, de folie, & de férocité[3]."

These characteristics pass over into literature. That is their significance. "*Ils sont dans leurs écrits à peu près comme dans leur conduite.*" This explains Shakespeare, and the "défaut général" of his tragedies,

défaut qui choqueroit les autres Nations infiniment plus que la Nation Angloise—c'est qu'elles excitent la pitié & la terreur par des cruautez épouvantables qu'on ne songe point à dérober à la vue des Spectateurs. Cela va si loin que, dans une pièce on voit sur le Théâtre un homme roué tout vif qui se plaint pathétique-ment de la barbarie de ses Tyrans.

Van Effen was not, of course, the first to analyse the English character and literature in this way. Réné Rapin's work, Dryden's critical bible, contains the following passage as translated by Rymer in 1674:

The English, our Neighbours, love blood in their Sports, by the quality of their temperament: These are *Insulaires* separated from the rest of men; we are more humane. Gallantry moreover agrees with our manners....The English have more of Genius

---

[1] *Vide Misant.* no. LXXXVI, 2nd ed.
[2] *Misant.* no. LXXXVI.   [3] *Bagat.* no. XXXVI.

for Tragedy than other People as well by the spirit of their Nation, which delights in Cruelty, as also by the Character of their Language, which is proper for Great Expressions.

But these views required much reiteration before they penetrated to the general intelligence, and Van Effen's contribution was probably as independent as it was influential on later criticism. Several other national traits explained certain things in English literature. The English furthermore failed in *pièces galantes* because they were materialistic and commercial. Even marriage was for them a business proposition rather than a romance[1]. Their very language appraised a man by his worldly goods, since they spoke of a man being *worth* so much[2]. Van Effen deprecates such an expression. In the *Hollandsche Spectator*[3] the same point is taken up by a correspondent who professes to "understand the English language properly." He defends the usage stoutly. It is simply a case of the wrong use of a *word*, which does not express the materialistic concept some people attach to it.

The English stage was run on strictly commercial lines, which had the evil result, only too apparent to-day, that a somewhat stupid public had to be catered for and the drama injured accordingly. On the other hand, the handsome profits were a stimulus to playwrights[4]. Needless to say, the English character did not necessarily depreciate in his mind on account of its commercialism. Indeed, in a good passage on commerce, Van Effen strongly recommends his countrymen to imitate their neighbours overseas:

Nothing is more carefully cherished and built up by them than trade and shipping. Their state parliament, in which a considerable part of the legislative power is vested, is open to merchants with whom sons of the most distinguished fathers are classed without their being provoked at it. They are not infrequently glorified by knightly titles, which pass to their descendants, and they enjoy the familiar society of the highest nobility and even of imperial dukes without the least suspicion of slavish submissiveness. There one does not hear any talk of people rising from beggary; they have not the least curiosity as to a man's pedigree. A man

---

[1] *Journ. Lit.* 1717, p. 167. [2] *Bagat.* no. LIX.
[3] No. 89. [4] Cp. above, p. 220.

of undistinguished parents, who has enriched himself by an honourable and wise trade, is there treated on the same footing and with the same respect as a distinguished General, who is a soldier of fortune and who can show no other noble scutcheon than his deeds. No wonder, therefore, that commerce, which opens the way to honours and greatness, daily increases there, and that it will soon decline into a wasting decay in lands where the least contempt is associated with it.

But other national characteristics were reflected in English literature and language. To the popular imagination in France, the English were for a long time a nation of gloomy regicides. They now had to satisfy the craving for romance by being made a nation of gloomy philosophers. There was hardly an eighteenth-century author, from Muralt to Prévost, Voltaire, Montesquieu, Holberg and many others who did not make the English character consist chiefly of melancholy or power of reflection; or, generally, of both. The English do not understand badinage, they are too glum and serious:

ils sont posez, sérieux, & même portez à la mélancholie; quand ils sont dans leur état naturel ils ont tout l'air de gens extraordinairement sages. On le voit parfaitement bien dans les Caffez qui sont ici les rendezvous des plus honnêtes gens:...on y voit les Anglois lier ensemble des conversations réglées sans s'interrompre les uns & les autres, & presque sans que chaque Compagnie puisse s'apercevoir qu'elle n'est pas seule....Le génie d'un La Fontaine ne se rencontre point chez eux:...ils prennent trop de l'imagination & pas assez du cœur; & l'on peut dire qu'ils pensent trop pour penser avec cette naïveté touchante qui embellit la Nature en restant de niveau avec elle[1].

In the *Hollandsche Spectator* Van Effen gives a sketch of coffee-house manners in England. These institutions are a blessing to large towns, especially London "stuffed with people as it is." Everything is ordered with the greatest method and propriety, no party interfering with another. Poets and other authors, who are often insupportable tatlers among other nations, "appear to come together to see who can keep his peace best." Except when diametrically opposed parties encounter one another—for Whigs and

---

[1] *Journ. Lit., loc. cit.*

Tories are such mortal enemies that although at the theatre the Tory side may be almost deserted, the Whig side would sit like "packed herrings" rather than cross over—or when the young men are playing hazards with great clatter, one may truly say that "twenty young British gentlemen are not as noisy in a coffee-house as ten Dutch or as one single French petit-Maître fresh up from Paris." "We aren't exactly gloomy like the English and the Spaniards," says the *Hollandsche Spectator* elsewhere[1], and in no. 270 gives another coffee-house sketch which must be quoted:

I have always deprecated in my travels the argumentative manners of the French and the English fine wits in their coffee-houses and other public gathering places. The former appear as the most intolerable rowdies and tatlers, and are continually mixed up in disputes among themselves about poems and plays that appear daily, whose merit is examined before the high tribunal of these witty gentlemen with a deafening din.

The English great spirits, on the contrary, one would take for statues, if it were not for the tobacco smoke they blow out intermittently. So they sit for hours at a stretch, without letting a word escape them, and a stranger who has purposely gone there in order to make the acquaintance of such great men, must satisfy himself with this mere sight.

No wonder, then, that Van Effen gives such an unflattering account of the pleasures of association with great wits[2]. As a young man he imagined that great honour and profit were to be derived from it; but he was speedily disabused; for men whose name and renown were never mentioned in any part of Europe except with the greatest reverence, were, he found, at their best in their writings and most disappointing when encountered at close quarters. Most of them were nauseatingly vain, proud and intractable; while poets, whose works were read throughout Europe with ecstasy, could not carry on a logical conversation properly or pleasantly. These remarks almost certainly apply, for the most part, to English writers. And they could be as cold as they were glum. They could be sincerely generous; "mais il faut les saisir dans le moment favorable pour tirer quelqu'usage de

[1] No. 169.   [2] *Holl. Spect.* no. 86.

leur générosité. Si vous laissez échaper l'heure où ils sont
pleins de chaleur pour vous, vous les trouverez bientôt tout
glacez & celui qui paroissoit entièrement dévoué à vos intérêts, vous regarde comme si jamais il ne vous avoit connu."
But we fear that eighteenth-century foreigners played the
part of fool gudgeons to the bait of English taciturnity. This
quality was regarded as the inevitable accompaniment of
English profundity of thought, and for such profundity Van
Effen felt the highest reverence, though, as we have seen,
he came very near to suspecting the truth. The English,
like other people, were foolish enough to hang themselves,
but then they did it with thoughtful deliberation[1]. Even the
language reflects their wisdom[2]:

However much it has been abused by foreigners as the scum
of all languages, it remains a fact that provided it be well handled,
it has no equal for expressing all subjects concisely, succinctly,
with energy, abundant variety and propriety according to the
nature of a thing, so that it deserves above all others, the title
of a philosophical language.

Except for some overstatement, this estimate agrees very
well with modern finding on the point, and certainly proves
that Van Effen had made a close study of English, which was
doubtless of as much use in guiding his own search after a
new style, as he wished it to be in curing his countrymen of
their excessive purism. "Here, too, let us imitate the English,
for they are a wise nation," he says in effect. The only word
Van Effen adopted from English is *Honigmaand*; "as the
English call the first month after marriage[3]."

But Van Effen's most complimentary words were
spoken when he compared the English and the French, not
only in literature but also in other things, to complete the
whole parallel. In fact these two nations are the *Antipodes
Moraux*[4]. The French are enquiring spirits, but are brilliant
and superficial. "Les Anglois[5] qui s'adonnent à l'étude ont
au contraire une attention infatigable pour les sujets les

---

[1] *Bagat.* no. xciv.   [2] *Holl. Spect.* no. 202.
[3] *Holl. Spect.* no. 298: *Honigmaand.*
[4] *Misant.* no. lxxxvi, 2nd ed.   [5] *Ibid.*

plus épineux. Leur raison ne se contente pas d'une légère teinture d'habileté, elle creuse jusqu'au fond des sciences & leur pénétration ne se laisse arrêter par aucun obstacle." They were, as we have quoted above[1], rather "grands Esprits" than "beaux Esprits."

In the *Bagatelle*[2], Van Effen quotes from the *Spectator*, and says:

Cet Auteur a certainement raison, pour peu qu'on connoise le génie des Anglois. Ce sont la plupart les plus sots *Rationalistes* du monde; ils se moquent ouvertement du stile des *François*.... Ils ne rejettent pas tout-à-fait un badinage, une raillerie, mais ils veulent que cela ne tombe pas entièrement sur rien; & quand on parle sérieusement, ils veulent, non seulement des choses, mais la substance & le suc des choses.

This latter part is a sample of *Bagatelle* irony and again shows Van Effen's admiration for English style, which he at first thought somewhat unpolished. English wisdom was not confined to a few only:

Je crois que toutes les personnes capables de réflexion, & qui ont eu occasion d'examiner de près les habitans de l'Angleterre avoueront sans peine qu'il n'y a point de peuple au monde où le Bon-Sens & l'imagination se trouvent plus universellement dans les Personnes de tous les ordres. On entend souvent avec surprise sortir de la bouche d'un Batelier de ce Royaume, des paroles, où la Raison & la Vivacité s'accordent avec une harmonie si juste & si naturelle, qu'un Bel-Esprit de profession pourroit s'en faire honneur sans se ravaler trop[3].

The only further praise that remains is to say recklessly with Holberg: they are "a nation of heroes and philosophers"!

Other traits which characterize their style and distinguish them from the French are freedom and imagination. Liberty appeared to the eighteenth-century mind to have become an English handmaiden. The very word recalled England to some minds. "Protestantism," says a correspondent, "must prevail, provided other sects are not ill-treated and are left in the full enjoyment—to speak in English-wise—of liberty and property[4]." Van

[1] Chap. ii.   [2] No. v.   [3] *Bagat.* no. lxxx.
[4] *Holl. Spect.* no. 276.

Effen, too, felt the unrestrained freedom and force of English literature and considered that "le caractère qui distingue le plus ces deux peuples" is that the French were servile to a Prince and to the mode, while the British nation was "souverainement jaloux de sa Liberté[1]." This is a fundamental idea of the critique in the *Journal Littéraire*, and elsewhere[2] Van Effen returns to it. "Their imagination was allowed free play and brought, out of the various nooks of their brains, ideas, which appear quite foreign to the French genius, and which they nevertheless are able to connect so well, that they keep the amazed reader in one continuous suspense." "English humour is somewhat stiffer" than French and "not nearly so natural and unforced."

Yet they can always, by an admirable fecundity, render themselves novel and distinctive. The spirit of the English gains a certain independence from their disposition, which makes every one of them adopt his own particular way of thinking. The national cast of their minds consists properly in a certain whimsicality which seems at first sight to have neither rhyme nor reason but which when examined more closely has the closest fitness and correspondence with Reason and Truth.

Van Effen clearly realized the extreme conventionality of French literature, and fully appreciated the originality of English; but the polished *naïveté* of La Fontaine he considered to be quite foreign to the English genius as, for instance, in Prior, "un des meilleurs Poëtes Anglois de nos jours."

In satire the English have nothing to equal Boileau's *Lutrin*, but have done some good things.

Dryden, contemporain du Comte de Rochester, avoit encore des talens extraordinaires pour la Satyr, qu'il gâtoit tout de même par une indignité odieuse & par une dégoûtante obscurité. Les mœurs licencieuses de la Cour de Charles II ne fournissoient que trop de matière au libertinage de cette plume qui a bien osé jetter tout son venin sur ce Prince, sur ses favoris & ses favorites, sans prendre d'autre précaution que de cacher Charles, Monmouth & Londres sous les noms de *David*, d'*Absolon* & de *Jerusalem*.

---

[1] *Misant.* no. LXXXVI, etc. 2nd ed. and *Dissert. sur la Poës. Ang.*
[2] *Holl. Spect.* no. 129.

This easy evasion of the *scandalum magnatum* and the licence allowed to scurrility was a thing Van Effen deprecated in the English character. He was shocked to find that their literary men even approved of it. "One of the privileges that the English set most store by, and which they imagine could not be taken from them without an actual violation of their liberty, is the unlimited freedom of the press." The press must, of course, be free, but there are limits, and these are exceeded:

The British nation will not suffer the least limitation, and the freedom which they arrogate to themselves in this regard, is daily seen to break out into such an excess of unheard-of mischievousness, that no one, however honourable and blameless, can be sure that he will preserve his just reputation. The laws find good to watch over the life and goods of the subjects, but appear to have neglected the maintenance of their cherished honour.

The greatest officers of state are constrained to see defamatory newspapers daily dispersed "in which they are decried for the most God-forsaken rogues that have ever sold and betrayed their fatherland." It is true that the *scandalum magnatum* exists, but it appears to have been made only to be evaded and wantonly scoffed at. It is sufficient if only some letters of a name be omitted.

Nowhere have I seen this execrable unseemliness—in company with which human society scarcely seems to be able to subsist at all, and which is nourished by the powerlessness of the laws— more wantonly and heedlessly pursued than in a public print which has at stated times appeared in London for years, and is even despatched throughout the whole of Europe. In it, everything that wit, invention, grace, eloquence, understanding and even learning can produce to make such venom appetizing, is employed always to express the same thing—though continually in a new way and in fresh metaphor—to wit: that one of the most prominent statesmen combines all evil inclinations and hellish vices in his bastard mind.... Now as I was an eye-witness, and palpably saw, at the very time when this pleasant poison was being vented in great streams upon the minds of the inhabitants, that the Kingdom, under the direction of that same great man, was daily increasing in power, wealth and formidableness, I could not consider such a criminal abuse of the most glorious gifts of the human understanding without the greatest indignation.... I could not resist expressing these opinions of mine to sensible people of that country, and particularly to a certain excellent poet whom I suspected, not without ground, of occasionally lending a hand to that paper, and who, though otherwise of good character and led astray by the force of habit and partisanship, dared to protest the innocence of a matter fraught with such grave consequences.

Their conversation is then related, and Van Effen convinces everyone except his friend the poet that the almost unrestricted scurrility of controversial literature is a disgrace to English society and an outrage to that true liberty which the English boast[1]. This unbridled nature of the English was expressed in their poetry too. It is "trop licencieux[2]" and even the *Rape of the Lock* "pèche un peu de tems en tems du côté de la modestie[3]." In *Absalom and Achitophel* there is, besides the political freedoms taken, "du feu infiniment des pensées fort neuves, mais en récompense bien de l'obscénité & de profanation. L'on y voit un portrait d'une affreuse force des infamies d'une Cour qui...." etc.

Oldham is known as the *Juvenal Anglois,* and the *Dispensary,* we are told, "plusieurs Anglois préfèrent à celui de M. Pope" (i.e. the *Rape*). And for Pope the *Journal Littéraire* had great admiration. In the literary news from London, 1714[4], he was introduced to the continental public:

M. Pope, fort estimé ici pour son talent dans la poësie Angloise, va publier aussi par souscription une Traduction de l'Iliade de Homère en vers Anglois avec des Notes....Entre les Pièces de Poësie qu'on a vu de ce M. Pope, il y a un Essai sur la Critique, *Essay on Criticism,* qui est fort estimé, mais ce qui lui a attiré le plus d'aplaudissemens, c'est un Poëme Héroï-Comique en quatre Chants, qu'il a fait sur une boucle de cheveux enlevée... on en a fait diverses éditions.

This is followed up a year later by:

On voit ici un autré Auteur Anglois qui dans un âge fort peu avancé se distingue extrêmement par la justesse & par le brillant

---

[1] *Holl. Spect.* no. 220.   [2] *Journ. Lit.* 1717.
[3] *Ibid.*   [4] May–June.

de son esprit. C'est M. Pope, âgé d'environ vingt-six ans. Il a fait des églogues admirables....The Temple of Fame...est encore une pièce qui lui a attiré des applaudissemens.....Je pourrai bien vous envoyer dans quelque tems d'ici des Extraits de deux belles pièces de cet Auteur dont il est parlé dans votre *Journal*. Toutes ces productions ne sont que de foibles essais, en comparaison de l'entreprise qu'il a formée de donner au public l'Iliade d'Homère traduit en vers Anglois....On est fort curieux de savoir si, malgré toute l'étendue de son génie, l'Auteur fera goûter aux Anglois ce Poëte Grec sans l'habiller un peu à la moderne.

Then follows some small talk about the young Burnet's satirical *Letter* on Pope's enterprise.

The long account of Pope's Homer in vol. VIII of this journal[1] is very appreciative. The preface is described as excellent, and written in a style almost "trop belle"; "les comparaisons y sont admirables & marquent une imagination digne de communiquer *Homère* aux Anglois." The translation itself has all the beauties of which the English language is capable and follows the original so faithfully that any extract "seroit un Extrait du Poëme d'Homère & non pas de celui de M. Pope." In spite of what Bentley had aptly said, the reviewer found it both a "pretty poem" and "Homer," too. He is surprised that Pope did not avail himself of the freedom which Milton used—blank verse. In 1717 came the criticism of the *Dissertation*: "Nous avons eu occasion de nous étendre d'avantage sur son mérite en parlant de la traduction de l'Iliade." The *Rape of the Lock* is analysed: "toute l'ordonnance en est entièrement neuve, les pensées vives & brillantes, le stile soutenu par toute la versification aisée, & le rime plus riche que dans la plupart des Poëmes Anglois." The description of the ombre party is "magnifique" and "sans doute un chef-d'œuvre." In fact Pope "égale tous les Poëtes Anglois de son tems, en fertilité & en force d'imagination," surpasses all of them "en correction & en justesse," and deserves the praise, equally with Homer, of changing all that he touched into gold. With all this praise and advertisement, it was not long before Pope

---

[1] 1716.

became one of the best-known and most famous of English authors in Holland. In 1717, his *Essay on Criticism* had already been imitated in French[1]. The reviewer in the *Bibliothèque Ancienne et Moderne*[2] is honest enough to say: "Comme je n'ai pas lu ce que Mr Pope a écrit en Anglois, sur cette matière, je ne puis pas comparer cette Imitation à l'Original; mais il faut qu'il soit bon puisque la Copie l'est...." In 1728, the *Journal Littéraire*, reviewing the *Guardian*, quotes Pope's prologue to *Cato* in full and in English "pour l'amour de ceux qui entendent cette Langue." A French translation follows, for it is a *chef-d'œuvre* "dans sa sorte." But this was not written by Van Effen, who had long since been dissociated from this journal. In February 1734[3], he mentioned Pope as follows: "One of the wittiest and most judicious English poets has managed to express the danger of insufficient learning, with the greatest concentration and sprightliness in four lines of his forceful diction." He then gives a Dutch rendering of *A Little learning...*, etc.

The connection of Swift and Van Effen has been mentioned above. This English author was much advertised by Van Effen. From the time that he appeared as editor of Sir William Temple's works he was of course not unknown on the continent, and although Bernard had noticed the *Tale of a Tub* in his *Nouvelles Littéraires* in 1705, its author, like Steele, was better known as a political writer. Dr Sybil Goulding[4] puts the position thus:

Pendant la première vingtaine d'années du XVIIIe siècle Swift est à peine connu à l'étranger. On peut supposer qu'il est bien connu de la société réfugiée en Angleterre & d'un certain nombre de littérateurs français et hollandais aux Pays-bas, qui ont des rapports avec l'Angleterre, mais sa grande renommée parmi un public français est encore à conquérir.

This is largely true for Holland also, whence Swift's reputation spread to other countries. Yet, before his best seller appeared in 1726, the basis of his fame had been laid. Van

---

[1] A Amsterdam chez l'Honoré & Chatelain.
[2] 1717, p. 234.　　　　　　　　　　[3] *Holl. Spect.* no. 240.
[4] *Swift en France*, p. 11.

Effen again was a useful agent in this process. He admired Swift greatly. In the *Bagatelle*[1] he versified Swift's story of the "gros homme" saying: "Un des plus spirituels Hommes de toute l'Angleterre a, selon moi, fort plaisamment turlupiné la sotte vanité de ces Messieurs.... [2]" He had to defend himself over this, and in no. LXVIII says: "J'ai cru franchement que ce petit conte, que toute l'Angleterre admire dans un de leurs plus beaux Génies, valoit la peine d'être traduit. Le sujet en lui-même est bas, j'en conviens; mais le sens en est excellent, & de dernière justesse." In no. LXXI, Swift is referred to as "un célèbre Auteur Anglois." In 1720, the *Bibliothèque Angloise* reviewed Swift's *Proposal for Correcting...the English Tongue* in terms which show that he must have been fairly well known.

L'auteur de cette Lettre n'auroit pas eu besoin de se nommer pour se faire connoître. A son stile, & à son tour d'esprit, on pouvoit déviner que c'étoit le Docteur Jonathan Swift.... Il y avoit déjà bien du temps qu'il s'étoit acquis la réputation de penser & d'écrire d'une manière à se faire distinguer de la foule. Le caractère de ses Ouvrages avoit toujours quelque chose de singulier, & ce caractère distinctif n'étoit pas une chose que l'on peut aisément contrefaire....

At last, in 1721, Van Effen's translation of *A Tale of a Tub* appeared. The reason why he had taken such a long time over the work becomes clear when we see that he had translated practically all Swift's best pieces up to date, and added copious notes, explanations and introductions. Furthermore, he complained at length of the "difficulté terrible" of translating English, and especially Swift. Here and there he found it necessary to "adoucir" the expressions; or, again, to blunt the edge of Swift's wit by ingenious circumlocutory renderings[3]. Otherwise the translation is adequate, and, for the period, excellent. He felt at the same time that he had to meet the captious criticisms of the English, who were never satisfied with any translation of their books.

---

[1] No. LIV.   [2] The writers of prefaces, etc.—*Tale of a Tub*.
[3] Cp. Bisschop, chap. VIII, and Dr Sybil Goulding, *op. cit.*

Ce sont des gens spirituels, & judicieux, s'il y en a au Monde, & il y auroit de la Sottise à leur disputer des qualitez, mais ils excellent du Côté de l'amour-propre autant que du Côté du mérite....Il faut avouer que leur vanité se conduise à cet égard avec beaucoup de finesse: si un Ouvrage dont ils font grand cas, déplaît aux Étrangers, c'est la faute du Traducteur; & s'il est approuvé, ils donnent la plus haute idée de l'Original en faisant croire qu'il a été affoibli par la Traduction.

Their attitude will make the world suspect that whatever is most striking in their literature consists "plutôt dans l'Expression, que dans le sens," which he, for one, does not for a moment believe. On the merits of the work Van Effen is less equivocal.

Les Anglois le considèrent avec raison comme un chef-d'œuvre de fine Plaisanterie &...je crois que le Lecteur conviendra, qu'il est difficile de trouver dans aucune Langue un Ouvrage si plein de feu, & d'imagination. Il est vrai en même tems, qu'il ne se peut rien de plus bisarre. La Narration est interompuë continuellement par des Digressions, qui occupent plus de place que le sujet principal; mais cette Bisarrerie n'est point d'effet d'un Esprit déréglé...; ce Désordre est affecté pour tourner en ridicule les Auteurs Anglois....Ces Digressions, d'ailleurs, sont d'un Tour si particulier, & pleines d'un Badinage si ingénieux, & si peu commun...[que]...l'Opinion générale le donne au Docteur Swift, ministre Anglicain, & un des plus beaux esprits de la Grande-Bretagne.

The *Modest Proposal* translated in Part ii is considered to be another *chef-d'œuvre*.

The *Boekzaal*[1] devoted two reviews to this translation and expressed its appreciation in terms borrowed from Van Effen's preface. It uses his defence of Swift on the charge of impiety, but leaves to the translator's account what he has said with regard to English cavilling over translations. In 1735, P. le Clerc produced a Dutch translation and again kept to Van Effen's words in his preface. The *Boekzaal* reviewer largely repeats le Clerc in turn. We have thus an instructive example of how Van Effen's judgment influenced subsequent criticism. But another authority is followed also,

---

[1] March–May, 1721.

namely Voltaire, whose endeavours on behalf of English literature are fully as important for Holland as for France.

He has been named the English Rabelais, but Mr Voltaire is of opinion that he is not done justice to when he is so named, because he by far excels Rabelais in common sense. He is not as jovial as Rabelais but possesses all the fineness, the reason, the choiceness and sound judgment in which the curé of Meudon is lacking. Entertaining badinage is characteristic of him; but, as Mr Voltaire says, it is necessary to take a trip to his country to understand his works properly.

Useful notes have therefore been added, for this work was not written for "unredeemed simpletons." The digressions are so full of the "wittiest jest," that in the "conciseness and aptness" of their "fine raillery," "the reader will have no desire to return to the main theme." Referring to the *Battle of the Books*, the reviewer says that Swift is at least the first who fought the moderns with their own weapons of raillery. The reader is assured that the *Tale* is a most singular production in which not a single serious word is to be found. Le Clerc also reviewed[1] Van Effen's translation, but he does not seem to have cared much for Swift. "Il turlupine tout....Il faut avouer qu'il leur dit souvent fort bien leurs véritez quoi-qu'en stile aussi caustique, que burlesque; mais il y a eu des gens qui ont cru que l'Auteur cherchoit plutôt à détruire qu'à édifier." In the *Battle of the Books*, "la Hardiesse de la fiction ne pouvoit guère être portée plus loin," while the *Modest Proposal* is full of a "sanglante ironie," and everywhere "l'auteur arrive à son but par des détours qu'on ne voit guère ailleurs, & par un langage auquel les Peuples de deçà la mer ne sont point accoutumez." When *Gulliver* appeared, and, as one might expect, was issued by an Amsterdam press, Swift became perhaps the most famous English writer among the continental public[2]. The *Journal Littéraire*, however, thought fit to say in its review that their copious extracts were enough to prove "que notre auteur est un homme d'Esprit qui fait mordre & badiner, mais qui pourroit infiniment mieux

---

[1] *Biblioth. Anc. et Mod.* 1721.   [2] *Vide* also Dr Goulding, *op. cit.*

employer son Génie qu'au Badinage & à la Satyre[1]." Later[2] it added: "On donne aujourd'hui de même au Docteur Swift tous les Livres comiques ou burlesques auxquels on veut assurer quelque Débit en Angleterre." When, in 1735[3], the *Boekzaal* reviewed a Dutch translation of the *Tatler*, it says of the letter on the Frogs: "In this letter one easily discovers the genius of the Dean of St Patrick (the famous Dr Swift)." Van Effen's last reference to Swift occurs in the *Hollandsche Spectator*[4]. The most characteristic elements of English humour are exemplified in the *Spectator*, and "chiefly in the wonderful writings of the renowned Doctor Swift who can even see a chance of making a comparison, as apt as it is significant, between a human being and a broomstick."

Van Effen also criticized English pastoral poetry for which, it appears, he had little taste. No. LXXV of the *Bagatelle* is translated from the *Guardian* (no. 84) on this subject, and it is noticeable that the sentence which describes Philips as the "eldest born" of Spenser is not translated. In no. XC, the subject is resumed: "Les habiles gens de cette Nation, si raisonnables d'ailleurs, ne raisonnent pas trop juste, à mon avis, sur le vrai caractère de ce genre de Poësie. Il me semble qu'ils le veulent plutôt Villageois que Pastoral...." He concludes, in fact, that English pastoral[5] is too artificial.

Van Effen's opinion of the *Spectator* is evident from what has been said above in other connections. But he has left a few studied and noteworthy appreciations of this work which remain to be considered. The first occurs in the *Bagatelle*[6]:

Comme je me suis rangé de nouveau dans le Parti des *Rationalistes*, j'ose dire hardiment que *je ne crois de l'esprit aux gens qu'à mesure qu'ils admirent le Spectateur.* Je sais bien qu'on y trouve par-ci par-là des Pièces fades & plattes; ce qui peut venir de ce qu'elles sont faites ou trop à la hâte, ou par celui entre les Auteurs qui a moins de génie. Mais ce qu'on y trouve de bon dans les principes de tous les Spectateurs du Bons-sens, est si

---

[1] 1727.   [2] 1729.   [3] March.   [4] No. 129.
[5] I.e., the pastoral poetry of Pope and Philips.   [6] No. LVII.

excellent, *que je ne conçois pas que l'Esprit humain puisse aller au-delà.* Je ne découvre pas seulement cet excellent dans certaines réflexions profondes & neuves sur les Vérités de la Religion, & dans ces caractères qui nous représentent la Vertu de son côté utile & aimable; je le trouve surtout dans la manière dont il traite certaines choses, basses & communes de leur nature, mais fertiles en réflexions & en lumières qu'il nous en fait tirer, sans presque que nous nous en appercevions. Telles sont certaines circonstances petites & ordinaires de la Vie, qui font infiniment mieux connoître le cœur humain, que ces actions éclatantes, qu'il produit ordinairement par des motifs qui lui sont étrangers.

The *Nouveau Spectateur François*[1] pays the following tribute to its great prototype:

C'est un Livre qui plaît également à tout ce qu'il y a de sensé dans toutes les classes des Esprits, & qui a su réunir en sa faveur tous les différens caractères, & tous les goûts différens des Lecteurs capables de réflexion; l'instruction & l'agrément s'y trouvent dans un mélange si bien ménagé qu'il s'empare des gens les plus livrés au simple badinage, & qu'il force ceux qui ne songent qu'à s'amuser, à devenir plus éclairés & meilleurs, sans qu'ils s'en appercçoivent presque eux-mêmes. Des qualités que d'autres productions de l'Esprit font considérer en quelque manière comme incompatibles, paroissent là dans la plus brillante union. La nouveauté y est solide, l'invention y est compagne inséparable du jugement; le burlesque même y est guidé par la justesse d'esprit, et dirigé vers une utilité qu'on cache avec prudence, pour la faire trouver d'une manière plus sure & plus agréable. En un mot le Spectateur Anglois contient, pour ainsi dire, la fleur de l'Esprit, & la force de la Raison des plus beaux Génies de la *Grande-Bretagne.*

When the Hollandsche Spectator takes up his pen for the first time, he also pays a tribute[2]. After the *Tatler,* the *Spectator* appeared, he says, with a somewhat different aim. Something less facetious and more moral, but properly enlivened, was to be attempted:

This demanded a far greater exertion of mind and a rare variety and combination of talents and knowledge. Here the Philosopher, the Divine, the Scholar, and the Poet had to join hands. Here were required a rare penetration of judgment, a singular liveliness of wit, an extended imaginative power, natural and

---

[1] No. 1.   [2] No. 1.

merry pleasantry, a style which is free and easy and could bend itself with flexibility to all subjects, heightening and lowering itself to suit the needs of each. All this did not seem to be enough. Even the jester had here to found his jests on sound Reason, while the philosopher required an unforced wittiness in order to drive home his teachings and arguments. The pleasant supported by usefulness, and the useful adorned by the pleasant, had to appear together. All these demands were abundantly satisfied.

Its enormous vogue in England is not strange:

One cannot deny without doing the English an injustice that even the humblest of them, though unlettered, seem as if by nature formed to be critics and lovers of wit and intellect. The talented Spectator Society also had such tender indulgence for their countrymen, that it frequently published something connected with the life and thought of the humblest working people. But such subjects, however low in themselves, were depicted in such a way that they were beautiful and ennobled.

Van Effen justly appraised the *Spectator* and appreciated its quality. Nothing struck him more than its wholesome bourgeois atmosphere and its clear familiar style, and these were the things he successfully attempted to realize for Dutch prose literature. We are now prepared for the following criticism on the *Tatler*: "Dans le Jazeur, la Gayeté & le Feu de l'imagination dominent, mais on y sent presque partout la direction d'une raison exacte. L'Agrément y tient le premier rang, mais d'ordinaire il mène à l'instruction[1]." That Van Effen was partial to the *Guardian* may be inferred from the fact that he translated it. In the *Hollandsche Spectator* he borrows from the *Guardian*, saying that "it is not in the least inferior to the Spectator, both having been very well translated into Dutch," and containing "many witty drolleries covering wholesome teachings." In the *Bagatelle*, too, Van Effen drew upon the *Guardian* with appreciative remarks, and we may be sure that he did not relish the injurious estimate of the *Journal Littéraire* when, in 1723, it reviewed his translation of this work. "La différence du Spectateur au Guardian est trop considérable

---

[1] Introduction to translation of *Guardian* (*Le Mentor Moderne*, La Haye, 1723) (cp. *Holl. Spect.* no. 81).

pour qu'ils puissent être les productions de la même plume." Happily there are exceptions from which extracts are given, and on the whole the work will sell well because "la réputation de ces Auteurs est si belle, qu'on doit naturellement s'attendre à quelque chose d'excellent quand ils y ont mis la main."

We have seen how their fame had grown. It was still to grow. "England, Germany, France and Holland have filled the libraries of an innumerable multitude of people with such moralizing writings, and the frequent printing and reprinting of them shows the universal approbation which they have received[1]." "The English Spectator, so honoured and loved throughout the whole of Europe," wrote another correspondent[2]. The reviewers apparently never tired of discussing this favourite subject. The *Boekzaal*, e.g., reviewed one edition after another, both French and Dutch, in terms consistently laudatory. The *Freeholder*, too, was duly translated and reviewed[3]. It is everywhere irradiated by the "cleverness of invention and exactness of judgment so characteristic of Mr Addison...one of the cleverest heads in England." Three reviews were devoted to le Clercq's Dutch translation of the *Tatler* in 1733, and the great reception accorded these works by the world is once more recalled. A part of the *Campaign* is translated, and the reader is reminded of the effect which it must have produced when the subject was still "fresh in the memory of everyone." The *Tatler* is described as "the fruit of the youth" of a great mind[4]. Both Van Effen's and le Clercq's translations of the *Guardian* received much space. It is "one of the most pleasant works that could be desired." The translator's introductory appreciation is quoted and supported. "The essays on pastoral poetry are all by the famous Pope, one of the best English poets[5]." In 1763, the *Guardian* and the *Tatler* are advertised as the works of the "universally, world-famous knight Richard Steele[6]," and an issue of the

---

[1] *Holl. Spect.* no. 147.
[2] *Ibid.* no. 329.
[3] Dec. 1726.
[4] *Boekzaal*, March–April, 1735.
[5] *Ibid.* March, 1731.
[6] *Ibid.* Nov. 1763.

Ladies' Library is accompanied by a full panegyrical account of Steele[1]. The dozens of imitations in Holland[2] naturally added their contribution to the paean of praise, in which Van Effen was honoured equally with his predecessors. By the translation of *Robinson Crusoe*, Van Effen added another important tributary to the stream of English literary influences. The point as to who the translator was should be definitely settled by Van Effen's statement in the letter to Camuzat[3] that he had completed the second half of vol. I and all the rest; but later writers do not appear to have noticed this[4]. The prefaces of Van Effen make good reading. In the *Misantrope* he had exclaimed against the romances which flout all verisimilitude. Here was a book that satisfied him in this respect. Not only the variety and the extraordinary character of the adventures, but also its "vraisemblance habilement ménagée," explained the immense popularity of the work. Indeed, it has been said that the story is literal fact. "Ce que je puis soutenir pourtant avec sincérité, c'est qu'il y a de très-honnêtes gens dans nos Villes, Marchands qui assurent avoir vû notre Voyageur au retour de ses derniers Voyages, d'avoir mangé avec lui, et de lui avoir entendu réciter une partie des Aventures qu'on voit dans ces deux volumes." Although it is obviously to the bookseller's advantage to be able to substantiate this, the "Editeur de cette Traduction" has "trop d'intégrité pour décider positivement là-dessus." Van Effen had to be cautious. The book promised to be a first-class business proposition, so public opinion had to be propitiated:

Je conviens qu'il paroît beaucoup d'industrie dans la description qu'on voit dans cette Histoire de tout ce que notre Aventurier a fait pour sa conservation & pour rendre sa solitude la moins désagréable qu'il étoit possible.... On sait à quels efforts la nécessité porte l'Esprit humain,

and we are astonished even at what animals will do "pour se procurer le bien & pour éviter le mal."

---

[1] *Boekzaal*, Nov. 1764.
[2] J. Hartog, *De Spectatoriale Geschriften van* 1741–1800 (Utrecht, 1872).
[3] Appended to the *Je ne sais quoi* of Cartier de St-Philip (Utrecht, 1730).
[4] Cp., e.g., W. E. Mann, *Robinson en France* (Paris, 1916).

Van Effen is, of course, touching here on the real significance of the book for literature, viz. its close, detailed realism, without which the modern novel would have been impossible. "Cette observation aiguë du détail, cette vraisemblance du plus petit fait, cette main-mise sur la réalité qui donne au roman anglais tout le relief d'une relation authentique, il ne paraît pas que les lecteurs de St Hycinthe et de Van Effen en aient saisi toute l'originalité[1]," says Jusserand, quoting partly from J. Texte[2]. While Van Effen fully realized the immense advance represented by *Robinson Crusoe*, he, like Addison, gave his opinion cautiously so as not to offend readers. Some readers, says Van Effen in the preface to vol. II, have objected that the amount of detail is boring, and

quoique je croye que c'est leur faute plutôt que celle de l'Auteur & que ces particularitez petites en elle-mêmes doivent être intéressantes pour tous ceux, qui ont assez d'imagination & de sentiment pour se mettre à la place de notre aventurier & pour s'approprier sa situation & ses pensées, j'ose leur promettre qu'ils ne rencontreront pas ici une pareille source d'ennui & de dégoût.

The last part of the sentence seems like a concession to would-be critics but is really an ironical comment on their obtuseness. There were other equally important and novel features of the book which Van Effen recognized. Jusserand has said[3] that "la vraie cause de son immense influence littéraire est toute dans la puissance de son style simple; chez lui, et pour la première fois peut-être dans l'histoire des lettres anglaises, aucune trace d'art n'est visible." Van Effen observes:

On y voit rien qui sente l'homme de Lettres. On y découvre plutôt un pauvre marinier.... Il est vrai qu'il n'affecte pas ce stile concis & sententieux par lequel nos Auteurs François tâchent de relever leurs réflexions & leurs caractères. Voulant être utile à toutes sortes d'hommes, il est simple, uni, familier; c'est un stile de conversation dénué de tout ornement & propre à faire briller la Vérité par la seule splendeur naturelle. Il est vrai même qu'il outre un peu quelquefois cette simplicité, & qu'il donne dans une

---

[1] J. A. Jusserand, *Le Roman Anglois et la Réforme Littéraire de Daniel Defoe* (Bruxelles, 1887).
[2] *Jean Jacques Rousseau*, etc.   [3] *Loc. cit.*

diction proverbiale & bourgeoise, qui dans l'Original sent un peu trop le Matelot pour satisfaire à la délicatesse Françoise.

For French readers, therefore, the style is duly polished up. But a third element, in which *Robinson Crusoe* constituted a distinct advance in the history of the novel, was the realistic depiction of character in situation, a localizing of character which is not found even in Richardson.

L'ouvrage dont il s'agit ici n'est pas seulement un tableau des différentes Aventures de Robinson Crusoe. C'est encore une Histoire des différentes situations de son esprit et des révolutions qui sont arrivées dans son cœur. Les unes & les autres répondent avec tant de justesse aux événements qui les précèdent qu'un Lecteur capable de réflexion sent de la manière la plus forte, que dans les mêmes circonstances il est impossible de n'être pas agité par les mêmes mouvements. Il est difficile de décrire d'une manière naturelle & pathétique les différentes situations du cœur si on ne le copie après ses propres sentiments; mais j'avoue qu'il n'est pas impossible, et que de ce côté-là, l'art & la force de l'Imagination peuvent mettre à peu près la fiction au niveau de la Vérité.

Van Effen, then, as if he had conceived it to be his mission to interpret the significance of English literary art to his contemporaries, pointed out to them wherein the real value of *Robinson Crusoe* lay. That they did not see it clearly is hardly surprising. The book produced its usual crop of imitations in Holland also, but, as with *Gulliver*, not one of them is of any literary value[1]. The public saw it mostly as a narrative of adventures rather better than the usual story, and later, with Rousseau, read a philosophical conception into it on which Defoe had not insisted; but which was an inevitable corollary to the book—namely, the idealization of the natural state.

"Malheureusement," says Van Effen, in paraphrase of Defoe, "la conversation se ressent de la corruption humaine qui semble prendre d'âge en âge de nouvelles forces[2]." In a quarto of twelve pages to which the name of Selkirk is appended, the thought is expressed that we can supply our

---

[1] *Vide* W. H. Staverman, *Robinson Crusoe in Nederland* (Groningen, 1907).
[2] Preface, vol. III.

wants "in a very natural manner so as to maintain...life, though not so conveniently yet as effectually as we are able to do with the help of all our Arts & Society,"etc. As Professor C. B. Tinker[1] has demonstrated, speculation on this subject was exceedingly common in the eighteenth century, and we may well believe with Prinsen[2] that people did not wait for Rousseau to philosophize for them over Defoe's remarkable work.

Verwer says in his *Life* of Van Effen that in 1722 there appeared his translation of the *Free Thoughts* "of the notorious Dr Mandeville of London," and that Van Effen's translation was long held to be the original, which shows that Mandeville was not well known at that time. In the *Hollandsche Spectator*[3] Van Effen refers to Mandeville, saying, "a certain foreign writer has composed a great and humorous dissertation..."; which again indicates that Mandeville was not generally known. Here, too, Van Effen acted as an advance agent to theses that are an important ingredient in eighteenth-century philosophy emanating from England[4]. The *Bibliothèque Angloise* published a good review on the *Fable of the Bees* in 1725[5]. "La Pièce n'a été que trop bien reçue & que trop applaudie....Il fait grand bruit en Angleterre, & comme on l'a déjà honoré de quantité de Réponses je suis en plein droit d'en rendre compte aux Estrangers." It evinces a decided distaste for the views, but acknowledges: "On y voit partout un Homme qui se croit un Esprit brillant & capable de devenir à quelque heure le Bayle de la Grande Bretagne." It asks pertinently: "Peut-il croire ce qu'il dit?"; and, if not, "Peut-il dire ce qu'il ne croit pas?"

The connection between Shaftesbury and Van Effen has been mentioned. In the preface to his translation of the *Essay* he defended the freedoms which foreigners accused English philosophers of taking and seems to show some admiration for Shaftesbury's style: "Bien des gens croyent qu'on n'a encore rien écrit dans cette langue de si correct,

---

[1] *Nature's Simple Plan.* [2] *Handboek de Geschiedenis...Ned. Let.*
[3] No. 36. [4] *Vide* Marchand, *Dictionnaire.* [5] Vol. xiii, p. 97.

de si vif & de si poli...." De la Roche noticed this translation[1]:

> The *Essay on the Freedom of Wit and Humour* has been esteemed a masterpiece of its kind. Purity of Diction, Delicacy of Sentiments & a Manly Vein of Reasoning runs through the whole: no wonder then an ingenious pen has attempted to represent the beauties of the original in a foreign dress. The Performance indeed was difficult, but the greater is the reputation of his success. Perhaps he has made the Author more intelligible, for besides the Notes which embellish and explain the text he has added a preface....

Reviewing Van Effen's critical opinions, we shall see that he was, on the whole, a discerning, independent and, except for some pardonable enthusiasms, judicious critic, not free from, but yet well in advance of, the ideas of his time. Among his remarks on Voltaire's *Henriade* he shows his distaste of rigid classical formalism: "M. de Voltaire a fait tort à la fertilité de son génie en suivant avec une timidité si scrupuleuse les poëtes épiques de l'Antiquité et surtout Virgile[2]." He was determined not to submit blindly to authority, but to reject "tout jugement qui s'appuie sur la tradition[3]." He would judge for himself:

> Certains chefs de parti fameux pour la supériorité de leur génie, semblent imposer à la multitude la loi de trouver un ouvrage mauvais sous peine d'être déchu de toute prétention à l'esprit & au bon goût. Chacun se donne un air de lumière par la hardiesse de ses décisions.... Que fera la Raison contre cette impérieuse extravagance? Elle s'écarte du chemin; elle laisse passer à côté d'elle l'impétuosité de cette opinion populaire.

As for the journalists, "ces grands hommes ne parlent point, c'est le Public qui s'exprime par leur bouche" and "je crois pouvoir soupçonner même, que quelquefois le Public est le Journaliste lui seul." Van Effen knew; he was a journalist himself. It is clear that he had made a special study of English literature[4], had a sincere if not always just apprecia-

---

[1] *Memoirs*, Article no. xx, April 24, 1710.
[2] *Nouv. Spect. Fr.* no. xviii.
[3] Cp. Oomkens, *op. cit.* x, p. 1024.
[4] Cp. preface to *Le Conte du Tonneau*: "Pour moi qui suis au fait, & qui ai lu avec attention ce qu'ils ont produit de plus estimé...."

tion of it and consciously exerted himself to effect a salutary orientation of what he conceived to be its best qualities with the literature of his fatherland. His views on English life and character which were displayed for imitation or condemnation in his own country, were equally studied and carefully formed. They were, moreover, after the uncritical fashion of the time, allowed to influence his literary judgment indiscriminately. To qualify as critic of a foreign literature one had to take a trip to that country. Van Effen was an intelligent traveller. Most travellers are satisfied to know "comment sont faits le Régent, le Roi George, Fontenelles, Newton, Hamptoncourt & Versailles." Dutchmen play the gallant abroad, go to the *Comédie* and the *Opéra*, frequent a certain *Café*, "rendezvous de tous nos compatriotes, où nous pouvons jouir de la satisfaction de parler notre Langue maternelle....Ils voient peu de chose, n'apprennent rien...; ils voient l'extérieur des François ou des Anglois[1]." Van Effen claimed to know the English "au fond," and rebuked people like Prévost[2] and Pavillon[3], who ignorantly romanticized over them. The copious notes to the translation of *A Tale of a Tub* reveal, as Dr S. Goulding remarks[4], "les excellentes connaissances qu'il a acquises de première main sur les institutions, l'histoire et la topographie anglaises." English men and women interested him. Innocent of and untrammelled by any formal education, the women exhibit all the healthy originality and diversity of the English character[5].

J'ose dire qu'elles ne sont pas généralement aussi belles, que le prétendent leurs Compatriotes prévenus, mais assurément on ne sauroit rien voir de mieux fait & de meilleur air depuis la Duchesse jusqu'à la Blanchisseuse. Ce sont des tailles pas trop déliées, mais droites & aisées; des épaules bien placées, un jarret tendu, & un pié tourné à merveille; leur démarche seule est capable de triompher d'un cœur, l'art & l'affectation y sont parfaitement cachés; & les Belles semblent sortir des mains de la Nature, telles qu'on les voit....Les Angloises n'ont pas un abord

---

[1] *Bagat.* no. xlvii.   [2] *Holl. Spect.* no. 274.
[3] *Bagat.* no. xxxvii.   [4] *Op. cit.*
[5] *Bagat.* no. xxxviii.

aisé & ouvert. Au contraire, leur air est froid avec les in-connus: mais ce froid n'est pas plat & fade, il est plutôt fier & approchant du dédain.

He proceeds to give a humorous account of the trials of English lovers, counselling them that "le souverain remède contre les bizarreries de la Belle, c'est d'affecter une bizarrerie supérieure." He was probably speaking from experience. "La Conversation des Dames est encore d'un grand secours contre la sécheresse," he advised the young men in his remarks on education[1].

On English politics he had little to say. "Les Anglois agissent par conséquent en hommes véritables, lorsqu'ils punissent des ministres, qui, trop obéissants aux Souverains, violent les loix fondamentales de leur Patrie," was his comment on ministerial responsibility[2], which article of government most text-books on the English constitution regard as the product of a much later time. The *Misantrope* for December 19, 1712, was written with a deep sense of disappointment at the attitude of the English over the peace negotiations. It seemed to him to be a defection from the Dutch, their trusted allies, towards the French, their traditional enemies. He animadverted freely on their excessive political partisanships, the cruel abuse of their leading men, but believed their state to be flourishing and daily increasing in power[3]. But in the *Misantrope*[4] he had said merrily: "Faisons voir, par exemple, que les Torys ont plus à cœur les véritables intérêts de leur Patrie que les Whigs. C'est un paradoxe très paradoxe... & je ne me sens pas assez de génie pour me tirer de cette affaire-là à mon honneur[5]." There are a few references to English ways of living, dress and manufactured articles. When he was entertained aboard the English man-of-war, he remarked: "Le Vaisseau se ressentoit fort de la magnificence de la Nation Angloise," and in the same account he remarks that when the game was started of throwing one another's articles of dress over-

[1] *Misant.* no. LXXXVII, 2nd ed.
[2] *Voyage en Suède*, Let. XIII.
[3] *Vide*, e.g., *Holl. Spect.* no. 220.
[4] No. LIV, 2nd ed.
[5] *Misant.* no. LIV, 2nd ed.

board the English lost more than the Swedes, who were not as "magnifiquement coïffés." English fashions were coming into vogue. A man boasts of his English watch[1]; a dilettante scientist has his English microscope[2]—a significant touch. A correspondent reports[3] of "masquerades à la anglaise" in his town, and Van Effen expresses his disapprobation of the *contre-danse* which has been introduced from England and Scotland[4]. But the day of anglomania described by the *Vaderlander* had not yet come, or those at the end of the century when "the liberally educated young gentlemen formed themselves into Sterne Clubs, familiarly calling each other by the names of distinguished characters in Sterne's writings, and marking even their apparel with some peculiarity from Sterne[5]."

The form of education in vogue amongst them he regarded with suspicion not free from contempt. The correspondent[6] who tells of his upbringing in England, whither his parents had gone for business purposes, writes:

Against the unbridled licence, which seems to be an inborn part of the English character, and whereof the unrestrained passions are daily seen and lauded as a characteristic of theirs, the Dutch carefulness of our mother had armed us with continual instruction, and implanted in our bosoms a longing desire for the restrained and not unbounded freedom of our country....

"Les Anglois sont outrez, & libres à l'excès dans leur tour d'Esprit, comme dans leur conduite, & dans leurs Manières: leur Imagination pétulante s'évapore tout entière en Comparaisons & en Métaphores...," yet "malgré la bisarrerie d'imagination qui s'y découvre," they usually exhibit "un sens admirablement exact." But nowhere was their licence more excessive than in religion.

I know, amongst others, a certain rich and prosperous country only too well, where among the upper classes religion is so much

---

[1] *Holl. Spect.* no. 144. [2] *Ibid.* no. 207.
[3] *Ibid.* no. 125. [4] *Ibid.* no. 321.
[5] N. S. Naylor, note 37, p. 33. *Op. cit.*
[6] *Holl. Spect.* no. 227.

out of fashion that a respectable man will as little dare to vent his religious feelings in company as appear in a pair of wide breeches with ribbons. There they do not scruple in the most illustrious society to break out into sacrilegious utterances fit to make an honest heart shudder with cold horror; and this not merely in the madness of a gambling game, but actually without the least passion and with the coolest indifference.... With regard to the common people in the same kingdom, they are brought up so barbarously and bestially, that their reason is confined to an animal desire to the satisfaction of their immediate necessities of life and that their thoughts cannot extend to the future. Honour and shame are scarcely known by name amongst them and...throughout they have not the least conception of the teachings prescribed by the established Religion. So that if any religion can still be found in the whole body of the whole nation, it will be amongst the bourgeois middle classes and in some wise and intelligent ministers of religion...so that it may be attested with truth that there is no country in the world where religion is more heinously despised and at the same time more strikingly maintained[1].

He gives a terrible picture[2] of the decay of the English clergy:

I know...that one should do that Nation the greatest injustice if one did not acknowledge that they excel in Divinity as well as in other weighty sciences above all other peoples, and that nowhere books more suited to put the Christian religion in her most beautiful light, and to inspire the observance of its supreme duties, are published. It is also incontrovertible that among the *higher Clergy*...we have with admiration seen the greatest lights of the true Religion of any time since the Reformation.

As for the lower clergy, although

striking examples of wisdom and piety are found amongst them, it is only too well known that the great majority by their looseness, lack of restraint, wantonness, ignorance, pride and scandalous conduct have brought upon themselves the general contempt of the whole nation. To drink in public taverns, to gamble, by their desires addicted to both those dangerous recreations, to allow themselves to be carried to irregular acts and expressions are their daily occupation, and people are so used to it, that it gives scarcely the smallest offence. It is not even regarded as a

---

[1] *Holl. Spect.* no. 47.   [2] *Holl. Spect.* no. 51.

rare occurrence, that one sees some of these brethren, overcome with wine, willy nilly emulating the movements of a ship tacking against the wind. Their whole reverence consists in their holy dress and all their love for religion consists in a wrongheaded adherence to the bare name of the High Church....

This ghastly account, which bears traces of the writer's acquaintance with Swift[1], is continued in the same strain and followed by a contrast in favour of the Dutch clergy. But however much Van Effen deplored certain vicious abuses in English life, culture and literature, he was convinced that the nation was sound to the core. Perhaps his attitude is summed up in no. 59[2], where he speaks of England, "which I have pitied on account of the decay of religion in her bosom, though the nation otherwise shows itself in a thousand ways to be one of the wisest and most reasonable Nations on the face of the earth."

When his *Spectator* appeared England had won both fame and notoriety. Indifference had passed. She had made a permanent impression on the minds and imaginations of men abroad. It was added to by the *Essay on Man*, the *Seasons* and *Paradise Lost*, the translation of which was, of course, an epoch-making event in every country. In Holland, J. van Zanten performed this necessary task for his countrymen, and he was induced to do it by the criticisms of the English *Spectator*[3].

The *Journal Littéraire*[4] reviews it together with a French prose version published "avec les Remarques de M. Addison." The words "magnifique" and "inimitable" are among the epithets used.

In 1730 appeared an imitation by Durand and a rhymed version by Paludanus.

Shakespeare was admitted much later, but was receiving increased attention. In 1748, the *Boekzaal* was apparently

---

[1] Cp. *Project for the Advancement of Religion.*
[2] *Holl. Spect.* May 19, 1732.
[3] Preface by translator. Speaking of Addison's papers, the translator says: "I should really say that the praise and applause accorded to it, kindled a desire in me to read through the poem attentively a second time...."
[4] 1729.

the first to notice that he was the original to which the "monstrous" play of Jan Vos must be traced. It gives a full comparison of *Titus Andronicus* and *Aran en Titus* with remarks on Shakespeare that reflect, on the whole, a growing appreciation.

Indeed, a signal victory had already been achieved. English literature had fought for a place beside French literature and had won it in Holland at least. Van Effen is appropriately our witness.

That much wit is to be found in French writers no one can deny, who has regarded with attention the estimation which all nations commonly evince for thousands of books from that country. It is also impossible to deny that the English rightly dispute the pre-eminence in this respect with their neighbours, since a great number of their writings, translated into other languages—theirs being not so common—are sought after with the greatest eagerness and read with the greatest pleasure. The good repute which English books enjoy even goes so far that some authors, in order to add distinction to their works, pretend and assert that these have been translated out of English[1].

It must be said again that this rivalry was no mere idle controversy, but was vital to the later development of European literature and the amazing outburst of the late eighteenth and early nineteenth centuries. Van Effen's share in it all has been assessed. He was a pioneer, but a necessary and distinguished one. In his work almost all the strains of English influence that had been working on the Dutch and other continental nations for nearly half a century before the *Hollandsche Spectator* was written, flow together. These were, in his last work, transfused into a native medium, and by the sum of his activities, largely, consolidated and established in Holland to become thenceforth one of the permanent moulding principles in Dutch literature for more than a century after, if not up to the present time.

[1] *Holl. Spect.* no. 129, Jan. 19, 1733.

APPENDIX

JUSTUS VAN EFFEN was born February 21, 1684, at Utrecht, of Dutch parentage (Melchior v. Effen married Maria Bom). He received his early education at the Latin school and later at the University, Utrecht. His father died in 1701 or near that date. He became tutor, probably towards the end of 1707, to the son of a Huguenot lady, Madame de Limeville, and from about 1709 formed a connection with the house of Count Wassenaer van Duivenvoorde at the Hague, being tutor to his son, until 1716. Meanwhile, Van Effen translated Shaftesbury's *Essay on the Freedom of Wit and Humour* as *Essai sur l'usage de la Raillerie* (A La Haye, 1710). On May 19, 1711, appeared his periodical *Le Misantrope*, which ran to December 26, 1712 (89 numbers). During this time he became a member of the fraternity which issued the important *Journal Littéraire*, 1713–22, to which he was the chief contributor.

The *Parallèle* or *Dissertation sur Homère et sur Chapelain* (written about 1707 or later) was published with St Hycinthe's famous *Chef-d'œuvre d'un inconnu* in 1714.

From February 1715 to about February 1716 Van Effen visited England as under-secretary to Baron Wassenaer, his employer. He became a member of the Royal Society in 1715. On his return to Holland he was offered the post of Secretary "der Heerlijkheit Geervliet in den lande van Putten," a post which he was allowed to sell. His pupil, the young Wassenaer van Duivenvoorde, having died, Van Effen proceeded with a new pupil, son of the Baron van Welderen, to the University of Leyden, where they registered on March 15, 1716, and remained for three years.

His periodical *La Bagatelle* appeared on May 5, 1718, and ran to April 13, 1719, comprising 98 numbers. During the first half of 1719 he wrote two plays, *Les Petits-Maîtres* and *La Critique des Petits-Maîtres*, and considered various projects—a tutorship in Paris, entering business, continuing the review *Nouvelles Littéraires*—all of which came to nothing. He also wrote the *Journal Historique, Politique, Critique et Galant*, 1719, and had a share in the review *L'Europe Savante*, 1718–20. The second half of the year 1719 was occupied with Van Effen's journey to Sweden as companion to Prince van Hessen Philipsthal. On his return to the Hague, Van Effen wrote or contributed to the review *Courrier politique et galant*, 1719–21, and prepared several important translations for the press. In 1720–21 appeared in succession the three parts of *Robinson Crusoe* in French, and in 1721 *A Tale of a Tub* as *Le Conte du Tonneau*. In that year he became tutor to the son of J. M. Huysman, a prominent merchant at Rotterdam, where he remained for three years and published the translation of Mandeville's *Free Thoughts* as *Pensées Libres*, and the *Guardian* as *Le Mentor Moderne*, La Haye, 1723, 3 vols., omitting, however, 29 of the English papers. He also contributed some items to the *Je ne sais quoi* of Cartier de St-Philip, 1723, a book over which he had to defend himself against Camusat, editor of the *Bibliothèque Française*. In 1724 he again proceeded to the University of Leyden, where, at the end of three years, both his pupil, Huysman, and he gained the Doctorate, Van Effen's dissertation being *De poena furti manifesti*. While at Leyden he issued *Le Nouveau Spectateur Français*, 1725, which struggled on into 28 numbers and stopped, as a collaborator had failed him. In 1726 appeared the review *Histoire Littéraire de l'Europe*, and in the same year a second edition of the *Misantrope* was issued, which contained the account of his journey to Sweden in 1719, as *Voyage en Suède*.

From October 1727 to May 1728 Van Effen visited England as secretary to his old pupil Van Welderen, who was the Dutch representative at the coronation of George II, an event which Van Effen celebrated with a panegyric in French verse. After their return Van Effen lived at the Hague with his patron. In 1730 he intervened in a theological dispute on behalf of an old school friend, and there appeared from his pen an *Essai sur la manière de traiter les controverses en forme de lettre adressée à M. de la Chapelle*; also *Suite de l'essai sur la manière de traiter les controverses*. Soon after he defended another friend against Dr Massuet.

On August 20, 1731, appeared the *Hollandsche Spectator* which continued up to April 8, 1735, running into 360 numbers.

In 1732, through the influence of his host and patron Van Welderen, Van Effen obtained the post of "kommies by 's lands magazynen van oorlog" at 's Hertogenbosch, and in the same year appeared the first two volumes of Van Loon's great work on medals, *Historie der Nederlandsche Gedenkpenningen*, translated by Van Effen into French as *Histoire Métallique*.

Towards the end of the same year, probably, Van Effen married a Dutch lady, Elizabeth Sophia Andriessen, whom he had long wooed. Two children were born of the marriage. Van Effen died on September 18, 1735.

INDEX

Numbers refer to pages

For EU product safety concerns, contact us at Calle de José Abascal, 56–1°, 28003 Madrid, Spain or eugpsr@cambridge.org.

www.ingramcontent.com/pod-product-compliance
Ingram Content Group UK Ltd.
Pitfield, Milton Keynes, MK11 3LW, UK
UKHW010343140625
459647UK00010B/793